Land Warfare: Brassey'
Weapons Systems & T

## Volume 1

# Guided Weapons

**Land Warfare:** Brassey's New Battlefield Weapons Systems
and Technology Series

*Executive Editor:* Colonel R.G. Lee OBE, Former Military Director of Studies,
Royal Military College of Science, Shrivenham, UK

*Editor-in-Chief:* Professor Frank Hartley, Principal and Dean, Royal
Military College of Science, Shrivenham, UK

The success of the first series on Battlefield Weapons Systems and
Technology and the pace of advances in military technology has prompted
Brassey's to produce a new Land Warfare series. This series updates subjects
covered in the original series and also covers completely new areas. The books
are written for military men who wish to advance their professional
knowledge. In addition, they are intended to aid anyone who is interested in
the design, development and production of military equipment.

Volume 1    Guided Weapons — R. G. Lee *et al*

Volume 2    Explosives, Propellants and Pyrotechnics — A. Baily and
S.G. Murray

Volume 3    Noise in the Military Environment — R.F. Powell and
M.R. Forrest

Volume 4    Ammunition — E. Archer and P.R. Courtney-Green

**Other titles of interest from Brassey's**

GARNELL            Guided Weapon Control Systems, 2nd edition

PERKINS            Weapons and Warfare

SHAKER & WISE    War without Men

SLOAN              Mine Warfare on Land

# Guided Weapons

**Colonel R.G. Lee, T.K. Garland-Collins,**

**D.E. Johnson, E. Archer, C. Sparkes,**
**G. M. Moss and A.W. Mowat**

*Royal Military College of Science, Shrivenham, UK*

**BRASSEY'S DEFENCE PUBLISHERS**
(a member of the Maxwell Pergamon Publishing Corporation plc)
LONDON · OXFORD · WASHINGTON · NEW YORK
BEIJING · FRANKFURT · SÃO PAULO · SYDNEY · TOKYO · TORONTO

| U.K.<br>(Editorial) | Brassey's Defence Publishers Ltd.,<br>24 Gray's Inn Road, London WC1X 8HR |
| (Orders) | Brassey's Defence Publishers Ltd.,<br>Headington Hill Hall, Oxford OX3 0BW, England |
| U.S.A.<br>(Editorial) | Pergamon-Brassey's International Defense<br>Publishers, Inc.<br>8000 Westpark Drive, Fourth Floor, McLean, Virginia<br>22102, U.S.A. |
| (Orders) | Pergamon Press, Inc., Maxwell House, Fairview<br>Park, Elmsford, New York 10523, U.S.A. |
| PEOPLE'S REPUBLIC<br>OF CHINA | Pergamon Press, Room 4037, Qianmen Hotel, Beijing,<br>People's Republic of China |
| FEDERAL REPUBLIC<br>OF GERMANY | Pergamon Press GmbH, Hammerweg 6,<br>D-6242 Kronberg, Federal Republic of Germany |
| BRAZIL | Pergamon Editora Ltda, Rua Eça de Queiros, 346,<br>CEP 04011, Paraiso, São Paulo, Brazil |
| AUSTRALIA | Pergamon-Brassey's Defence Publishers Pty Ltd.,<br>P.O. Box 544, Potts Point, N.S.W. 2011, Australia |
| JAPAN | Pergamon Press, 5th Floor, Matsuoka Central<br>Building, 1-7-1 Nishishinjuku, Shinjuku-ku, Tokyo<br>160, Japan |
| CANADA | Pergamon Press Canada Ltd., Suite No. 271, 253<br>College Street, Toronto, Ontario, Canada M5T 1R5 |

First edition 1988

**Library of Congress Cataloging in Publication Data**

Guided weapons/R.G. Lee (et al)
p. cm. (Land warfare: v.1)
Bibliography: p.
Includes Index
1. Guided missiles. 2. Antitank weapons,
I. Lee, R. G. (R. Geoffrey) II Series
UG1310.G83 1988 623.4'519 dc 19 88-10543

**British Library Calaloguing in Publication Data**

Guided weapons
1. Guided missiles
I. Lee, R.G. (R. Geoffrey)
623.4'519

ISBN 0-08-035828-4 Hardcover
ISBN 0-08-035827-6 Flexicover

Cover photograph: High Velocity Missile — Starstreak
(Courtesy Short Brothers Ltd)

*Printed in Great Britain by A. Wheaton & Co. Ltd., Exeter*

# Preface

This series of books is written for those who wish to improve their knowledge of military weapons and equipment. It is equally relevant to professional soldiers, those involved in developing and producing military weapons or indeed anyone interested in the art of modern warfare.

All the texts are written in a way which assumes no mathematical knowledge and no more technical depth than would be gleaned from school days. It is intended that the books should be of particular interest to army officers who are studying for promotion examinations, furthering their knowledge at specialist arms schools or attending command and staff schools.

The authors of the books are, or have been, military or civilian members of the staff of the Royal Military College of Science, Shrivenham, which is comprised of a unique blend of academic and military experts. They are not only leaders in the technology of their subjects, but are aware of what the military practitioner needs to know. It is difficult to imagine any group of persons more fitted to write about the application of technology to the battlefield.

**This Volume**

Over the past forty years, guided weapons have developed faster than any other form of weapon system. They now influence international politics, strategy and tactics to a dominating extent. This volume is based on the Guided Weapons book published as part of the original Battlefield Weapons Systems and Technology Series. It has been re-written, up-dated and considerably expanded. In particular the subjects of Electrical Power Supplies and Electronics Warfare have been added. Consequently it now provides an up-to-date description of the technology involved in the design of modern guided weapons. It then moves on to describe how they are used as weapon systems on the world stage as a deterrent and on the battlefield against armoured vehicles, ground targets and aircraft.

*January 1988*                                    Frank Hartley
*Shrivenham*                                      Geoffrey Lee

# Acknowledgements

The authors would like to record their gratitude to their colleagues at the Royal Military College of Science for their generous co-operation in the preparation of this book. They would also like to thank all those who have so readily provided illustrations to enhance the text.

Finally they would like to thank Judith Fisk for her help preparing the manuscript for publication.

Shrivenham
January 1988

R.G. Lee
T.K. Garland-Collins
D.E. Johnson
E. Archer
C. Sparkes
G.M. Moss
A.W. Mowat

# Contents

# List of Illustrations

## Chapter 3 — Electrical Power Supplies

## Chapter 4 — Airframes

## Chapter 5 — Guidance

**Chapter 6 — Control**

## Chapter 7 — Electronic Warfare Applied to GW

## Chapter 8 — Payload

## Chapter 9 — Anti-tank Guided Weapons and Light, Unguided Anti-tank Weapons

## Chapter 10 — Surface-to-Air Guided Weapons

## Chapter 11 — Surface-to-Surface Guided Weapons

# 1.
# Introduction to Guided Weapons

## The Rise of Guided Weapons

During the 1939–45 war, Germany developed and brought into service the V1 and V2 long range guided weapons (GW); they had also reached the drawing board stage in the development of an anti-tank guided weapon (ATGW), the XH7, by the end of that war.

Since then, over the past forty years, GW have developed faster than any other form of weapon system. Now they influence international policies, strategy and tactics to an enormous extent. They may yet spell the end of manned strike aircraft and the current concept of the Main Battle Tank (MBT).

The technology involved in GW electronic counter measures (ECM), and counter counter measures, (ECCM) is advancing at an ever increasing rate. Indeed, it can be said that the successful use of GW will be the decisive factor in a future war, as air battles in the Middle East and naval actions in the South Atlantic have indicated. Today, no member of the Armed Forces nor anyone involved in the development of weapons can afford to ignore a study of them.

## Definition of a Guided Weapon

A guided system may be described briefly as a weapon system in which the warhead is delivered by an unmanned guided vehicle.

In most cases, the guided weapon systems available to the armed forces of the world are readily recognisable as such. The long range strategic rockets, the dog-fight missiles carried by the aircraft, the short range anti-tank missiles, and the surface-to-air anti-aircraft defence systems are readily brought to mind by anyone interested in military equipment. However it is prudent to avoid an unduly restrictive definition of the term 'guided weapon' for there are several examples from the past of systems difficult to identify as guided weapons. This is also true of some current systems. In the future, the different types of weapon may be expected to expand considerably, particularly in the use of guided projectiles.

1

To give some examples of such unfamiliar systems the case of the 'beetle tank' may be taken from the Second World War. This was a miniature tank packed with explosive and remotely controlled by a wire cable. It was guided to its target by an operator who observed both tank and target and who steered the crawling bomb as it moved away from him (cf 'Manual Command to Line of Sight' (MCLOS) in the chapter on guidance).

An example of a system which was developed, but not put into production, was a spherical ball which once launched could move in any direction and could hover in response to commands sent to it. The idea was to position it carefully over the target and then command the warhead to detonate.

A more modern and interesting design of guided weapon produced by the West German firm MBB consists of a small remotely piloted vehicle (RPV) carrying a warhead which may be used for anti-aircraft defence suppression.

During the Vietnam War the United States airforce introduced a guidance kit which when fitted to their conventional 'iron' bombs transformed them into guided weapons. Notice that this was a case of a GW which did not have a propulsive system: the motive power was provided entirely by gravity and the launch velocity.

Many of the more unusual GW of the future may have unfamiliar forms of motive power such as projectiles fired from ordinary guns, rotating discs (or flying saucers!) or 'sleeping' GW in earth orbit.

The warhead, too, may not be of the conventional or nuclear type. A nation prepared to resort to chemical warfare might well stock GW capable of spraying toxic gas or powder while the vehicle moved along some desired path. Suggestions have been made that suitable carrier missiles might distribute anti-tank mines, jammers, or remote ground sensors into some designated area.

Having made the point that the term 'guided weapon system' may cover a considerable range of weapon concepts, some of which may be highly unusual, it is emphasised that the bulk of the discussion in this book will be concerned with existing conventional GW systems, and developments in their technology which may be expected to enter service with land forces within the next few years rather than naval, air force, or space force activity.


## Terms and Classifications

Over the years, many different systems have been used to classify GW. Most of them are still used to a greater extent, so it is desirable to mention the more important of them here.

## Launch Point – Target Location

Originally there were four groups, Surface-to-Surface (SSGW), Surface-to-Air (SAGW), Air-to-Surface (ASGW) and Air-to-Air (AAGW). This was sufficient to describe the early systems where the conventional winged aircraft was the only form of airborne launch platform or target and no distinction was made between land and sea. Today the spectrum of launch points and targets must be extended to include airborne Remotely Piloted Vehicles or tethered platforms, helicopters, gliders, paravanes and, perhaps, airships. Submarines may launch missiles or suffer attack by a GW, and targets or launchers in space must be considered as well as anti-missile missiles. The discussion in this book will concentrate on surface-to-surface, surface-to-air and air-to-ground systems which are the main concern of the land forces.

## Classification by Target and Method of Carriage

From the point of view of the nation which has to pay the bill for the introduction of a weapon system, it is an unfortunate fact that general purpose GW have seldom proved satisfactory in the past. In spite of many attempts to introduce such systems, eg an infantry-portable weapon for the attack of tanks and aircraft, it has always turned out that a weapon system is not effective in one role or the other – or both. Thus it is nearly always the case that a GW system is optimised to attack a particular class of target.

It is of particular interest therefore that the careful design which has resulted in the Oerlikon ADATS weapon offers a new system, incorporating the latest technology, which has both an air defence and an anti-tank role. A further development in the search for dual purpose weapons is the current intense interest in the possibility of bringing new technology to bear on the problem of using existing guns which are required anyway, to launch guided projectiles. This is of particular interest in the case of the naval gun, the main armament of the main battle tank (MBT) and 155mm field artillery.

It has become common practice to describe systems in such terms as anti-tank GW (ATGW) anti-helicopter GW (AHGW), anti-RPV GW and so on. In view of the increasing number of airborne platforms which require confrontation it is certain that further attempts will be made to produce general purpose systems – at least in the ground-to-air role.

The land forces are greatly concerned with mobility, so the type of vehicle used for the transport of a system is a matter of some importance. Many GW systems are therefore given such titles as 'Man-portable anti-tank GW'. 'Tracked Rapier', 'Towed Rapier' or 'Swingfire on Striker'.

In some cases GW systesm are designed in single integrated units which may be fitted to tracked, wheeled or rail transport. Such systems are usually called 'pod mounted' systems.

### *Classification by Flying Mode*

There are several aspects of the flight mode which are used to describe particular missiles. The term 'boost-coast' is used for a missile which is rapidly accelerated to flying speed and which then has no further propulsion power throughout its flight.

A 'boost-sustain' system has a two-stage propulsion system which tends to maintain speed after the initial acceleration is over. These matters will be explained in detail in Chapter 2, which includes propulsion systems for both subsonic and supersonic missiles.

The trajectory or path of a GW is also used in its description. The main terms used are 'Ballistic Missile', 'Cruise Missile'. 'Line of Sight Missile' and 'Proportional Navigation system'. These trajectories and some less common ones will be discussed in Chapter 4.

In the case of very long range GW, the altitude of the missile above sea level in successive phases of flight may be used to describe its path. This is a method borrowed from the world of conventional aircraft and results in such terms as 'HI-LO-LO' and 'LO-HI-LO'.

GW are often labelled by the method used to control them. In addition to the two main categories of control, i.e. aerodynamic or thrust vector control, a missile may be called a 'twist and steer' missile, a 'roll position stabilised' missile or a 'wire controlled' missile. These terms will be explained in detail in Chapter 5.

A further description of flying mode may be made at the encounter with the target. The importance of matching the fuze and warhead to the target to obtain the greatest possible Single Shot Kill Probability (SSKP) is affected greatly by the accuracy of the missile, usually expressed in terms of its Root Mean Square miss distance (RMSMD), a precise statistical metric which relates to the most likely lateral distance by which the missile will miss the target. If the missile is very accurate the RMSMD is so small that virtually all the missiles launched against the target (except of course engineering failures) will strike it. These missiles do not require a proximity fuze and rely on a contact fuze to initiate the warhead. Such GW are sometimes called 'hittiles' as opposed to 'missiles' which do require a proximity fuze.

Some mention should be made of the so called 'smart' munitions. This type of weapon includes projectiles or warheads suspended from slowly falling parachutes which are not GW in that the path of the weapon is not controlled by a closed loop system. However a sensor detects the presence and direction of a target. The warhead is then triggered and a lethal slug or jet is directed over a distance of several tens of metres at the target. The slug itself is not guided. Such a system might be described as a polarised warhead munition with a long range proximity fuze.

Finally, the point should be made that new modes of classification of GW systems are continuously coming into fashion. For example, the terms TGSM (Terminally Guided Submunition) and PGM (Precision Guided Munition) have recently become much used to describe GW in which accurate guidance for the last part of the trajectory is of particular significance.

# 2.
# Propulsion

Over the great range of missile systems employed today, from the giant long-range Intercontinental Ballistic Missile (ICBM) to the small Anti-Tank Guided Weapon (ATGW) and even the smaller unguided Light Anti-Tank Weapon (LAW), there is one feature at least which is common to them all: it is jet propulsion, which is provided either by a rocket motor or by an air-breathing engine.

## Engine

At the outset it will be helpful to explain briefly what is meant by jet propulsion. There is a widespread tendency to regard a rocket as a device which is totally different from the type of propulsion unit, the jet engine, which is employed in nearly all today's large aircraft. At first there would appear to be some truth in this. For example, the rocket motor is completely self-contained whereas the aircraft jet engine relies on breathing the surrounding atmosphere. However, in respect of the fundamental manner in which a useful propulsive force is generated, the rocket motor and the air-breather are the same. This fundamental principle is that of reaction propulsion and is embodied in Newton's Second and Third Laws.

Thus, despite various important differences in operation and construction between rocket motors and air-breathers, it is clearly important to appreciate that each is a device particularly suited to specific applications but nevertheless relies wholly for its effect on reaction propulsion obtained by the generation of a stream of propulsive medium, ie in general, a high-velocity jet of propulsive gases. That is what is meant by jet propulsion.

## Basic Principles

### General Applications

The most obvious use of a propelling force, whether it is applied to a land, sea, air or space vehicle, is to accelerate the vehicle; it is the force used to effect a change in the vehicle's velocity. Another important function for the propelling force, certainly in a land, sea or air vehicle but not in a space vehicle, is to overcome the drag which resists its motion. This resisting force may be variously due to rolling resistance, aerodynamic resistance, wave-making resistance, or perhaps a combination of them. The third use, which is often necessary, is the provision of a lifting force: this may not be provided solely by the same source as the accelerating and resistance-overcoming forces, but may be provided, partially or wholly, by other means such as the wings on an aircraft. This aspect does not require elaboration at this stage.

In the case of missiles, we need to look in detail at the form of propelling force which they use, which is jet propulsion.

## *Jet Propulsion*

In jet propulsion a jet or stream of fluid, always gaseous in practical propulsion systems, leaves the missile through a suitably shaped and positioned orifice. In a rocket, a momentum change in the propulsive gas is produced merely by ejecting it from the rocket motor. In an air-breathing engine, the gas must be ejected at a velocity greater than the forward speed of the engine through the air for a momentum change to take place. This rate of change of momentum of the leaving gas is proportional to the force being applied to the gas; it can be seen that this is effectively a statement of Newton's Second Law of Motion. The reaction to this accelerating force is equal in magnitude and opposite in direction and therefore is the useful propelling force on the missile. The latter sentence is in effect a statement of Newton's Third Law of Motion. The laws of applied mechanics thus are of fundamental importance in missile propulsion.

So far, no mention has been made of the means by which a propulsive jet of gas is produced for missile propulsion. These matters are governed by the laws of applied thermodynamics, which are equally important in propulsion.

## Jet Propulsion Methods

### *Classification of Motors*

Before examining the types of propulsion unit available to the missile designer, it is worth looking at jet propulsion systems in a very fundamental way, according to the origin of the fluid medium which forms the jet. There are two main systems. The first is a rocket in which the medium is carried along with, and in due course discharged from the missile. The second is an air-breather which picks up its medium, the surrounding air, and also, in due course, discharges it. Both burn fuel in their operation and so, generically, they can be called thermodynamic devices. We can go further in propulsion systems for missiles, because the original source of energy is always chemical; this means we can refine our definition of the systems to call them thermochemical.

## Net Effect of Propulsive Forces

A study of Figure 2.1 will produce a simple understanding of the net effect of the forces acting on a rocket motor. In general the lateral forces on the missiles are self cancelling. The axial forces are not, so according to Newton's Laws this provides the net propulsive force. $U_e$ = Exhaust gases velocity.

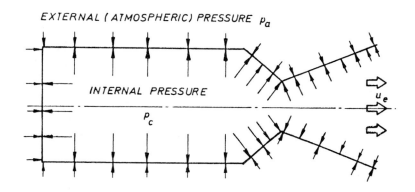

FIG. 2.1 Pressure distribution in and around an ideal rocket motor

# Types of Jet Propulsion Unit and their Main Features

## Basic Types and Features

Thermochemical propulsion systems can be classified in various ways. The following chart shows the principal types available. It is interesting, incidentally, in that, from a common starting point, two main branches grow. Later, these branches join up to form a hybrid system, No. 6, the ram-rocket.

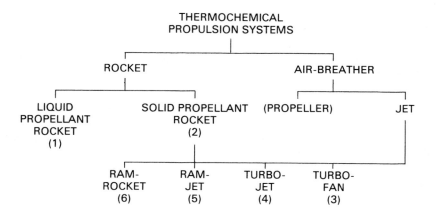

The main characteristic feature of the jet, from the performance point of view, is its velocity. Typical jet velocities for the systems shown in the chart are:

| | |
|---|---|
| Subsonic turbofan (3) at 36,000 ft | 350 –  500 m/s |
| Static turbojet (4) at sea level | 500 –  750 m/s |
| Supersonic turbojet (4) at 36,000 ft | 900 – 1,000 m/s |
| Supersonic ramjet/ramrocket (5/6) at 36,000 ft | 1,000 – 1,200 m/s |
| Solid propellant rocket (2) | 1,500 – 2,500 m/s |
| Liquid propellant rocket (1) | 2,000 – 3,500 m/s |

The most obvious feature of this table is the wide spread of magnitudes of jet velocity. Also obvious is the steady progression through a range of propulsion units from moderate jet velocity to high jet velocity. It is no accident that such a wide range of jet velocities is at the disposal of the designer of the missile propulsion system. As will be mentioned later, the efficiency of the propulsion process is intimately associated with the magnitude of the jet velocity in relation to the magnitude of the flight velocity. Of course, the attainment of a high efficiency of propulsion is not necessarily a requirement in the design of a propulsion unit. Convenience, lightness or cheapness may be more important considerations.

### Solid Propellant Rocket

The solid propellant rocket motor is by far the most widely used unit in missile propulsion. Essentially it consists of four components: they are the motor case, the nozzle, the solid propellant charge and the igniter. A typical loose-charge, solid propellant motor is shown in Figure 2.2.

The operation of this type of motor is superficially very straightforward. The igniter, behaving like an energetic firework, starts the solid propellant charge burning on the desired surfaces. Gaseous products of combustion are rapidly generated, filling the void space in the motor at a considerable pressure, typically 70 atmospheres, enabling combustion to be sustained at the surface of the propellant. The case is thus a pressure vessel. The hot gases vent through the characteristically shaped convergent-divergent nozzle at a high speed, which can be 2000 m/s or more at the exit plane. For steady-state operation the gases must be generated in and escape from the motor at a fixed rate. This is normally achieved by arranging for the burning surface area of the charge to remain very nearly the same throughout the majority of the burning time. As discussed previously, the ejection of the gases at high velocity is the reaction to the creation of an imbalance of forces on the gas within the motor as illustrated in Figure 2.1.

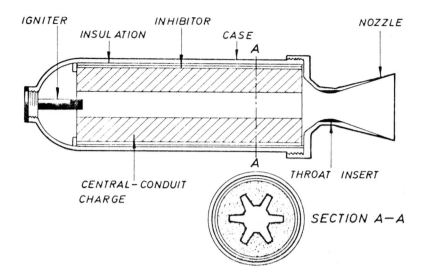

FIG. 2.2  Typical loose-charge solid propellant rocket motor

## *Liquid Propellant Rocket*

The liquid propellant engine generates thrust in exactly the same way as the solid but the operation and construction are rather different.

In the liquid engine the fuel and the oxidant are usually tanked separately. The combustion chamber, shown in Figure 2.3, to which the fuel and oxidant must be delivered, is not the propellant store as in the solid propellant type; so the fuel and oxidant can be stored remotely from the combustion chamber at normal pressures. However, the fuel and oxidant must be supplied to the chamber at specific rates and under specific pressures. There are various ways of pressurising the liquids, some of which involve pressurising the holding tanks, others of which do not. Clearly the liquid propellant type offers certain advantages which the solid propellant type cannot. For example, the propellant flowrates, and hence the thrust, can be varied on demand. The duration of the firing is dependent only on the capacity of the tanks, in the first instance. Disadvantages are the likely expensive engineering of the engine, the complication and hence the reduced reliability. There are circumstances, however, in which these drawbacks must be borne in order to gain the other advantages.

As indicated earlier, the feature of the rocket which distinguishes it from other propulsion units is its almost total independence of the surroundings. This is in direct contrast to the air-breather.

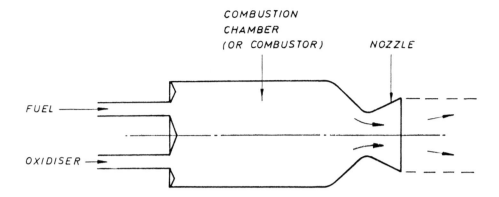

FIG. 2.3 Diagrammatic bi-propellant liquid rocket engine

## *Turbojet*

The fundamental air-breathing jet propulsion unit is the turbojet and it is easiest to understand. It is illustrated in Figure 2.4

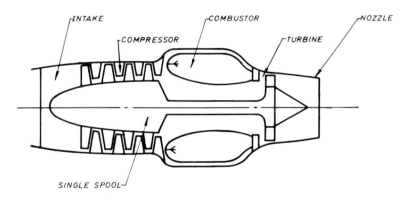

FIG. 2.4 Component arrangement of a typical turbojet engine

The function of a nozzle is to accelerate a high pressure gas from rest or low velocity to a high velocity. The components of a turbojcet upstream of the nozzle have the primary function of supplying the propulsive medium in a suitable quantity and at suitable pressure and temperature to the nozzle.

The intake's role is to capture the air and deliver it to the compressor as efficiently as possible and at an appropriate velocity. When the engine is propelling a vehicle in flight, significant pressure increase is produced in the intake.

This is usually called the ram pressure rise. At static conditions, when the engine is at rest, the air pressure entering the compressor is slightly less than that of the surrounding atmosphere.

The compressor pressurises the air for delivery to the combustor where the temperature of the air is raised greatly, typically up to about 1200 K, by burning kerosene in the air stream. The air, or products of combustion and air, are now at a suitable pressure and temperature for entry to the turbine, through which the gas passes, losing energy. That energy is transmitted to the turbine rotating parts which, by means of a connecting shaft, drive the compressor upstream. The partially spent gases then flow into the nozzle where they are accelerated.

It has to be emphasised that there is a regenerative principle built in to the turbojet. The compressor supplies the air to the turbine (which drives the compressor) via the combustor, where, by burning fuel, the temperature is raised at nominally constant pressure. The hot, high pressure gas flows through the turbine, which produces the power to drive the compressor.

It should be noted that although the turbojet engine, supercially at least, is a simple device, the individual components must be designed and developed to a high level of performance if it is to operate efficiently. This is particularly true of the compressor and turbine. Consequently it is an expensive item and requires high level engineering production.

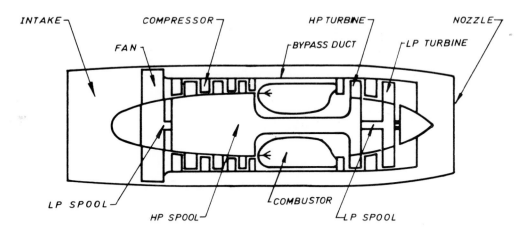

FIG. 2.5  Component arrangement of a typical turbofan engine

## Turbofan

The turbofan, as can be seen in Figure 2.5, is a very close relative of the turbojet. It will be briefly dealt with and compared with the turbojet, in the sections dealing with efficiency of propulsion and choice of turbojet or turbofan. For the moment, it will be sufficient to say that the turbofan is a derivative of the turbojet that employs the by-pass principle (see Figure 2.5) so as to develop the same thrust as an equivalent turbojet but with a reduced jet velocity. This, in general, gives an improved level of performance. In its essential parts, the turbofan employs the same components as a turbojet.

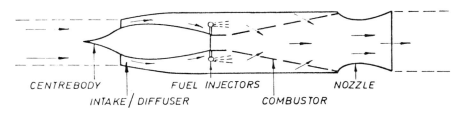

FIG. 2.6a  Liquid-fuel ramjet with axisymmetric nose intake (podded)

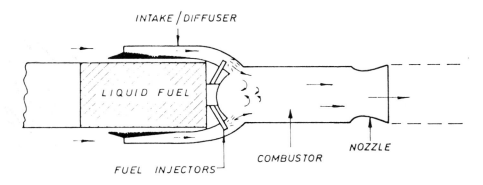

FIG. 2.6b  Liquid-fuel ramjet with multiple side intakes

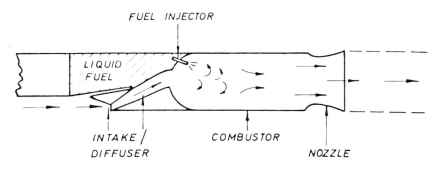

FIG. 2.6c  Liquid-fuel ramjet with ventral intake

## Ramjet

In introducing the turbojet, the reader may recall that mention was made of the pressure rise that could be obtained in the intake solely by virtue of the forward motion. It was mentioned that the name given to the pressure increase is 'the ram pressure rise'. It is a fact that, at subsonic velocities, the ram rise is fairly modest. However, at supersonic velocities, say Mach 2 to Mach 4, the potential ram pressure rise is great. The ramjet engine hinges on this characteristic.

A ramjet therefore relies wholly on its forward motion through the atmosphere to develop a sufficient pressure rise in the intake. As will be seen from the diagram in Figure 2.6a the intake is rather different from the conventional subsonic turbojet intake: this is to deal with supersonic airflow. The intake's job is to collect and diffuse, or slow down, the air to a low velocity before it enters the combustor; there is no mechanical compressor. Much as in a turbojet, liquid fuel is normally sprayed into and burned in the airstream in the combustor, raising the temperature at nominally constant pressure. Immediately downstream of the combustor, the flow is directed to the nozzle where, as usual, the gas accelerates at the expense of the pressure (and temperature): there is no turbine or compressor required. Provided there is sufficient ram pressure rise, a sufficiently high temperature produced in the combustion chamber and a sufficient level of efficiency obtained in these three processes, the ramjet will produce a net forward force or thrust, ejecting a high velocity jet in the process.

The main disadvantage of the ramjet is that it is non-operational at zero and low forward speeds and so it must be boosted from rest to a suitable velocity, usually around Mach 2, when it can then accelerate if desired. On the other hand it is much simpler than a turbojet or turbofan.

## Ramrocket (or Ducted Rocket or Air-Augmented Rocket)

Finally, the ramrocket, which is the subject of considerable current interest, is a hybrid unit employing both rocket and air-breather features. In the form used in the Soviet S-A 6 missile and in various feasibility studies, the so-called ramrocket is more properly described as a ramjet employing a solid propellant.

From Figure 2.7 it can be seen that the rocket part of the whole unit is providing a supply of fuel to the air-breathing part downstream. To achieve this, the rocket propellant is particularly fuel-rich and so provides the fuel for combustion with the air which has been captured by the intake and directed to the combustor. The ramrocket then behaves like a conventional liquid-fuel ramjet and should be viewed as a variant of it rather than as a true hybrid device. In the form described, the ramrocket may be said to have the virtues of a dense propellant and an ability to avoid flame-out. Countering those advantages however, is the inherent difficulty in varying the thrust level of the ramrocket. It has to be done by varying the flow rate of the gas from the rocket part and techniques for doing so are difficult to devise. There is the

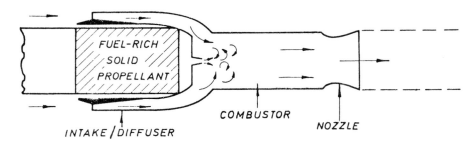

FIG. 2.7 Solid propellant ramrocket with side intakes

added problem that, even if an alternative satisfactory method by altering the gas generator nozzle throat could be devised, the rate of response of the unit to given thrust changes would be poor, particularly towards the end of the thrusting period when the gas generator combustor would be largely full of gas, rather than solid propellant, as it is at the start of the burn.


## General Propulsive Performance

Having briefly described the main types of propulsion unit employed in missiles, the next stage is to discuss their relative performance, how they would be used in practice and how their efficiency can best be assessed.

Provided one is careful in setting up one's model, it is not very difficult to establish an equation for the thrust or force developed by a generalised propulsion unit. The diagram at Figure 2.8 shows a typical layout.

Making use of Newton's Laws, it can be established that the following simple equation gives the approximate thrust developed by the typical idealised unit:

$$F = \dot{m} \, (u_e - u_a)$$

ie Thrust F = Propellant Flow Rate $\dot{m}$ x Velocity change $(u_e - u_a)$.


### Application to a Rocket Engine

When this equation is applied to the rocket engine there is an immediate simplification because, of course, no mainstream flow enters the rocket. The approximate thrust equation for a rocket engine therefore is:

$$F = \dot{m}\,(u_e - u_a)$$

ie Thrust F = Propellant Flow Rate $\dot{m}$ x Velocity change $(u_e - u_a)$.

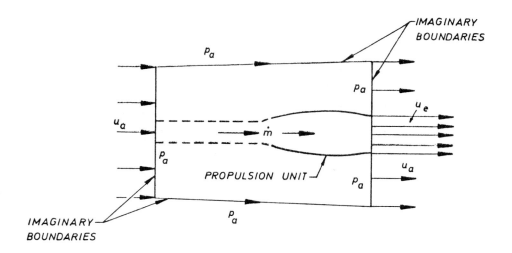

FIG. 2.8 Ideal generalised propulsion unit

## Application to a Rocket Engine

When this equation is applied to the rocket engine there is an immediate simplification because, of course, no mainstream flow enters the rocket. The approximate thrust equation for a rocket engine therefore is:

$$F = \dot{m}u_e$$

ie Thrust F = Propellant Flow Rate $\dot{m}$ x Exhaust Velocity $u_e$.

A widely used criterion of performance is the thrust developed per unit mass flow rate of propellant gases, the specific impulse. Referring to the basic thrust equation, specific impulse I can be shown to be given by:

$$I = \frac{F}{\dot{m}} = u_e$$

There is an alternative way of visualising the concept of specific impulse. Since a rocket motor's function is to provide a thrust for a certain time, ie an impulse, the impulse can be evaluated from a knowledge of the variation of thrust over the known burn time. If this impulse is then divided by the mass of propellant consumed over the burn time, we get the specific impulse. This definition and technique of evaluation are particularly suited to the solid propellant motor whose mass flow rate is difficult to evaluate because it may well vary with time.

What might be confusing to the reader is the widespread practice of quoting specific impulse in 'seconds'. This practice arose through defining specific impulse as thrust per unit weight flow rate which has units of seconds. In SI units it is convenient to remember that since at sea level gravity g is approximately 10 m/s², a specific impulse of 250s is very nearly 2500 m/s or 2500 Ns/kg.

### Application to an Air-Breathing Engine

In the case of the air-breathing engine, the appropriate thrust equation is the generalised thrust equation. Various criteria of performance are used. The ratio thrust/air flow rate is the specific thrust and is comparable to specific impulse in rocket motors. When air-breathing engines alone are under consideration, it us usually fuel flow rate/thrust, the specific fuel consumption, that is quoted.

Close examination of the approximate thrust equation for the air-breather reveals that the term additional to that in the rocket thrust equation is $-\dot{m}\,u_a$. The significance of this term is considerable and therefore merits discussion.

The negative sign attached to the product $\dot{m}\,u_a$ indicates that it represents a force term in the direction opposite to the desired thrust direction; such a force is a drag force and so $\dot{m}\,u_a$ is known as momentum or ram drag. It can be visualised as the momentum rate associated with the approaching propulsive stream. In order to develop a useful reactive forward force using this stream, its momentum must be increased in a rearward direction. Thus it is the momentum increase of the stream which gives the propulsive force. The term $\dot{m}\,u_a$ is not then, in any way, mysterious. It is merely the measure of the momentum of the airstream prior to acceleration. Thus, for an engine at rest, the term disappears, since the air is accelerated from rest.

It's also worthy of mention that when the thrust equation for an air-breathing engine in motion is written in the following way, the ideas of gross thrust and net thrust are emphasised:

$$F = F_{net} = \dot{m}\,u_e - \dot{m}\,u_a$$

$$= F_{gross} - D_{ram}$$

This highlights the fact that since, in an air-breather, the net thrust is generally the difference between 2 large quantities, a decrease in the

magnitude of F gross (perhaps through deterioration of component performance etc) can lead to a disproportionately large decrease in the net (ie useful)
thrust. Air-breathers thus tend to be fairly susceptible to comparatively small
changes in intrinsic engine performance.

While the rocket motor is more or less independent of flight conditions, the
air-breather is very much influenced by both ambient pressure and flight
speed, as the curves in Figures 2.9 and 2.10, each for a given engine type,
illustrate. The curves in Figure 2.11 are rather different, illustrating the
approprimate best specific fuel consumption that could be expected for an
engine designed for a given flight Mach number. For convenience of comparison of the rocket and air-breather, the corresponding specific impulse in Ns/kg
is quoted also.

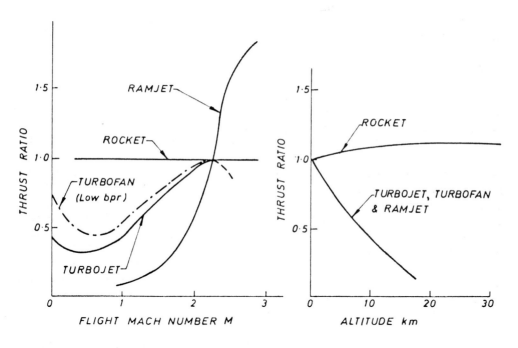

FIG. 2.9 Variation of thrust with flight Mach
number for different types of engine

FIG. 2.10 Variation of thrust with altitude for
different types of engine

## Propulsive System Efficiencies

An alternative approach to the problem of assessing propulsive system
performance is available if one considers first how efficiently the engine
converts the heat released in combustion of the fuel into a high-velocity jet,
and second how efficiently this jet is employed in propelling the vehicle. The

former idea leads to the concept of thermal efficiency while the latter leads to the concept of propulsive efficiency. These two efficiencies multiplied give the overall efficiency of propulsion. The better the overall efficiency, the lower is the specific fuel consumption.

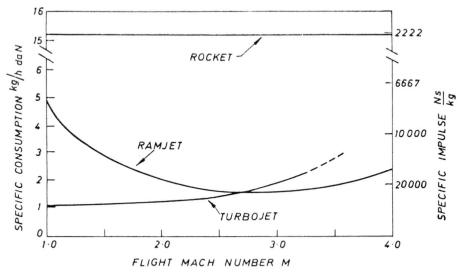

FIG. 2.11 Variation of best achievable specific fuel consumption with flight Mach number for different propulsion units

## Turbofan or Turbojet? — The Influence of Propulsive Efficiency

The over-riding objective behind the development of the turbofan engine was to reduce specific fuel consumption (at a given flight speed and thrust) in order to increase range. In the turbofan this is achieved by increasing the propulsive efficiency considerably at some small cost in thermal efficiency. The overall efficiency improves and so the specific consumption reduces.

The effect is obtained by developing the given thrust with a reduced jet velocity by increasing the flow rate of the propulsive gas. Reducing jet velocity also reduces the kinetic energy of the propulsive stream dissipated in the surrounding atmosphere, hence raising the propulsion efficiency. This increase is reflected in a reduction in fuel consumption. There are consequential effects, some of which are not desirable: these aspects will be discussed in the section dealing, in some detail, with air-breathers.

## Rockets

It was mentioned in an earlier section that solid propellant rocket motors were by far the most widely used means of missile propulsion. Thus it might be appropriate to deal with them in detail first. Before doing so, however, it should be appreciated that there are principles and performance criteria which are common to all types of rocket, in particular to the two types to which we shall confine our attention. These features in common will be briefly dealt with now.

## Performance Criteria and Thermodynamics

In addition to the specific impulse, two other parameters of rocket performance are frequently used. They are thrust coefficient $C_F$ and characteristic velocity $c^*$.

Considering thrust coefficient first, its significance is that for a fixed geometry nozzle it is very much dependent on pressure ratio $P_c/P_a$ and is almost independent of combustion temperature. Thrust coefficient is thus closely controlled by nozzle performance and is therefore used as a measure of nozzle performance.

On the other hand, characteristic velocity can be shown to be independent of pressure ratio but dependent on combustion temperature. Characteristic velocity is thus independent of nozzle performance. Just as $C_F$ is used as an indicator of the quality of the nozzle performance, so $c^*$ is used as an indicator of the quality of the combustion process. Thus the rocket engineer has at his disposal two parameters which enable him to isolate nozzle performance and chamber performance.

The thermodynamic performance of a rocket engine can be evaluated relatively easily provided several reasonable assumptions are made. Among these are the assumptions of steady, one-dimensional, frictionless flow of a perfect gas. It would not be appropriate, in these brief notes, to cover the detail but, remembering that the velocity of the gas at the rocket nozzle exit is the most important feature, application of basic principles can reveal that the exhaust velocity (which can be taken to be close to the specific impulse) is a function of combustion pressure ratio, combustion temperature and gas properties. That specific impulse should be so dependent is not surprising since the product of $C_F$ and $c^*$ is specific impulse I.

Given the dependence of specific impulse on various parameters as detailed, it is interesting to inquire into how sensitive I is to variations in these parameters.

Increasing the pressure ratio improves the specific impulse but over a value of about 40/1 the gains are marginal. There are other reasons for operating at pressure ratios greater than 40/1, but specific impulse increases are small for relatively large pressure ratio increases.

Increasing the combustion temperature raises specific impulse but there are associated practical disadvantages and limits to this procedure, as there are with increasing pressure.

### Nozzle Performance

The function of the nozzle in a rocket motor is to accelerate the propulsive gases to a high velocity in an expansion process. As has been discussed, a high pressure upstream of the nozzle is a necessary feature. One would readily expect a converging duct to be adequate for that purpose, however owing to a phenomenon known as 'choking', there is a limiting velocity to which the gas can be accelerated. This limiting velocity is the local velocity of sound, ie the acoustic velocity of the expanding gas at the exit plane of the convergent nozzle. Under these circumstances, the ratio of upstream pressure (the combustion pressure) to pressure at the exit plane is approximately 2 only. Since this is a very small portion of the typical pressure ratio available in a rocket motor, one must endeavour to make use of all (or nearly all) of the remaining available pressure ratio. The only way in which this remaining pressure drop can be employed is to provide a diverging section downstream of the exit area of the converging section to enable the flow to accelerate to a velocity greater than the local value of sonic velocity, at any plane. Such a process is acceleration to supersonic velocities. The need to provide such a shape to the nozzle is hardly possible to arrive at intuitively. But theory can be devised to show that a continuous flow passage which is to accelerate a subsonic flow to a supersonic flow must first converge and then diverge. Hence the characteristic shape of a rocket motor nozzle.

## The Solid Propellant Rocket Motor

### Shape of Motor

A solid propellant motor case usually has a cylindrical external form, as illustrated in Figure 2.2. This simple shape is convenient in several respects. It is generally a satisfactory shape for a pressure vessel, which the chamber must be; it is a fairly good shape for accommodating the desired burning surface area; aerodynamically the cylindrical shape is convenient; and for manufacturing, storing and transporting it is a generally good shape.

### Advantages of Solid Rockets

To the user the chief advantages of the solid rocket in missiles, are the avoidance of field servicing equipment, the straightforward handling and the easy firing, usually with simple electrical circuits. These features contrast clearly with the employment in the early days of liquid propellant engines, particularly those using cryogenic propellants, as will be seen in the later section on liquid propellants. The use of the packaged liquid-propellant rocket today, in the Lance system, is much more straightforward and is, practically, on a par with the use of a solid motor.

## Factors Affecting Performance

It was noted earlier in the text that, essentially, the solid motor consists of four components; they are the pressure vessel case, the nozzle, the combustible charge and the igniter. In practice, designing and making solid motors is much more complicated than this crude enumeration suggests. Considering first the propellant, ignoring for the present its composition, the shape of the surface at which burning must take place is a matter which requires very careful consideration. It can be seen from the cross-section of the typical solid motor in Figure 2.2 that the burning of the solid propellant at its exposed surface at a high pressure will generate gaseous products. These accelerate through the exhaust nozzle with a velocity at the exit plane of the order of 2000 m/s or more. Solid propellants in motors burn away at a definite rate and do not explode, so the thrust developed is proportional to the mass flow rate of the gases produced. Consequently, a large thrust requires a large mass flow.

While there is some scope for mass flow variation, by choice of the linear rate of regression of the burning surface of the propellant, the main variable at the disposal of the designer is the amount of burning surface area of charge that can be designed in to the relatively restricted space in a cylindrical pressure vessel.

For a large thrust there must be a large burning surface area in order to produce a large mass flow rate. The rapid consumption of propellant therefore tends to give rise to a large thrust for a short duration, typically from 10 milliseconds up to 3 or 4 seconds only. Conversely, small thrusts for long durations take place with small burning surface areas, giving the required low consumption rate. Long burning times could be from about 5 seconds to 100 seconds.

Within the case of a solid-propellant rocket motor the pressure level is strongly dependent on the ratio of the burning surface area of the propellant charge to the nozzle minimum cross-section area amongst other parameters.

Since most motors are designed to give nominally constant thrust, the propellant charge is described as homogeneous. When the propellant consists of a suitable mixture of fuel and oxidant, it is described as heterogeneous. In particular the two main ingredients of the former type are nitrocellulose and nitroglycerine; such a combination being frequently referred to as double-base propellant. The best known type of heterogeneous propellant consists of crystalline ammonium perchlorate as the oxidiser, one of a range of poly-merisable binders and, possibly, powdered aluminium also, as the fuel. This type is often referred to as composite propellant and is of a rubbery nature.

There is also a third type based on a combination of the double-base and composite types. This consists of ammonium perchlorate and powdered aluminium in a matrix of nitrocellulose/nitroglycerine. This combination is very energetic but suffers from the production of dense white smoke, as do most of the composite propellants.

In general double-base propellants are preferred for UK-designed missiles. While somewhat less energetic than the composite type, they are smoke-free in operation and can be made flash-free also. Their manufacture falls into two techniques – casting and extruding. Casting is usually reserved for large charges and for geometries impossible to extrude. Extrusion (see Glossary) of charges is confined to the smaller sizes, because there is a limit to the size of press that can be economically made and operated.

### Advantages and Disadvantages of Solid Propellant

A major advantage of solid propellant, compared with liquid propellant, is its high density; this is an asset in volume-limited designs. Another is its instant readiness. It is also chemically stable for several years. Finally, the basic materials are readily available, well tried and tested and already proved in service.

When compared with liquid propellant designs solid propellant motors do, of course, have some disadvantages. Typical solid propellant specific impulses are somewhat inferior to those of many liquid propellant combinations; there is a fundamental difficulty in varying thrust level on demand; smokey exhausts may be produced; radio signal attenuation is more severe; and performance is affected by variation in ambient temperature. However, their simplicity, ease of handling and superior reliability greatly outweigh their bad points. These factors account for the preponderance of solid motors in missiles.

### The Liquid Propellant Rocket Engine

As was mentioned earlier, the liquid propellant engine relies totally for its operation on a feed system since the propellants are stored outside the combustion chamber, unlike the solid propellant motor. In the initial stages of design of a typical bi-propellant engine, a decision must be made as to whether or not to pressurise the tanks in order to achieve propellant injection into the combustion chamber. The alternative to pressurising tanks is to employ pumps between tanks and combustion chamber; the obvious advantage of this is that the tanks need only be made to sustain ambient pressure (see Figure 2.3).

It has long been recognised that there is an upper limit to the size of pressurised tanks that can be employed because of the severe weight penalty associated with their construction. Hence, for large total impulses the so-called pressure feed system has to give way to the lighter turbopump system: this is employed in many satellite launching vehicles. For the smaller systems, in which UK GW market is primarily interested, there is a case for the pressurised tank system. It is a simpler system and should be more reliable. We shall therefore not discuss the turbopump system further but will expand a little on the details of the modern packaged liquid rocket concept, which features pressurisation of the propellant tanks during motor operation.

Assuming that the bi-propellant type of engine is under consideration, it has already been estabished that the pressurised tank feed system is the lighter. If in addition hypergolic propellants, in which oxidant and fuel ignite on contact, are employed, we have simple starting and ignition systems. Finally, if the propellants are pre-packed into their respective tanks, to avoid filling just before launch, another simplification is obtained. These are the characteristic features of the so-called packaged liquid rocket engine.

Considering the various aspects in turn briefly, the bi-propellant type is always preferred when high specific impulse is an essential requirement. Thus fuel and oxidant need to be tanked separately. The tanks are pressurised only during motor operation. The expulsion system may employ high pressure gas stored in bottles; an alternative is gas produced from a cool-burning solid propellant gas generator or a liquid mono-propellant. The gas acts on pistons or diaphragms, or directly, to force the propellants through their respective injectors into the combustion chamber. The injectors themselves may or may not be any more elaborate than simple holes in a plate. With self-igniting propellants, where liquid-phase mixing is desirable, the pattern of the holes will probably be designed to ensure that a stream of fuel impinges directly on a stream of oxidant.

Pre-packing the fuel and oxidant into their tanks, and sealing them until use, requires tank materials which are compatible with their contents. Considering the corrosive nature of some propellants this may not be achieved easily; so it creates storage problems.

Noting the relative simplicity of the pressurised tank feed system compared with the turbopump system and also noting the characteristic features, such as sealed tanks and hypergolic propellants in packaged liquid rocket engines, there still remains the following question. On what gounds would one choose a packaged liquid-engine rather than a solid propellant motor?

First, when volume is a problem, as in SAMs and AAMs, a packaged liquid engine has a large specific impulse and is competitive with most solid propellants. When the propellant system can take up more space, liquid propellant engines have an overall superior performance.

Perhaps the most important advantage provided by liquid propellants is the ease of control. Where missile trajectories require thrust modulation, control becomes very important and can not be provided by solid motors. Solid motors are confined to built-in pre-programmed thrust variations such as the simple two-level high-boost phase followed by a much longer low-thrust sustain phase. Additional advantages gained from liquid propellants are the wide temperature ranges they can sustain, in storage, their exhausts' low resistance to electromagnetic transmissions and their low smoke emission levels.

On the other hand, liquid propellants are more expensive and less reliable than solids, they often give off a toxic exhaust and the motors tend to be fragile.

Concluding this section on rockets, it is emphasised that there are very many practical aspects of design and development that make both solid and liquid rockets very special. For example, the high temperatures in the thrust chamber present great difficulties in the choice of materials and cooling techniques. The high pressures require the solution of stressing and weight problems. Long-term storage necessitates the development of propellants and tanks which will not deteriorate as time elapses. And above all, perhaps, both types must be safe for the user, reliable and as cheap as possible.

## Air-Breathing Engines

### Turbojets and Turbofans

The past few years have seen the development of new types of missile employing turbojets for propulsion. For example, there is the McDonnell Douglas Astronautics Harpoon anti-ship missile and the British Aerospace Sea Eagle anti-ship missile, the successor to Martel. In addition the long-range theatre/strategic Tomahawk or Air Launched Cruise Missile (ALCM) may employ either turbojet or turbofan. It seems likely that various additional projects involving turbojet propulsion may well be underway.

The Soviet Union has for many years employed air-launched anti-ship or bombardment missiles with aeroplane configurations. Certainly the early versions of these used turbojet propulsion and modern types may also do so. There can be little doubt that various weapon systems are under development in the USSR which will employ turbojet or even turbofan propulsion.

At this stage it is pertinent to ask under exactly what circumstances a turbojet or turbofan would be employed in missile propulsion. Tactical missiles, because of the developing ability of defenders to detect both airborne and seaborne launch platforms at greater ranges than hitherto, must be launched much further from their targets. In addition, to minimise the likelihood of detection, such missiles should be smaller and possibly faster than before. Since supersonic flight at low level tends to necessitate a large missile, there is much to be said for a moderate-to-high subsonic missile velocity. At the required ranges the low specific fuel consumption of the turbojet compares well with that of the rocket engine and is therefore a very important factor. Only when ranges become very large does the better specific fuel consumption of the turbofan give it favour over the turbojet.

There is a band of supersonic flight velocities around Mach 2.5 where the specific fuel consumptions of the ramjet and turbojet are comparable. At the lower end of the speed bracket, there are ranges at which the combined weight of power plant and fuel is approximately the same for the turbojet and ramjet installations. Thus, the final choice of propulsion unit may have to be made on other grounds. For example, its self-acceleration ability after air-launch at perhaps Mach 0.8, or its ability to undertake high g terminal manoeuvres, which necessitate an increase of thrust. A turbojet would probably fulfil those neds better than a ramjet; however, it is clear that for a missile flying at about Mach 2.5, there would have to be exceptionally good reasons for specifying a comparatively expensive turbojet rather than a cheaper ramjet.

The turbofan will probably not be used much in missile propulsion. Only for very long ranges or for great endurance, such as the loiter of a remotely piloted vehicle, will the extra complexity and cost of the turbofan be justified. The cruise missile is such a case.

## Performance Criteria

In judging the suitability of a turbojet or a turbofan for a missile's propulsion, one must use various performance parameters that can be calculated at the project stage. The main concerns are the magnitude of thrust required, the rate of consumption of fuel to give the thrust, the diameter and weight of the engine for the desired thrust and the weight of fuel for the required duration or range. Since, as was mentioned earlier, the forward speed of the engine through the air and the altitude of operation have important effects on the engine's performance, they also must be taken into account in assessing performance.

Foremost among the various possible performance parameters are specific fuel consumption and specific thrust.

### Specific Fuel Consumption

Specific fuel consumption (sfc) is a measure of the rate of fuel consumed per unit of thrust developed. This parameter is analogous to specific propellant consumption (spc) which is the reciprocal of specific impulse for the rocket motor. Direct comparisons between sfc for the air-breather and spc for the rocket motor are therefore possible. On rare occasions, a fuel specific impulse which is the reciprocal of sfc is met. Then fuel specific impulse for an air-breather can be compared with propellant specific impulse for a rocket motor.

### Specific Thrust

Specific thrust is defined as thrust developed per unit of air mass flow entering the engine. Occasionally, when comparisons are being made with rockets, it is referred to as air specific impulse. It is used as a criterion of engine size, and therefore also of engine weight, provided certain restrictions are applied, for a given thrust.

Restricting remarks to turbojets at this stage, before one can specify that a turbojet has a certain propulsive performance for a given application, one must choose an appropriate thermodynamic cycle. In order to do this, a parametric study must be undertaken. In this process the critical engine performance parameters are varied systematically in order to find the combination which gives the most suitable values of sfc, specific thrust, engine weight etc. for a 'design' flight condition. If the missile is required to operate at a substantially constant flight speed, altitude and thrust, this optimisation process will probably be adequate. If, in addition, the missile must operate at other flight conditions, calculations must be undertaken to determine the performance at those other conditions and assessments made to show whether the performance is adequate.

Apart from pure propulsion considerations, what is certain is that in missile propulsion one is seeking a simple, light, expendable engine. It should have a designed-in short life, excellent starting reliability, high g loading resistance, good inlet distortion resistance, probably a signature of low detectability and above all it should be reliable and offer value for money.

### Turbofans for Missile Propulsion

Having considered briefly the turbojet for missile propulsion, we can now examine the turbofan. It was pointed out earlier that the turbofan was conceived as a means of reducing specific fuel consumption by raising propulsive efficiency. This was achieved specifically for application in aircraft propulsion. In particular, the greater the ranges requiring to be flown the better is the case for reducing sfc, because, despite a likely increase in engine weight for a given thrust and a certain increase in diameter and therefore pod drag, the overall weight of engine and fuel can be reduced. The case in short range aircraft propulsion is much less strong and this is reflected in the modest by-pass ratios of around two compared with about five in engines employed in the wide-body long-range airliners.

In missile propulsion it is generally true that until recently, airborne missiles have not been required to fly ranges up to those comparable with medium range aircraft. Therefore the need to diminish sfc to maximise range has not necessarily been the prime requirement in choosing a propulsion unit for a missile. Availability, cost and reliability are very often the factors which finally govern the choice of propulsion unit. In addition, airborne missiles are small compared with medium or long-range aircraft, so the size of engine suitable for a typical missile is usually of a different order of magnitude compared with that for even a medium-sized aircraft. The consequence of this is that a small turbofan engine of missile size is not likely to be in existence. Consequently, a specific programme would be necessary to develop one. Technically a scaling-down exercise from existing aircraft designs is unlikely to be ideal.

### *Small Turbine Problems*

That last point highlights some of the difficulties inherent in producing a small turbine engine. Small turbo-components suffer from an intrinsic low level of efficiency compared with large ones. This is a consequence of both the governing internal aerodynamics and mechanical design constraints. Missile engines are mostly limited in diameter to something slightly less than the diameter of the missile body itself. In contemplating a turbofan under these circumstances, the situation is aggravated because the core of the turbofan is even smaller than a corresponding turbojet to develop the same thrust. This depresses potential compressor and turbine efficiencies even more, and has an adverse effect on the sfc. Mechanically the turbofan is likely to be more complex and expensive because a two-shaft configuration is virtually certain to be a feature in order to meet design limitations. Avoidance of the two-shaft configuration is probably only possible by the incorporation of a reduction gearbox between fan and compressor. Such a solution does not seem to be the best for an expendable engine.

It is fairly safe to predict that the turbofan will not be used extensively in missile propulsion, except possibly when the prime requirement is very long range or great endurance. Then its cost and complexity may be justified. The Tomahawk and ALCM appear to be in the former category. Optimisation of the turbofan cycle is rather more complex than that of the turbojet, However, in missile propulsion, as compared with long-range aircraft propulsion, moderate maximum cycle temperature, pressure ratio, and by-pass ratio and a two-shaft arrangement are the most likely turbofan characteristics. These conclusions arise from the certain prime requirements of smallness, cheapness and expendability. It is doubtful whether sfc will ever be the all-important feature of a missile engine.

## Intakes

Most of the preceding remarks about turbine engines have applied to subsonic missile applications. Subsonic engines invariably have Pitot intakes. This is essentially a forward facing hole in a carefully shaped duct, the function of which is to collect and decelerate the appropriate airflow quantity efficiently. Generally these intakes are able to provide adequate performance in terms of efficiency and stability over a range of subsonic velocities, if required to do so. While it is important that they meet these performance criteria so that the overall propulsive performance is adequate, they are not of such critical importance as intakes for high supersonic velocities of Mach 2 or more, which present very severe problems of efficiency and stability and off-design speed operation. In the next section, therefore, we shall discuss aspects of air intakes which particularly apply to supersonic missiles. As will now be understood, this topic is absolutely fundamental to the ramjet and will therefore provide a suitable lead-in to ramjets and ramrockets.

### Gas Dynamics of Intakes

When a Pitot intake is operating at a subsonic forward speed for which it is designed, the captured airstream is decelerated in a controlled, efficient manner with the minimum of disturbance and is presented to the next component, the compressor, in the case of a turbojet, at an increased static pressure and at the desired Mach number (see Figure 2.12a). The air which is not captured and is necessarily diverted around the intake lip is speeded up somewhat locally and rejoins the main airstream. The design of the camber of the outside of the intake is important because of the need to avoid accelerating the diverted air up to and beyond the local velocity of sound. If this happens, extra drag is incurred in the development of shock waves as the air inevitably slows down to mainstream velocity. This situation can be aggravated if the intake is subjected to an approaching airstream whose direction is not coincident with the axis of the intake. Then the intake is said to be operating at incidence. Such problems can usually be handled quite satisfactorily by the Pitot intake, provided forward speeds are subsonic.

If this simple intake is subjected to supersonic foward speeds a completely different airflow pattern is produced. A normal shock wave is formed ahead of, just on or inside the intake lip (see Fig 2.12b). For greatest efficiency the shock wave should occur at the lowest possible Mach number. It must therefore not be allowed to occur inside the intake but must either be ahead of or on the intake lip. Even assuming such advantageous operation of the propulsion unit, at flight mach numbers greater than about 1.5 the simple Pitot intake is unacceptably inefficient. Thus a missile which had a

supersonic portion in a largely subsonic flight plan would be adequately
served by a Pitot intake in the supersonic phase, provided the flight Mach
number was less than about 1.5. The intake is stable and is simple and cheap
to construct. It is therefore an attractive proposition for any subsonic missile.

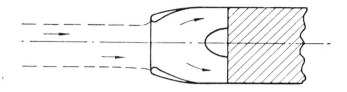

FIG. 2.12a  Pitot intake at subsonic forward speed

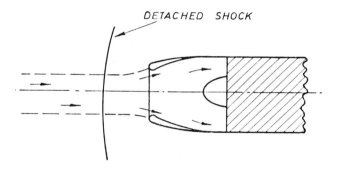

FIG. 2.12b  Pitot intake at supersonic forward speed

A missile which is wholly supersonic, say Mach 2 or more, must have an
intake so designed to be as efficient as possible throughout the flight. Such a
missile would not normally be designed for sustained speed at Mach numbers
less than 2. It has been established that the creation of the normal shock
upstream of the intake at such a Mach number results in a poor efficiency, so
the design must be such as to avoid the creation of the normal shock at the
flight speed. Such an intake is known as the external compression intake; an
axisymmetric type is illustrated diagrammatically in Figure 2.13.

The principle behind this configuration is one of slowing down the
supersonic airstream to a subsonic high pressure airstream in several stages
instead of in one stage through a normal shock. The mechanism by which
this can be done is the oblique shock, which is a weak form of shock wave
compared with the normal shock. As the flow is subjected to the oblique
shock, it is both turned and slowed down, but normally remains supersonic.
The principle of design incorporated into the type in the diagram is to create
a single oblique shock, then a single normal shock which is not particularly
intense, because it has occurred in a stream whose Mach number is much

less than the Mach number which occurs in free air (freestream Mach number). The overall effect is to collect and slow down the air to the desired subsonic velocity in a much more efficient manner than would be obtained by a normal shock alone occurring at freestream Mach number. This improvement is reflected in the high pressure of the air leaving the intake and flowing to the next component. It is normal to describe this as a good pressure recovery. Such a characteristic is essential for the efficient operation of a missile's propulsion unit at a sustained speed in excess of Mach 2. This observation is particularly true of the ramjet which relies totally on the intake to slow down the air efficiently, with a corresponding large rise in pressure. In a ramjet the intake is, in effect, the compressor.

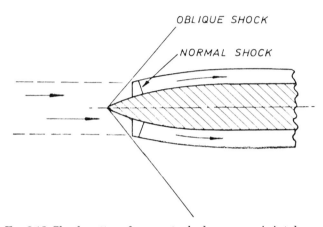

FIG. 2.13 Shock pattern for a centre-body supersonic intake

In the external compression intake, some of the compression takes place outside the lip of the intake. It is best operated at a single design flight speed. However it can operate satisfactorily over a narrow range of flight speeds and also when subjected to an oncoming flow at several degrees of incidence to the axis. If a missile were required to operate, say, from Mach 2 up to Mach 4, then it would not be ideal to operate the intake over such a wide speed range without incorporating variable geometry. Then, in the case of the axisymmetric type, for example, it would be desirable to have the capacity to move the centre-body axially to optimise the position of the oblique shock system with respect to the lip of the intake. In an expendable propulsion unit such a degree of complication is best avoided: so, to date, supersonic missiles sustained by air-breathing engines incorporate fixed geometry intakes and tend to operate over a narrow range of sustained flight speeds.

## Ramjets

Because of the relatively straightforward application of the solid propellant rocket motor in missile propulsion, the guided weapons industry has usually been reluctant to employ the ramjet engine, even when speed and range requirements have been well-suited to it. The consequence is that ramjet-propelled missiles are fairly rare, as the following brief but interesting history shows.

It was not until after the war that serious efforts were applied to ramjets for supersonic propulsion. Support from the military services in the United States for development programmes resulted in at least three ramjet-propelled missiles. Of these, the Navajo, a strategic airborne missile system was ultimately cancelled in favour of the Atlas, America's first intercontinental ballistic missile system. The Bomarc, a large surface-to-air system entered service in 1961 but was obsolescent by 1970. The Talos, a ship-launched area-defence surface-to-air weapon system entered service in 1959 and stayed in service until the early 1980s. In Great Britain, in the early 1950s, work started on the Bloodhound I continuing into the 1960s with the MK II and the start of the Sea Dart development. Other programmes failed to come to fruition.

Since then, in both America and Europe, interest in ramjets was confined to low-key research and there was a waning of interest in the practical applications of ramjets to missile propulsion. As far as tactical missiles are concerned, this decline was attributed primarily to the continuing suitability of the solid-propellant motor for the short ranges usually required. A secondary factor, frequently cited, was the unavoidable need of the ramjet for a booster motor or motors, resulting in a dual propulsion system, despite the fact that rocket-propelled missiles were often multi-stage vehicles or employed dual-thrust motors! Finally, the strategic intercontinental missile continued to be ballistic in nature and so there was no place for the ramjet in this category of missile.

What has led to the revival in the fortunes of the ramjet?. First and foremost, it can provide high speed and long range. These characteristics are acquiring ever-increasing importance for both defensive SAMs and offensive ASMs, AAMs and SSMs as detection techniques improve. For example, the long-range high-speed SAM offers the opportunity of a second interception if the first round is unsuccessful. Conversely, platforms launching ASMs or AAMs can stand off well outside enemy defences. The ramjet also offers benefits to the long-range low-altitude penetrator type of missile such as the next generation of anti-ship missile, for example, in terms of improved defence penetration (terminally powered manoeuvres), reduced mid-course vulnerability (high speed) and high kinetic energy at impact (high speed). Second, associated with the above changes in operational use, is a hardware advance in which the rocket booster and the ramjet sustainer are contained in a compact propulsive unit known as the integral rocket-ramjet. While this is regarded as a fairly novel concept in the West, it should be noted that the Soviet SA-6 Gainful missile employs an integral rocket ramjet and was deployed in about 1967.

## Ramjet Characteristics

The most important feature of the ramjet is its ability to provide high-speed propulsive thrust for a modest consumption of fuel. In addition, it is simply constructed, largely from sheet metal, and therefore, is cheap. These features alone merit consideration in matching a propulsion unit to a supersonic missile of medium or long range.

The ramjets basic operating principle was outlined earlier and is apparently straightforward. However, whereas a rocket motor's performance is almost completely independent of any atmosphere that may surround it, the ramjet's performance is influenced by the forward speed of the vehicle, the pressure recovery in the intake/diffuser, the incidence of the oncoming airstream to the axis and ambient pressure and temperature. These additional complications mean that analysis of ramjet performance over a range of speeds, heights and thrust levels is not straightforward.

The type of intake used for a supersonic air-breather has already been discussed at some length. One or two additional characteristics of intakes, and recent developments can be added here.

The symmetrical nose inlet of the type used in Sea Dart, as shown in Figure 2.13, is in general very satisfactory, but it does have several disadvantages. The ducting takes up a great deal of space; the propulsion unit gets in the way of other components; and the radar dish arrangements, which often form part of the system, are very restricted.

Alternatives are symmetrical arrangements of four side intakes near the engine at the rear, as in Figure 2.6b: a problem with this configuration is that some ducts will fail to scoop in air as the missile manoeuvres. A rear-mounted chin intake, as shown in Figure 2.6c, is simpler and efficient.

## Ramjet Performance

In the section on turbojet and turbofan performance it was said that to select a propulsion unit for a given task, an appropriate thermodynamic cycle would be chosen after carrying out a parametric study. In selecting a ramjet, a similar approach would be adopted, except that the velocity at which the missile engine has to operate may not be as closely defined at the outset as would be the case with, say, a subsonic turbojet. This is because the flight velocity of operation is absolutely fundamental to the performance of a ramjet. There may then be an opportunity to 'optimise' the flight velocity, since it is one of the major performance parameters. Rather than use maximum cycle temperature as an additional major performance parameter, in ramjet design-work it is normal to replace this with fuel-air ratio which is of greater practical significance. A secondary, but still very important parameter, which could be incorporated into these optimisation studies, is pressure recovery, which was defined in the introduction to this chapter. It is dependent on intake design, forward speed and the degree of incidence of the intake the freestream velocity. With a range of variables at his disposal, to enable them to assess the suitability of a particular combination of variables, the designer must use various performance parameters which are influenced by the choice of those variables and which can be calculated at this stage. Of primary importance are specific fuel consumption and the frontal area and weight of the engine.

Assuming that a missile is to be designed for a given speed, lift/drag and fuel mass fraction, then the range achievable is dependent on the sfc: the lower the sfc, the greater the range. The rocket motor performs badly on this basis because it must carry its oxidant in addition to its fuel. An air-breathing engine therefore has an inherent advantage. However, because the ram pressure ratio at subsonic and low supersonic speeds is small, the sfc of the ramjet is much inferior to that of the turbojet in that speed range. But around Mach 2 it is only marginally inferior to the turbojet while above about Mach 2.7 it is superior to it. There is thus a broad band of flight speed from about Mach 2 to Mach 4+ (see later remarks on speed limit) in which the lighter ramjet really comes into its own (see Figure 2.11).

Since a supersonic missile of a given all-up-weight suffers from a high drag compared with a subsonic missile, there is a need for a fairly large propulsive unit. This may well result in an additional drag penalty, particularly for a stub-mounted unit (eg as in the Bloodhound installation). Fortunately, the ramjet compares well with the turbojet in terms of thrust developed per unit of frontal area and so is quite well matched to a supersonic vehicle in this respect. It is also much superior to a comparable turbojet in terms of thrust developed per unit of engine weight. A brief consideration of the mechanical construction of the turbojet and ramjet will serve to emphasise this point.

Off-setting the above points, at speeds above about Mach 4.5, even at great height, the ram temperature rise has an adverse effect on the structural strength of the ramjet. Also, too low a pressure in the combustion chamber at some combinations of altitude and speed can make combustion inefficient. At near hypersonic speeds (Mach 4.5+) a phenomenon called disociation may depress combustor performance. And finally, at great heights, despite high speeds, the missile aerodynamics may be adversely affected by the low dynamic pressure.

On the basis of the outcome of the parametric study, a cycle will be chosen. This ultimate selection of governing performance parameters such as, for example, cruise speed, altitude, thrust, weight fuel consumption, results in a paper design being produced. These performance parameters then give the design point performance. Even a ramjet propelled missile after boosting does not operate at precise, unchanging velocity, height, fuel/air ratio etc, but must vary its performance to suit the missile flight trajectory. So it is necessary for the ramjet engine maker to provide numerous performance graphs showing, for example, the manner of variation of thrust and sfc with speed and height at several values of fuel/air ratio. A typical set of performance curves for a ramjet whose nominal design point speed is Mach 2.5 at an altitude of 11 km is shown in Figure 2.14

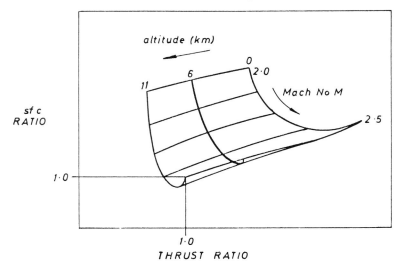

FIG. 2.14  Variation of thrust and specific fuel consumption with flight
Mach number and altitude for a given ramjet engine

This performance map indicates that, as the forward speed of the engine increases, so does the thrust, while the sfc decreases. These trends are in general true but this over-simplified picture is in fact complicated by performance variations. They result from throttled operation, which reduces the fuel/air mixture ratio and operation with the intake subjected to an asymmetric approaching air flow. More performance restrictions arise from unstable operation at too low a forward speed or from too low a pressure in the combustion chamber at adverse combinations of altitude and forward speed. Perhaps it should be mentioned however that in matching a fixed-geometry ramjet to a missile's trajectory every effort is made, consistent with meeting operational requirements and economic disciplines, to subject the ramjet to as little variation as possible from its nominal design condition. Such a restricted envelope of operation should result in a simpler, cheaper and more reliable engine.

### Solid Fuel Ramjet

The mention of simplicity and cheapness in the preceding paragraph provides a suitable lead-in to a brief exposition of the solid fuel ramjet. The general peformance characteristics discussed so far have been for the conventional hydrocarbon liquid fuel ramjet. An alternative configuration has attracted some attention in recent years. The solid fuel ramjet should not be confused with the ramrocket which is discussed in some detail presently. The solid fuel ramjet is illustrated in Figure 2.15.

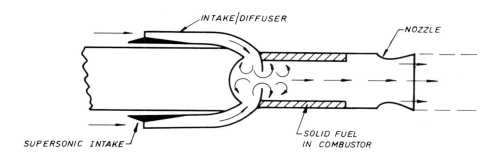

FIG. 2.15 Solid fuel ramjet with side intakes

The conventional liquid fuel ramjet uses standard turbojet combustion techniques: kerosine, usually, is pumped from tanks and carefully metered to the combustor. The solid fuel ramjet, on the other hand, employs a solid charge of fuel cast into the combustor. Once ignited, the fuel is ablated from the surface of the solid fuel and in the fuel port is partially burned in the air flowing through from the intake. The fuel surface regresses in a radial direction (as in a radial-burning solid-propellant rocket motor) and so the endurance of ramjet operation is governed by the thickness and regression rate of the fuel layer. Since the regression rate is influenced by the pressure within the fuel port and the air through-flow rate, which are both influenced by flight conditions, ie altitude, lateral acceleration and Mach number, the fuel/air ratio is a dependent variable not amenable to active control. It would seem, therefore that the performance of the solid-fuel ramjet is intimately tied up with the missile trajectory, a feature which may narrow the range of applications. A variant of the type illustrated is the bypass design which may be a more practical missile propulsion unit in that it provides a better combustion efficiency and an increased duration of operation.

## Ramrocket

The ramrocket is a hybrid which also employs a solid fuel but operates on a different principle. Reference to the diagrammatic figure below will help.

The principle of operation is straightforward. There is a solid propellant gas generator which is constructed like a conventional solid propellant rocket motor. After conventional ignition by a pyrotechnic igniter, the high-temperature fuel-rich gas stream generated within the gas generator is fed into the combustor. Here spontaneous ignition occurs when the ram air

mixes with the hot fuel-rich gas. The solid propellant charge differs from a
normal composite charge because it has a very small proportion of oxidiser.
Once ignited, the gas generator will operate until propellant exhaustion and
so potential flame-out, a perennial problem with liquid fuel ramjets, cannot
occur. This is a particularly important feature in a missile: its manoeuvrability requirements may result in the air approaching the intake at perhaps
$10^0$ of incidence. In a liquid fuel ramjet the disturbance to the air flow to the
combustor could easily cause a flame-out.

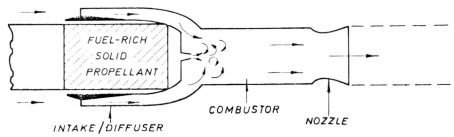

FIG. 2.16 Solid propellant ramrocket with side intakes

In terms of specific impule alone, the typical ramrocket with a medium-energy
solid propellant is somewhat inferior to the hydrocarbon liquid fuel ramjet.
Even a high-energy type with a high proportion of boron, which has a high
caloric value, is still somewhat inferior. This is a consequence of the propellant
being partly oxidiser and of the combustion efficiency in the main combustor.
However, the density of a boron-type gas generator propellant is about twice
that of kerosine and the product of specific impulse and propellant density is
then significantly greater for the former than the latter.

In a volume-limited design the high density feature could be important. A
drawback of the high-energy boron propellant (and medium-energy com-
posites with metal additives) is the smoke signature. Operational requirements
may necessitate no visible trail. Another more important disadvantage is the
difficulty of varying the magnitude of the thrust. Apart from very simple
applications, in many missiles with a ramjet engine there is likely to be a
need to vary thrust level in response to changes in altitude, speed and,
possibly, terminal manoeuvres. This task is much more difficult for a
ramrocket than for a conventional ramjet burning liquid fuel.

To vary the flowrate of the gas from the gas generator, the ratio of nozzle throat
area to propellant burning surface area must be altered. This alters the gas
generator combustion pressure and hence the rate of production of propellant
gases. In practice, the aim is to achieve the variation by reducing or increasing
the gas generator nozzle throat area by perhaps installing a translating plug in
the response to these area changes is, in general, unsatisfactory. Whatever
technique an engine maker may choose to incorporate into an engine, one can
be certain that the development of a satisfactory system will be very difficult.

This unfortunate difficulty associated with the ramrocket is recognised as a fundamental weakness. It may be that as a consequence, as hinted before, the solid propellant ramrocket will be confined to applications where thrust variation is not high on the list of priorities. In this form, therefore, the type could well turn out to be of simple design, cheap to produce, highly reliable in operation and easy to handle. Thus the liquid fuel ramjet, with its expensive fuel control system, pump, valves and tank, will probably continue to the best choice for a missile required to fly a trajectory requiring close control of the propulsive thrust.

### *Boosting*

It would not be appropriate to finish this section on ramjets without mentioning the methods of boosting on which ramjets are totally dependent.

Until a few years ago, ramjet-propelled vehicles were always boosted up to a speed close to their cruising speed by a rocket motor or motors. Typically, in a matter of 3 or 4 seconds, the boosters accelerate the vehicle to Mach 2 and then are jettisonned. The ramjet engine is ignited before the end of boost and so, at boost motor termination, there is a smooth take-over by the ramjet as it is fuelled up to the required thrust level. Provided there are no restrictions on the overall volume of the missile, this system of add-on boosters is very satisfactory, except that the added weight of the booster motor itself, in addition to the missile, has to be accelerated. Two configurations are generally in use: they are the wrap-around (Figure 2.17a) and the tandem (Figure 2.17b).

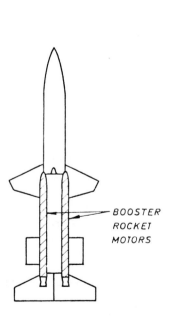

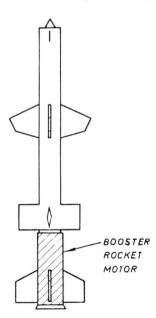

FIG. 2.17a  Ramjet-propelled missile with wrap-around booster rocket motors

FIG. 2.17b  Ramjet-propelled missile with tandem booster rocket motor

Where there are limitations on the total volume of the missile, it is advantageous to integrate the booster motor into the ramjet itself. This is called the integrated rocket ramjet (Figure 2.18).

In this concept, a dual-purpose combustor is employed for greater volumetric efficiency. The combustor is loaded with a solid propellant booster charge. In addition, because the booster propellant burns at a pressure much greater than the ramjet heat a specially inserted smaller nozzle is employed during a boost period. At the same time, the inlet or inlets are sealed with covers. At the end of the boost phase, the boost nozzle is ejected and the inlet covers are blown in allowing ram air to enter the combustor, which now undertakes its

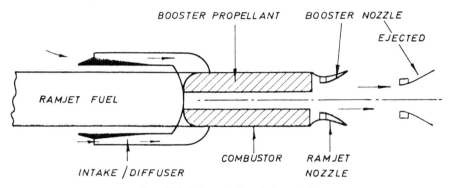

FIG. 2.18 Integrated rocket ramjet

second role, and to mix with fuel. The fuel may be liquid or gaseous depending on whether the basic design is conventional liquid fuel ramjet or solid propellant ramrocket respectively (see Figure 2.16). Since this integrated design avoids the need for a separate, jettisonable booster, it may well make possible a missile with only 60 - 70% of the volume of a comparable ramjet with a separate booster motor.

Among various development problems associated with this design, it should be noted that probably the most crucial phase of the operation of a propulsion system incorporating the integral booster is the transition from rocket boost to ramjet sustain. There must be the minimum of delay between end of boost and start of sustain in role to avoid excessive deceleration of the missile and the risk of it not even reaching the desired operating condition.

### Summary of Motor Uses

It is not possible to match the characteristics of motors to specific missile types, except possibly with the exception of air-breathers. The almost total versatility of the solid propellant motor precludes such a possibility. However the following table briefly indicates the typical areas of appliction of the various types with accompanying examples.

| Type of Motor | Type of Missile | Example |
|---|---|---|
| Solid propellant rocket | ATGW (light, medium, heavyweight) | LAW, MILAN, Swingfire |
| | AAGW (short, medium, long range) | Magnic, Skyflash, Phoenix |
| | SAGW (very low, low, medium/ high level) | Blowpipe, Rapier, Patriot |
| | ASGW | Martel, Maverick |
| | A Ship GW (short, medium/long range) | Sea Skua, Exocet |
| | SSGW (strategic, ballistic) | Polaris, Minuteman |
| | SSGW (strategic, cruise) | Pershing |
| Turbofan engine | SSGW (strategic, cruise) | Tomahawk, ALCM |
| Turbojet engine | SSGW (tactical, cruise, subsonic) | Harpoon |
| | ASGW (tactical, cruise, subsonic) | Sea Eagle, Harpoon |
| Ramjet engine | SAGW (medium/long range, high level, supersonic) | Bloodhound, Sea Dart |
| | A Ship GW (medium/long range, supersonic) | ANS |
| | ASGW (medium/long range, supersonic) | ASMP |
| Liquid rocket engine | SSGW (tactical, ballistic) | Lance |

## The Future

It can be stated confidently that in missile propulsion, up to the year 2000 at least, the solid propellant rocket motor will retain its predominant position.

First, assuming that strategic ballistic missiles remain deployed, there is no prospect of an alternative to the multi-stage solid propellant rocket vehicle. Second, in theatre weapons of a ballistic nature, a similar situation will prevail. Third, in the short-range air-to-air and anti-tank roles it is anticipated that the compactness, cheapness and reliability of the solid propellant rocket motor will justify its retention almost indefinitely.

As far as tactical ballistic missiles are concerned the situation is less clear-cut. Various NATO countries operate the Lance missile system which uses bi-propellant liquid rocket engine propulsion. It remains to be seen what system ultimately replaces Lance.

The theatre and strategic range has recently been invaded by a non-ballistic weapon, the subsonic cruise missile. That such missiles are now practicable is due primarily to advances in guidance techniques and progress in the design and making of lightweight expendable turbojects and turbofans. As defensive measures to these weapons improve, there may be a move towards supersonic versions of cruise missiles, but such a trend is thought to be doubtful on the grounds of the immense development costs.

However, there is increasing interest in air-breathing propulsion for supersonic tactical missiles. After years of stagnation in this area, there is now a demand for extending the range of air-to-air, surface-to-air, air-to-surface and anti-ship missiles while obtaining or maintaining supersonic velocities: these are sometimes required at low level. The ramjet and ramrocket have therefore undergone a kind of re-birth and have emerged in several interesting configurations. There is still no sign of such missiles with high-level speeds greater than about Mach 4 entering service, so it can be safely concluded that the ramjet-propelled hypersonic missile with a speed of Mach 5+ is still a long way. Interest in air-breathing propulsion systems for missiles has rarely been so intense.

Finally, apart from the Lance missile, no application for the packaged-liquid rocket engine as a main missile propulsion unit does appear to exist at present. This no doubt is due, among other reasons, to there being no vehicle which can make use of the packaged liquid engine's main attribute, which is an ability to provide a wide range of thrust level, on demand, over short and medium ranges.

# 3.
# Electrical Power Supplies

In any guided weapon system the greater part of the electrical power is generated and consumed on the ground, the ship, or the aircraft from which the missile is launched and controlled. This chapter is not concerned with such electrical supplies but only with those carried on board the missile itself.

## The Requirement

The Operational Requirements are very simply stated. They are

A VERY SHORT ACTIVE LIFE. Typical short flight missiles for ATGW or SAGW systems have flight times of less than 20 seconds. Such a short life makes difficulties in the provision of an efficient lightweight electrical power supply (EPS). The longer flight times of the cruise missile demand an EPS which can be satisfied by more familiar methods.

A VERY LONG PERIOD OF STORAGE WITHOUT ATTENTION. A storage life of up to ten years is desirable.

IMMMEDIATE AVAILABILITY ON FIRING. The EPS must be fully operational within a period of about one second or less after activating the weapon and before it leaves the launcher.

HIGH RELIABILITY. The EPS must match the reliability of all other components in the missile.

SMALL WEIGHT AND SIZE. The reduction in weight and size of modern electronic circuits has not been accompanied by a pro rata reduction in weight and size of their power supplies. Unfortunately, the basic principles of energy storage are against such dramatic improvements and the EPS must be critically designed if it is not to become an unacceptably large part of the total load.

### Electrical Requirements

The electrical power requirement of a typical missile is for electronic circuits only. Exceptionally electrical power is used to move control surfaces. (Examples of this are in EXOCET, HARPOON, MARTEL).

Compared with early designs, the modern weapon has become smaller and the improved efficiency of modern electronic circuits has resulted in quite modest demands for electrical power. Typical power requirements are 100 to 150 watts at 28 volts d.c. but, if powerful radars or electrically operated control surfaces are used, the power demand may rise into the kW range.

The energy requirement of the EPS naturally depends on the flight time. Short flight missiles have a requirement measured in fractions of a watt-hour but the more recent introduction of long flight cruise missiles now may require energies of kilowatt hours.

## Available Sources of Electrical Energy

Electrical Energy does not occur naturally in any convenient form and must invariably be converted from another form of energy. The diagram in Figure 3.1 shows the available process by which this may be achieved.

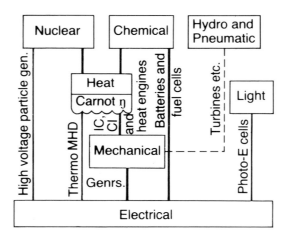

FIG. 3.1 Sources of electrical energy

Of the various possibilities shown, most have been considered but rejected as impractical for missiles.

Nuclear power could be used in some forms of missile in a manner similar to that used in satellites. Although capable of high power outputs, it requires extensive auxiliary equipment and poses logistic and safety problems.

Solar energy has obvious applications in space weapons systems but not in the missile. Its conversion requires large area collecting surfaces exposed to sunlight.

Energy stored in compressed gas has been used for short flight control surface actuation (SKYFLASH) but not for the generation of electrical energy.

Magnetohydrodynamic (MHD) generation uses the principle of passing a fluid conductor (rocket efflux) through a magnetic field to generate a voltage. Much investigation has been carried out with a view to using the propulsion blast tube of a missile for this purpose. Although attractive for long flight boost-sustain motors there are many problems which have not yet been solved.

Chemical energy may be used in two ways. The heat of reaction may be used to drive an engine or turbine and the mechanical energy thus obtained to drive an electromagnetic generator. If the main propulsion of the missile incorporates a turbo-jet or turbo-fan engine, a direct mechanical driven may be taken from this to the electrical generator. An even simpler method of converting some of the main propulsion energy into electrical form is to use a ram-air turbine driven by the forward motion of the missile through the atmosphere.

The second conversion from chemical energy depends on choosing a reaction which can take place electrochemically in a battery or a fuel cell. The conversion from chemical to electrical energy is direct, avoiding the intermediate form of heat with its inherent low efficiency of conversion to another form. Unfortunately, although more efficient, the specific energies of most electrochemical reactions are particularly low compared with those of the combustion of typical fuels such as petrol and kerosene.

In summary, the choice of the source of the electrical energy for a guided missile is currently chemical energy. The decision that remains to be made is whether to use direct conversion in a battery or to use a combustion reaction and an electrochemical generator.

## The Choice Between Batteries and Generators

Most well known electrochemical batteries are quite unsuitable for use in missiles but, before looking at this problem in detail, we should consider the general principles of choice. Weight is a very important consideration and, from this point of view, we may choose between batteries and generators for a given type of missile.

The graph, Figure 3.2 on page 46 shows the relative weights of an ideal battery and generator system for a given power requirement plotted against time. The turbo-generator will theoretically run for ever, given a supply of fuel, but the battery weight is directly proportional to the stored energy. The battery appears to be an obvious choice for short flight times but any practical battery has a lower performance at high rates of discharge. Depending on the type of battery the practical curves may well be as shown in Figure 3.3.

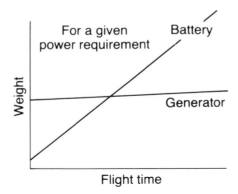

FIG. 3.2 Relative weights of ideal battery and generator systems

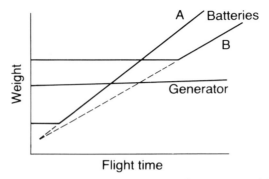

FIG. 3.3 Practical curves showing battery and generator weights for a
short flight time

At the other end of the time scale, the very long flight times of cruise missiles
suggest the choice of a generator and preferably a generator not requiring
fuel (Figure 3.4).

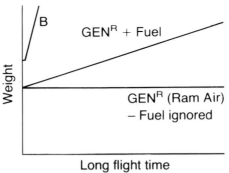

FIG. 3.4 Practical curves showing battery and generator weights
for a long flight time

It is not strictly correct to ignore the fuel required by an engine take-off or a ram-air drive. Both add an extra load to the main propulsion systems, albeit a very small one. A typical missile electrical load is considerably less than 1% of the engine output power and thus it is reasonable to assume that the extra fuel to be carried for the generator is not significant.

If a separate hot-gas generator is used to drive the turbine, the fuel required for this purpose is separately contained and burnt and the extra weight associated solely with the EPS must now be counted.

## A Method of Comparison of Batteries at Various Rates of Discharge

It has already been mentioned above that the energy delivered by a battery diminishes at high rates of discharge. This is because of internal losses in the cells which increase with the rate of discharge. Figure 3.5 shows a plot of Energy delivered in watt-hours against Power in watts for a particular type and size of battery.

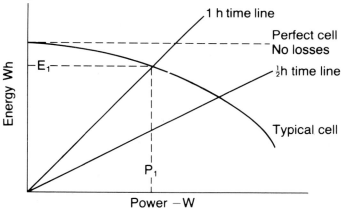

FIG. 3.5 Energy in watt-hours v. power in watts

It can be seen that, on such a graph, a straight line drawn through the origin has a slope of Energy/Power which is Time. The Time Line intersects the battery characteristic at a point where the delivered energy and the discharge power (as read from the axes) are those for the full discharge of the battery in that particular time. Thus, for the case shown in Figure 3.5, the battery will discharge in exactly one hour at the rate of $P_1$ watts, the total energy delivered being $E_1$ watt-hours.

Other time lines may be drawn and the performance compared at various times of discharge.

This now leads to the comparison of one type of battery with another. In order that comparisons may be made on a basis of weight, the values of

energy and power are divided by the weight of the battery. Such values are
known as *Specific Energy* (in Wh/kg) and *Specific Power* (in W/kg). These
values when plotted, as shown in Figure 3.6, can be compared with those of
another type of battery. The time lines are unaffected by the re-scaling of the
diagram and may be used as before.

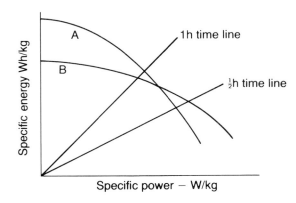

FIG. 3.6 Specific energy v. specific power

In order to present this information more compactly over a wide range of
values derived from a number of different batteries of varying performance,
the graph may be plotted with logarithmic scales. The time lines will now all
be of the same slope but can be used in the same way. Figure 3.7 shows a
graph of this type plotted for a number of well known batteries.

Such a graph may now be used to estimate and compare the weights of
different types of battery required for a particular electrical load over a given
time of discharge.

In most applications of batteries the discharge time is of the order of hours
and interest centres on those with high specific energies in this region. High
rates of discharge or high specific powers are not so important here although
all batteries are obviously limited in specific power and show a marked
deterioration in performance as this limit is approached.

For typical short flight missile applications, with discharge times of less
than a minute, the interest moves to those batteries best capable of high
specific powers. Figure 3.7 shows clearly that conventional types of battery
are in many cases quite unable to operate satisfactorily in this region.
Batteries specially designed for the purpose have evolved and Figure 3.8
shows the superior performance of:

▶ Thermal batteries.

▶ Silver-zinc Reserve batteries.

These batteries are described in the next section.

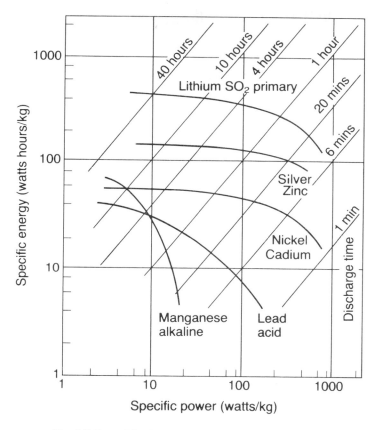

FIG. 3.7 Logarithmic plot of specific energy v. specific power

## Batteries Suitable for Short-Flight Times

The requirement for very high rates of discharge calls for cells with liquid electrolytes having a high state of ionisation. Dry cells are clearly unsuitable, as is shown by the characteristic for the Manganese-Alkaline cell in Figure 3.7. Lead-acid and Nickel-Cadmium cells show a progressive improvement in performance but it was the Silver-Zinc cell that first appeared to offer a solution to the problem. Whilst clearly capable of high rates of discharge, the silver-zinc battery in its normal form has some very undesirable features. It cannot be stored for long periods without deterioration, its useful storage life being of the order of weeks rather than years. Its performance at low temperatures is poor. These problems have been overcome by producing the battery in Reserve form.

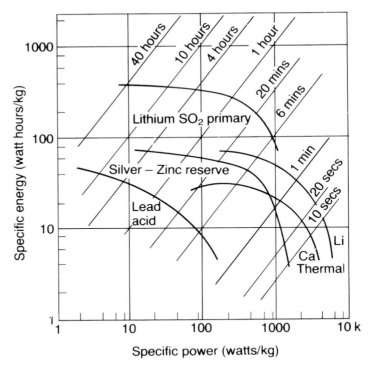

FIG. 3.8 Comparative performance of thermal batteries and
silver-zinc reserve batteries

## The Automatically Activated Silver-Zinc Reserve Battery

The silver-zinc cell uses the oxidation reaction:

$$Zn + AgO + H_2O \rightleftharpoons Ag + Zn(OH)_2$$

the electrolyte being an aqueous solution of potassium hydroxide. The cell voltage is 1.5V.

The reserve cell is assembled dry with the electrolyte stored in a separate reservoir. In this form a battery may be stored for some years without deterioration. When the battery is required for use, an electric squib is fired and the electrolyte is forced into the battery. In some designs the electrolyte is heated by a pyrotechnic mixture on its way into the battery. Activation times of less than one second can be achieved. Two designs of this type of battery are shown in Figures 3.9 and 3.10.

As can be seen from Figure 3.8, this type of battery has a specific power of about 1 kW per kg and is probably at its best when applied to missiles having flight times of greater than one minute. It is used in a number of U.S. missiles (e.g. PHEONIX, HARPOON and ICBM's), EXOCET, and in the Anglo-French MARTEL where it provides power up to 2 kW for several minutes.

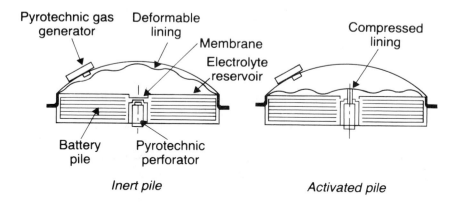

FIG. 3.9  The Saft (UK) auto-activated pile type silver-zinc battery

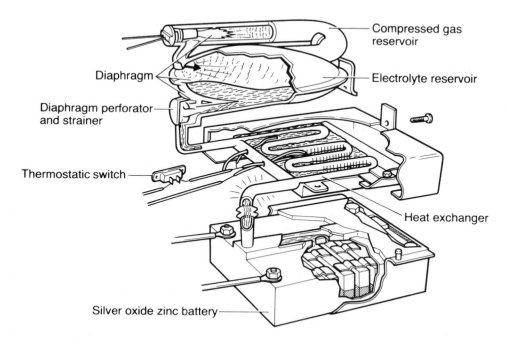

FIG. 3.10  Schematic view of the PS-502 chemically heated battery (USA)

### The Thermal Battery

The Thermal Battery is a reserve type in which the electrolyte, instead of being separated from the active electrodes, remains inert throughout years of storage in a solid non-ionised form. When the battery is required for use, it is activated by raising it to a temperature well above the melting point of the electrolyte. The hot molten electrolyte is now strongly ionised of the order of ten times that of acid or alkali electrolytes and the cells are capable of very high rates of discharge.

The electrolyte commonly used is a eutectic mixture of lithium and potassium chlorides. It is solid and chemically and electrochemically inert at room temperature but melts and becomes highly conductive at $352^0$C. Thermal activation is by built-in pyrotechnic heat sources fired by an electric squib and the electrolyte can be melted in a few tenths of a second in small battery sizes. Strongly reacting metals such as calcium, magnesium and lithium may be oxidised in such cells by chromates or sulphides and the resultant high activity gives high specific powers and the high cell voltages.

Early cells of this type were made with calcium anodes and calcium chromate cathodes i.e.

$$Ca \,|\, LiCl + KCl \,|\, CaCrO_4$$

Such batteries were fitted to many short flight missiles prior to the '80s. They have proved their stability in storage and samples of batteries from batches manufactured in 1960 discharged today show no deterioration in performance. However, due to parasitic reactions, the active life of these batteries is reduced and they are at their best when used for short flight times. See Figure 3.8 and also Figure 3.11 showing their construction.

The calcium thermal battery has now been superceded by batteries using lithium anodes. Over the last decade two types have evolved. One type uses lithium metal, molten at the battery operating temperature but immobilised using a special anode design, the other uses solid lithium alloy anodes. The electrolyte is a eutectic mixture of lithium halides (LiC1/LiBr/LiF), having a melting point of $430^0$C. The cathode is iron disulphide. The cell description is

$$Li \,|\, LiCl + Li\,Br + LiF \,|\, FeS_2$$

The working temperature is between 700 - $500^0$C, considerably higher than the old calcium cells. The temperature is raised by electrically fired pellets of gas-less thermite. Activation times are of a few tenths of a second to one or two seconds depending on the battery size and design. Figure 3.8 shows the improved performance of lithium thermal batteries. With a maximum specific power of about 5 kW/kg and a maximum specific energy of about

60 Wh/kg, the active life can vary between a few seconds up to about one hour. Storage life-times are expected to be as good as the calcium cells and accelerated life tests have confirmed these expectations.

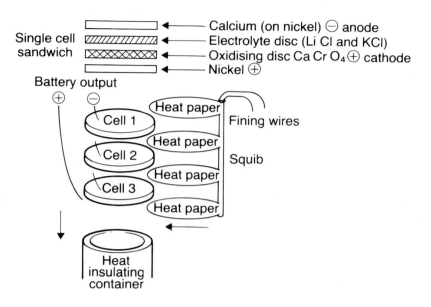

FIG. 3.11 Construction of a thermal cell

Today the great majority of all short flight missiles use thermal batteries. The use of lithium in the past ten years has reduced the size of these batteries to as little as one-tenth of that of earlier designs using calcium.

Lithium thermal batteries are now contenders for the demands of the longer flight missiles such as HARPOON and EXOCET. When these missiles were designed, their requirements were clearly best served by silver-zinc batteries. The longer active life and the improved performance of the lithium thermal battery now make it suitable for this type of missile. The high cost of silver-zinc batteries together with their poor low temperature performance may well influence a change here.

## Batteries for Long-Flight Missiles

The silver-zinc reserve battery, already discussed above, has a possible active life of several hours only limited by the inevitable internal short circuits of a reserve battery of this type. It has been used for a number of IBCMs.

More recent developments again using the metal lithium are now suggesting more attractive alternative battery EPS for these longer flight-times.

### The Lithium/Sulphur Dioxide Primary

This battery has been commercially available for some years and appears attractive from the characteristic shown in Figure 3.8.

The reaction between lithium metal and sulphur dioxide takes place in a non-aqueous organic solvent (such as acetonitrile) which is saturated with the sulphur dioxide. The internal pressure is about 3 atmospheres at normal temperature and rises to about 30 atmospheres at 100°C. The cells must clearly be very well sealed and are vented at 30 atmospheres. High rates of discharge are possible, up to 1 kW/kg at the 6 minute rate and the temperature range from –50°C to +70°C. Cell voltage is 2.8 - 2.9V. The construction is shown in Figure 3.12.

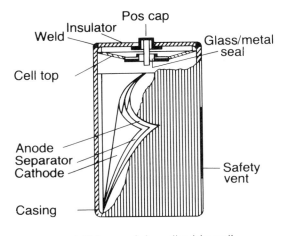

Lithium sulphur dioxide cell

FIG. 3.12 Lithium sulphur dioxide cell

The shelf life of the cells is good. It is claimed that less than 10% of capacity is lost during a five year period at room temperature. The fact remains that this is not a reserve cell. If installed in a missile, it is active and some form of isolation is needed to keep it from discharging during storage. There is also a problem due to passivisation during storage. This is the formation of a thin non-conducting film over lithium anode. It disappears once discharge begins but may delay full discharge after long periods of storage at low temperature.

### The Lithium/Thionyl Chloride Reserve

The problem of passivisation is avoided by any reserve system as is the need for isolation. The Lithium/Thionyl Chloride (Li-SOCl$_2$) cell is currently manufactured in reserve form and has a number of defence applications. Low rate primary cells of this couple have extremely high specific energies of over

600 Wh/kg but at higher rates and in a reserve battery this figure must come down to be comparable with the Li-SO$_2$ primary. Even then it has a specific energy about four times that of the silver-zinc reserve battery at the 1 h rate (see Figure 3.8).

A lithium-thionyl reserve battery may well replace the silver-zinc reserve in future long-flight systems and it is the only available battery to offer a serious challenge to the use of generators in long-flight missiles.

## Electrical Generators for Missiles

The electrical output of all rotating generators is directly proportional to speed and we should expect to find very high speed machines in missiles. The highest power densities and the most rugged and simple rotors capable of very high speed can only be achieved by alternators. Such machines can have no sliding contacts and must therefore be of the inductor or permanent magnet rotor type.

### Drives for High Speed Alternators

A simple solution bleeds off the hot gas from the main motor. This method was used in VIGILANT, a short-flight anti-tank missile, but is not regarded favourably because of severe contamination of filters. The provision of a gas generator removes any dependency on motor duration and allows the EPS to be operative before the motor lights: both liquid and solid propellant gas generators are used. Because of the considerable dead weight of the gas generator, the turbine and the alternator, this type of EPS is at a disadvantage when compared with high power density batteries for short flight times. For longer flight times, so long as the effective energy density of the fuel is considerably greater than that of the competing battery, the advantage of lighter weight will apply to the generator system.

It can be seen that, for very long flight times, the energy density of the fuel, modified by the appropriate conversion efficiencies and the necessary proportional weight of the fuel tank, is in direct comparison with the energy density of the battery system. With the availability of longer life reserve batteries based on lithium, the advantages of gas turbine alternators are no longer clear. See Figure 3.13.

### Drives from Main Engine or Ram Air

If, however, the drive for the alternator is taken from a turbofan or turbojet main engine or if a ram air turbine drive is used the consideration of fuel is unnecessary. The extra main fuel required to power the alternator is negligible compared with that required for propulsion. Now the alternator drive is free and the energy density of the system becomes higher as the flight time increases. See Figure 3.13. This advantage is not without qualification as we must now consider the time just prior and just after launch when the main engine may not be up to full speed or where the missile has not yet reached the speed to give the ram air drive. This period will have to be covered by a separate launch-phase power supply such as a thermal battery.

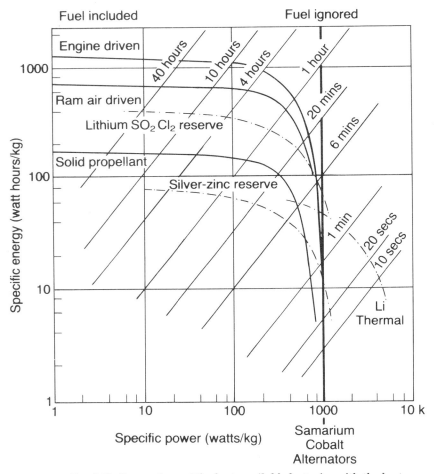

FIG. 3.13 Comparison of the best available batteries with the best available generator systems

Figure 3.13 makes a comparison of the best available batteries with the best available generator systems. It is convenient to show the generator on the same plot as has been used for batteries showing specific energy against specific power. It can be seen that a separately driven gas turbo-alternator cannot compete with a lithium battery but the main engine or ram air driven alternators become competitive at a flight time of about 20 minutes even if the extra weight of main engine fuel is taken into account.

## Types of Alternator

At the very high speeds demanded by the need for the highest possible power density and also to match the efficient speeds of small turbine drives, it becomes quite impractical to use a conventional design of alternator. Speeds of 20,000 to 80,000 rev/min are typical and necessitate simple rugged rotors carrying no windings and requiring no sliding contracts.

## The Inductor Alternator

Here the rotor consists of a simple bar or a toothed wheel which switches the magnetic flux from one path to another in the stator. Figure 3.14 shows the machine in its simplest form. The external flux path of the permanent magnets is carried by the bar rotor. As the rotor moves from one diagonal position to the other, the flux through the armature windings on the stator is reversed. A continuous reversal of flux linking the armature windings produces an alternating e.m.f. A complete cycle of a.c. is generated in the movement of one tooth pitch. Frequency will be tN/60 Hz where t = no. of teeth and N = rev/min. The six tooth rotor shown in Figure 3.15 is the optimum for small machines. The 1.5 kVA SEASLUG generator ran at 24,000 rev/min with a frequency of 2,400 Hz.

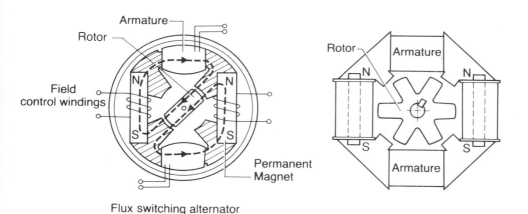

Flux switching alternator

FIG 3.14 Simple flux switching alternator          FIG. 3.15 Optimum flux switching alternator

The specific power of these machines including the gas generator is of the order of 100 W/kg and it can be seen from Figure 3.8 that this performance is low being roughly comparable to a lead-acid battery at the 6 minute rate. With such machines it is possible to control the output voltage by use of control windings added to or subtracting from the magneto-motive force of the permanent magnets.

### *The Permanent Magnet Rotor Alternator*

The very considerable improvements that have been made in permanent magnet materials in the last twenty years have made it possible to produce a permanently magnetised rotor in the form of a disc (see Figure 3.16). The disc is magnetised parallel to its axis with alternate poles appearing on the plane of the disc. This method of magnetisation gives the highest possible magnetic loading for a rotor of given size and weight but it would have been quite impractical to magnetise a shape in this configuration before the development of high coercivity magnetic materials such as Barium Ferrite and, even better, Samarium Cobalt alloy. All permanent magnets tend to demagnetise themselves and this tendency increases as the ratio of length to cross sectional area decreases. Further demagnetising effects are due to currents flowing in the armature windings of alternators which, at poor lagging power factors, directly oppose the magnetisation. Permanent magnet material must therefore have not only a very high coercivity to oppose these demagnetisation effects but also a high retentivity to provide a good working flux.

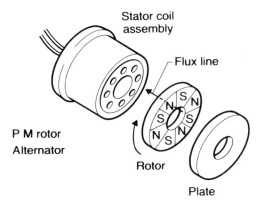

FIG. 3.16 Permanent magnet rotor alternator

Figure 3.16 shows the arrangement of such a machine. The plate, of soft magnetic material, forms a return path for the lines of magnetic flux.

The frequency of such a machine is pN/120 Hz where p is the number of poles on the disc and N is the rev/min.

There is no simple way of controlling the output voltage but it is expected that the output of such machines will be immediately rectified and the voltage limited to a constant voltage d.c. supply.

The power density of such machines complete with turbo drive and gas generator or ram air duct is dependent on the permanent magnet material used. With Barium Ferrite machines a figure of about 500 W/kg and with Samarium Cobalt machines about 1 kW/kg can be obtained at the 1 kW rating (see Figure 3.13). With long flight times the advantage of using the superior machine can only be realised with a ram air or main engine drive.

## Conclusions

In deciding on the EPS for a guided missile, a choice must be made between batteries and generators.

We have seen that, for short-flight missiles, an excellent power source may be found in the lithium thermal battery. These batteries hold unquestionable superiority for short flight times up to one minute. Even above this time they now compete with the silver-zinc reserve battery up to times of several minutes. They are made in single units up to powers in the kilowatt range and can be used in parallel for larger demands.

The silver-zinc reserve is still in use in many current weapons but, as can be seen from Figure 3.13 (repeated below for easy reference), the role of the

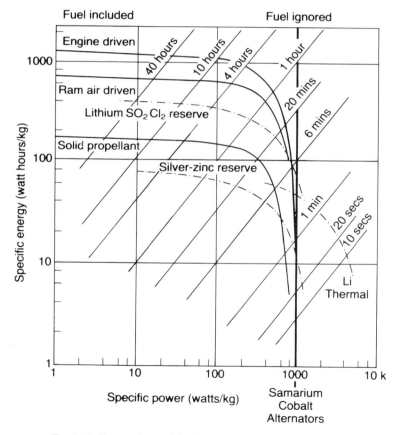

FIG 3.13 Comparison of the best available batteries with the best available generator systems

silver battery for longer flight times is now being seriously challenged by the lithium-thionyl reserve. This is still comparatively untried in missiles but may assume great importance in future long-flight systems.

At about a 20 minute flight-time the generator, driven from the main engine or by ram air, becomes competitive with the best lithium batteries. The hot gas turbine drive for generators is now clearly inferior to batteries at all times and is unlikely to be used again. The main engine and ram air drives unfortunately do suffer one important disadvantage. That is, before and immediately after launch, the engine speed or air speed will not be sufficient to drive the generator. During this period an alternative EPS must be provided. Thermal batteries are most likely to be used.

# 4.
# Airframes

## Introduction

Broadly speaking, the airframe of a guided weapon is the structure required to maintain the essential elements of the weapon system in the correct relative positions for the weapon to fulfil its mission. The external shape of the missile must enable it to be controlled on a particular flight path. It should also provide any aerodynamic force required to change from one flight path to another, for target interception for example. Finally, the air resistance or drag of the complete missile should be kept low. None of the forces acting on the missile in flight should significantly distort the airframe nor cause a lasting oscillation to occur to any part of it.

## The Missile Structure

### Basic Requirements

The airframe mut be as light as possible, consistent with the structural requirements described above. In order to ensure the integrity of the airframe, the structure must be both strong enough to carry any external and internal loads without collapsing or permanently bending and stiff enough not to distort or deflect sufficiently to change significantly its external aerodynamic shape.

The loads which the structure must withstand are the forward thrust from the motor and boost, the loads on each part of the weapon induced by missile accelerations, the lift from the wings and control surfaces, the local pressure forces on the surface of the weapon caused by its motion through the air and transport loads.

### Thrust Loads

Thrust loads, particularly if boost motors are used, are usually the largest loads which the missile has to withstand. The motor and boost fixings must therefore be very robust. The individual missile components must also resist the force which will try to push them towards the missile tail, as the motor accelerates the whole missile forwards. This force is aligned with the direction of motion of the missile and is proportional to the missile's longitudinal acceleration

61

## Acceleration Loads

Another force is produced on each component, at right angles to the direction of motion, if the missile is turning. This is proportional to the normal acceleration of the missile. The word 'normal' is used in its technical sense here, meaning 'at right angles to'. The use of the phrase 'normal acceleration' is therefore to be interpreted to mean 'those accelerations which act at right angles to the direction of motion'. Missile accelerations are often measured in multiples of the acceleration due to gravity (9.81 m/s²). They are then referred to as so many 'g'. An acceleration of 2g's therefore means 2 x 9.81 m/s². When subjected to a 2g acceleration, an object appears to weigh twice as much as it does when it is at rest.

The presence of loads due to missile normal accelerations can be illustrated by likening the missile, in a steady turn, to an object being whirled around one's head on a piece of string (Figure 4.1). Trying this out for yourself will soon show that the force in the string increases as the speed of the object is increased and decreases as the length of the string is increased. In the case of the missile, the force in the string is replaced by the aerodynamic lift. This must therefore increase if the missile speed increases or if the radius of the turn is to be reduced. It is the difficulty of providing sufficient lift which often limits the manoeuvring performance of a missile.

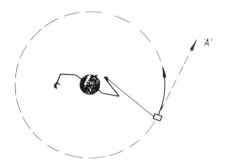

FIG. 4.1  Forces involved in circular motion

In Figure 4.1, the string provides the force needed to maintain the object in its circular path. If the string broke at this moment, the object would continue in direction 'A'.

As far as the structural loads are concerned however, it is the weapon airframe which acts as the 'piece of string' for each item which is attached to it. Again, the simple experiment described will show that the force in the string also appears to depend on the weight of the object being whirled round. In fact, it depends on the mass or inertia of the object, to which the weight is proportional.

The weapon airframe must therefore provide the force needed to 'whirl round' each component of the missile. The heavier, ie the more massive, the component is, the stronger and stiffer must be the local structure needed to hold it in place. Since the forces on the missile components caused by weapon accelerations are proportional to the inertia of the individual component considered, they are known as inertial loads.

It is also clear from this simple illustration, why it is important to keep the weight of the weapon as small as possible. The lighter the missile for a given forward speed and radius of turn ie for a given manoeuvrability, the smaller will be the lift force that is required. This means that smaller wings can be used. These are, in turn, lighter themselves, and so on. Unfortunately, this interdependence also works in the opposite way if the weight starts to rise, which is a common experience in the development programme for a new weapon. Strict weight controls are needed at all stages of design and development to prevent this from becoming a major problem.

## *Loads Created by Life*

Lift from the wings and control surfaces is aerodynamic in origin and comes from the difference in the pressures acting on the upper and lower surfaces of these components. In reality, therefore, the loads are spread over the whole area of the surface and the structure must be strong enough locally to support these pressures. The local pressures change significantly from place to place on the missile. They tend to be negative, ie lower than the ambient static pressure, on the wing upper surface, and positive on the wing lower surface, since this is what is needed in order to produce lift. They vary greatly with the height above ground, speed, shape and attitude of the missile.

When considering the fixing of the wing or control surface to the body, it is only necessary to represent this load distribution by a single force on each panel. The force is imagined to act at a position which produces the same moment about the fixing point as the actual load distribution. This position for the lift, which gives the correct moment as well, is known as the centre of pressure. This concept of a centre of pressure, as the point at which the lift acts to give the correct moment, will also be used when we examine the stability of the missile later in the chapter.

From a structural viewpoint, the missile may be considered to be made up of a series of beams. This is illustrated in Figure 4.2. The forces acting on the body due to missile normal acceleration, as in the turning manoeuvre discussed above, are distributed along the length of the body. The most significant forces will probably be due to the mass of the warhead and the mass of the motor and its fuel. In a steady manoeuvre, the sum of all the inertial forces is numerically equal to the lift force. The body is therefore subjected to transverse bending moments.

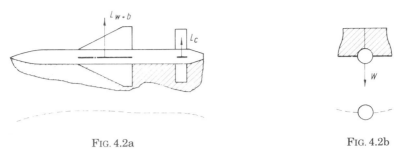

FIG. 4.2a                                    FIG. 4.2b

FIG 4.2 Loads on the missile

In Figure 4.2a, the lift on the wings and control surfaces opposes the weight plus any additional inertial loads, of the individual components. Since these are spread along the length of the missile, there is a tendency for the body to bend. The resulting centre line shape of the body is shown, with the deformations greatly exaggerated, in the lower part of the Figure. In Figure 4.2b, it can be seen that the wing lift, shown as a single force in Figure 4.2a, is distributed in the spanwise sense ie along the wings. This leads to bending of the wings as well.

A very efficient structural shape for resisting bending and also torsional, or twisting, loads, is a hollow circular cylinder. The structural properties of a hollow cylinder may be demonstrated by rolling up a sheet of paper. This resists bending much more than the original flat sheet but is only really effective if the free edge is fastened down as in Figure 4.3a. It is not therefore good practice to cut slots in the surface of the missile! If this edge is stuck down and the tube is bent, failure still occurs quite quickly because the tube flattens and then bends easily. In order to stop this happening, some local structural stiffening in the form of circular hoops, known as frames, or discs, known as bulkheads, is required.

### Local Loads

Even with stiffening in place, local buckling of the surface may still occur. This can be prevented by longitudinal stiffeners known as stringers. This type of construction, with a body of circular cross-section made up from a relatively thin skin supported by frames and stringers, is shown in Figure 4.3b.

Looking at the missile from the front (as in Figure 4.2b) makes it clear that the wings of the weapon must also be designed to resist bending. One half of the total wing lift required is provided by each wing panel. The spanwise centre of pressure position is some distance from the wing-body junction. The inertial loads on the body and its contents act through the plane of symmetry of the missile. There is therefore a bending moment acting on each wing panel.

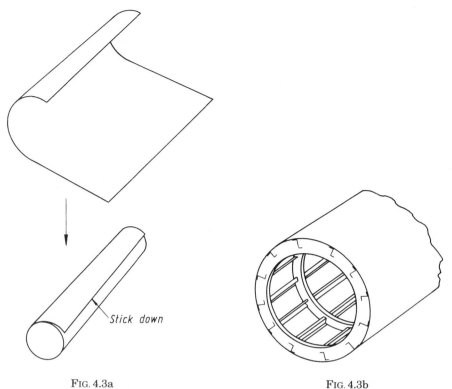

FIG. 4.3a                                    FIG. 4.3b

FIG 4.3  Body construction

In steady level flight, the missile is only subjected to gravitational acceleration. The inertial forces on the components are then equal to their weight and the total lift force on the missile is exactly equal in magnitude and opposite in direction to its total weight.

The main function of the wings is to develop lift. The cross-sectional shape of the wing in a plane parallel to the body centre-line must therefore be acceptable as an aerofoil. The shape implied by this statement will be examined later; at this juncture it is sufficient to appreciate that the wing thickness ie the maximum distance between the upper and lower surfaces, must be kept as small as possible. Since a grossly flattened tube has already been shown to have very little resistance to bending, another technique must be used to increase the wing strength and stiffness.

The trick here is to utilise two flat rectangular elements, called booms, positioned at the maximum thickness point of the aerofoil section where it is easiest to resist bending. These are held apart by a vertical plate called the web. The resulting cross-section of the member is therefore like a capital 'I'.

If this type of built-up construction is used, there is usually more than one
such I beam. They are known as spars and can be seen in Figure 4.4. The
aerofoil section is formed by covering them with a skin. This may again be
supported by a number of stringers and streamwise members called ribs to
prevent local buckling under load. On smaller missiles however, it is usual to
find that the wings are machined from solid. This is also standard practice
for the control surfaces, even on large missiles.

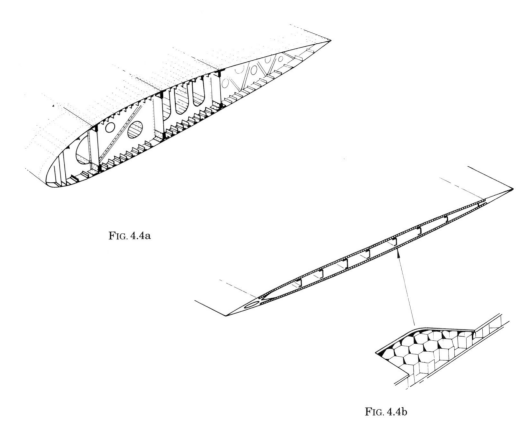

FIG. 4.4a

FIG. 4.4b

FIG. 4.4 Wing construction

Figure 4.4a shows a typical wing construction for a subsonic aircraft. A
similar construction would be used for a cruise missile. Figure 4.4b is a built
up wing for a supersonic vehicle using honeycomb sandwich skins.

## *Transport Loads*

In addition to the flight loads discussed above, the missile must also
withstand transport loads and be able to survive its logistic environment

without significant damage. The requirements are often severe but are also difficult to quantify realistically. An anti-tank missile, for example, may be carried for much of its life on a tracked vehicle or on a helicopter. Both types of vehicle are potent sources of vibration. The missile must also be reasonably 'soldier proof' and must function properly even after being man-handled under battle conditions.

Another example is the air-to-air missile. This could be subjected to many cycles of temperature change and aerodynamic and inertial loading as an external store on an aeroplane. It is still expected to perform properly when eventually it is required. Such considerations as these, whilst not unusually designing any of the major structural elements of the missile, often have a significant influence on the detailed design of the missile and its components.

## Overall Missile Configuration

### General Configuration

In plan view the missile will consist of a body, normally of circular cross-section, containing the guidance package, warhead, fuze and safety and arming device, motor and propellant, and control servos and power pack. It also usually has wings to provide aerodynamic lift and a set of control surfaces. The nose, and sometimes the tail, of the body is shaped to reduce drag. The missile does not normally have a preferred orientation in flight. Consequently, unlike an aeroplane which is essentially designed for efficient steady level flight at one attitude, the missile is symmetrical about the horizontal axis. For lateral manouevrability, another set of wings is usually provided at right angles to the horizontal pair.

The guided weapon therefore usually has a cruciform layout and is broadly identical in both plan and elevation. The cruise missile is an exception to this – as its name implies, it is designed for cruising flight, in the same way as an aeroplane. It therefore has a preferred flight orientation and this is reflected in its unsymmetrical layout.

### Lifting Surfaces

The wings, or main lifting surfaces, of a guided weapon, are usually fixed. The exception to this is where it is necessary to keep the missile body aligned with the oncoming airflow. This may be a requirement if, for example, ramjet engines have been used. Additionally, there will be another set of smaller lifting surfaces, again usually of cruciform layout, normally positioned as far from the wings as possible. These will be hinged along a spanwise axis so that their angle to the airstream may be altered. They may be located close to the nose of the missile. This is known as a 'canard' configuration. Alternatively, they may be rear-mounted to produce a tailed configuration. Some of the advantages and disadvantages of these two configurations will be enumerated later. The function of these additional lifting surfaces is to enable the flight path of the missile to be controlled. They are called control surfaces; each panel is known as a fin.

## *Effect of Performance Characteristics*

The external shape of the missile is largely dictated by the performance characteristics which the weapon must exhibit. These include properties like range, speed of flight, and rate and radius of turn. These, in turn, are determined, in part, by the aerodynamics of the missile. Both range and flight speed are determined, for a given propulsion package, by the resistance to forward motion of the missile ie its drag. The rate and radius of turn ie the manoeuvrability of the missile, are determined, at a given speed, by the lateral force available. This is the force at right angles to the direction of motion of the missile. This force will be called lift, regardless of its actual direction with respect to the vertical. The origins of these two forces, lift and drag, are examined in more detail below.

Before doing so, however, it is important to recognise that there are two regimes of flight which we will need to consider. They are delineated by the value of a dimensionless speed ratio, the Mach number. The Mach number of the missile is defined as the ratio of the forward speed of the missile to the ambient speed of sound in the atmosphere where the missile is flying. There is also a local Mach number for the flow. This is given by the ratio of the local flow speed to the local speed of sound. If, everywhere around the missile, the local Mach number is less than unity, then the weapon is subsonic. Because the airflow is locally speeded up by the passage of the missile, the missile Mach number is always less than the maximum local Mach number of the airflow. Hence, the maximum missile Mach number which will ensure that the airflow everywhere is subsonic, ie the missile's Critical Mach number, is rather less than one.

The exact value for this quantity, depends on the detailed shape of the missile. For a typical anti-tank guided weapon at low incidence angles, this value is normally between 0.7 and 0.8. The more streamlined is the missile, the higher is this critical value. Once the critical Mach number is exceeded, small shock waves begin to form around the missile and the overall drag of the missile starts to rise very rapidly with further increases in speed.

If the missile Mach number is greater than 1, which means that the missile is flying at a speed which above the local speed of sound, then the weapon is supersonic. When there is a mixture of subsonic and supersonic flow, the missile is said to be operating in the transonic regime. This flight regime, whilst practically important for many weapons, is difficult to deal with in a general manner and it will not be considered further here. Subsequent references to supersonic missiles will always assume that virtually the whole of the flow field around the missile is supersonic as well.

## Shock Waves

### Sound Waves

An inevitable accompaniment of flight at supersonic speeds is a system of shock waves. The way that these are produced is illustrated in Figure 4.5. Imagine a very small object moving through otherwise stationary air. At each instant, the object is pushing aside some of the air. Each of these impacts with the air generates a small pressure wave which travels away from the impact point in all directions at the speed of sound. This pressure wave warns the air of the approach of the object so that the air can adjust itself to flow smoothly around it. Figure 4.5a shows what happens when the object is moving at a speed which is one half of the ambient speed of sound ie at Mach 0.5. The circles represent the positions that the pressure waves, generated at various times in the past, have reached at the present time. It can be seen that although the waves travelling ahead of the object are closer together than those travelling behind it, the air still receives warning of the approach of the object.

### Supersonic Shock Waves

Now examine the situation when the object is moving at twice the local speed of sound ie at M=2. Instantaneously, it looks like Figure 4.5b. Now the pressure waves which are attempting to travel ahead of the object, coalesce into a straight line which intersects the line of flight of the object at the object itself. This line, which is a very weak pressure pulse, is known as a Mach line or, in three-dimensions, as a Mach cone. It is clear that any air to the left of this line/cone can receive no warning of the approach of the object. Since the speed of advance divided by the ambient speed of sound has been defined as Mach number and the individual pressure waves propagate out-wards at the local speed of sound, it follows that the included angle between the Mach line/cone and the line of flight can be found from the expression Main $\mu = 1$. This angle ($\mu$), is known as the Mach angle.

In the case of a larger object such as a guided missile, for example, the individual pressure waves are stronger and travel rather faster than the speed of sound. The included angle of the common tangent to the pressure pulses now produced is larger than the Mach angle and the air experiences a significant rise in pressure in passing through this region. This region of rising pressure is called a shock wave. It is physically very thin, typically less than one thousandth of a mm thick at sea level. It represents the first indication which the air receives of the approach of the missile. The air then

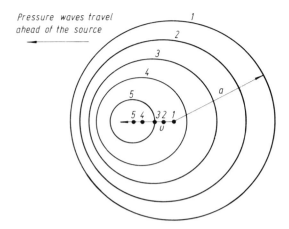

Source moving at $M = 0.5$ ie. $U = \frac{a}{2}$

FIG. 4.5a

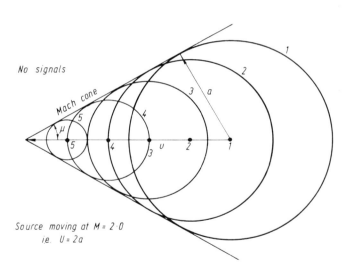

Source moving at $M = 2.0$
ie. $U = 2a$

FIG 4.5b

FIG. 4.5 The formation of shock waves

changes direction at the shock wave to flow around the nose of the missile. As the air moves back over the missile, it will encounter changes in missile shape. If the local slope of the missile surface increases, another shock wave will be produced. When reductions in surface slope are met, the air changes direction through a broader region. This is known as an expansion fan. A typical supersonic flow field is shown in Figure 4.6. This picture of a bullet was taken at a Mach number of 2.5, with a special optical technique being used to make the shock waves and expansion fans visible.

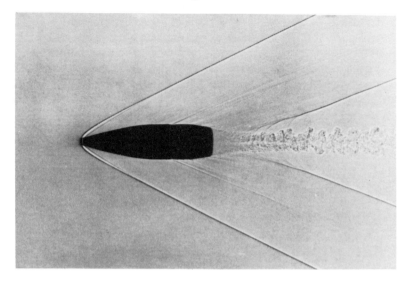

FIG. 4.6 Supersonic flow around a bullet

## Aerodynamic Lift

### Generation of Lift at Subsonic Speeds

Almost any unsymmetrical object moving through the air will generate a certain amount of lift. However, the generation of large amounts of lift, without the simultaneous production of large amounts of drag, requires specially shaped lifting surfaces; these are wings. They have carefully controlled shapes, both in cross-section where the resulting shape is known as the aerofoil section, and in planform.

### Large Span Wings

For efficient flight at subsonic speeds, it is necessary to use wings which have as large a span as possible. This is done in order to reduce drag, as explained later. Additionally, it is advantageous to use aerofoil sections which are slightly curved, or cambered, and wings which are twisted across the span. This type of wing is used on long-range aeroplanes and on cruise missiles. Most guided weapons however, need the ability to manouevre equally well in any direction. This dictates missile symmetry and symmetrical aerofoil sections and untwisted wings are the norm. The aerofoil section will have a rounded nose and tapered trailing edge. The lift, on a wing of this type, varies directly with the area of the wing, its angle to the airflow, which is known as the incidence angle, and the local air density; this is the density at the particular flight altitude being considerd. Lift also depends on the square of the speed of flight. If, at a fixed flight speed, the incidence is increased to too large an angle however, the lift generated by the wing will start to decrease again and the drag of the wing will rapidly increase. The angle at which the lift reaches a maximum, is known as the stalling angle and at incidence angles above this value, the wing is said to be stalled. Typical stalling angles are in the range $15^0$ to $20^0$ for an isolated wing. When a wing with a symmetrical aerofoil section is added to a body however, the stalling incidence is even lower than this.

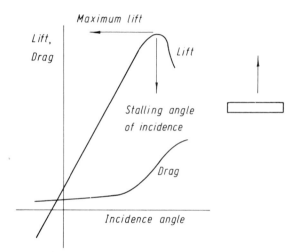

FIG 4.7a

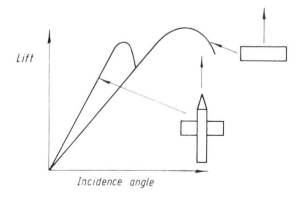

FIG 4.7b

FIG 4.7 Wing planform 1 – large span wings

Figure 4.7a shows the way in which lift varies with incidence angle for a large span wing. Figure 4.7b demonstrates how this behaviour is influenced by the addition of a circular body, when the aerofoil section is symmetrical and the wing is untwisted.

Although wings of this type are extremely efficient, in the sense that they generate significant amounts of lift for very little drag, they are not suitable for most guided weapons. There are several reasons for this. One is simply the handling, carriage and launch problem with large span wings. This is dealt with in the cruise missile by using flip-out wings. Another potentially serious disadvantage is the fact that, above a rather small incidence angle, the wing will stall and hence lose lift. With a simple autopilot of the type normally used in present-day guided weapons, the reaction of the autopilot to a smaller lift force than that demanded will be to increase the incidence of the missile still more. Since this will further decrease the lift produced, the situation now becomes distinctly unhealthy! To avoid this difficulty, tight limits on missile incidence must be applied in flight. Perhaps the most significant disadvantage of the large span aeroplane-type wing however, is its unsuitability for supersonic flight. The reasons for this will become clear later on, but are, in part, due to the very large forces generated in supersonic flight. These inevitably produce enormous bending moments when they act on long moment arms and these must be resisted by thick wing sections which produce large amounts of drag.

### Slender Wings

Another class of wing which is more suitable for most guided weapon applications is the slender wing. To be slender, the wing must be at least as long in the direction of motion ie in its chordwise direction, as in span. It is also often used with the leading edge of the wing swept back through a large angle. This class of wing, whilst it produces more drag at a given lift than the large span wing, does not suffer from the disadvantages listed above. In particular, its small span promotes ease of handling, carriage and launch. It is structurally simpler and more efficient to engineer this type of wing to fly at supersonic speeds. As will be seen, this type of wing also has aerodynamic advantages at supersonic speed. Finally, this class of wing does not stall in the way described above. If the wing has a reasonably large amount of leading edge sweepback (more than $60^0$, say) then the lift continues to increase as the angle of incidence is increased up to about $45^0$.

The general characteristics of slender wings are illustrated in Figure 4.8

### Aerofoils for Supersonic Speeds

At supersonic speeds, the type of aerofoil section which is used depends on the planform shape of the wing. If the leading edge is swept back at an angle

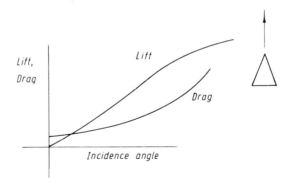

FIG 4.8 Wing planform 2 – slender wings

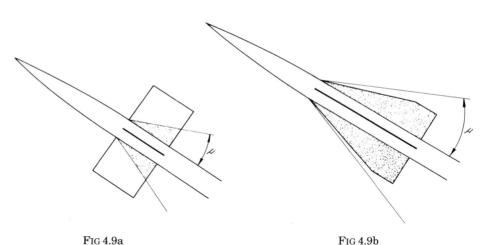

Fig 4.9a　　　　　　　　　　　　　　Fig 4.9b

FIG. 4.9 Wing planform 3 – wings at supersonic speeds

which is less than the angle produced by the Mach line from the wing apex (Figure 4.9a), then the air will receive no warning of the approach of the wing. Under these circumstances, an aerofoil section which has a sharp leading edge, such as a symmetrical double wedge (Figure 4.10a), is used. Another efficient supersonic aerofoil section is the bi-convex section (Figure 4.10b). This is rather difficult to manufacture, and a common alternative is the parallel double wedge, shown in Figure 4.10c. A wing with this aerofoil section will have quite a small span for the reasons discussed previously. It will also have quite a small area because the very high speed at which the missile is operating enables it to generate large amounts of lift quite easily. It may be noticed in passing, however, that the lift at constant incidence no longer increases as the square of the speed as it does at subsonic speeds. In supersonic flight, the lift at constant incidence varies much more nearly linearly with Mach number, particularly at high Mach numbers.

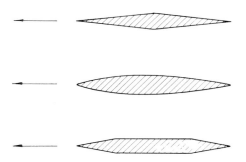

FIG. 4.10 Typical sections of wings with supersonic leading edges

The use of supersonic aerofoil sections is associated with wings that have small amounts of leading edge sweep-back. If the wing leading edge is swept back so that it lies inside the Mach line from the wing apex, then the air receives some warning of the approach of the wing (see Figure 4.9b), and subsonic wing sections are again appropriate. The slender wing described above has this property at low and moderate supersonic Mach numbers and wings of this kind will perform similarly at both subsonic and supersonic speeds. This will be discussed further with reference to their effects on the stability of the missile but it may be noted that this relative invariance of their lift and moment characteristics with Mach number is another reason for the use of slender wings on guided weapons.

If large amounts of lift are not required, or alternatively, if the missile is designed to fly at very high speeds, it may not be necessary to use wings at all. A typical missile body will produce some lift at incidence, though substantially less per unit plan area than a wing. Even if wings are not used, there will still normally be tail surfaces to provide stability and control.

### Wing Summary

A comparison of the lift and drag produced at the same subsonic speed by a large span wing, a slender wing and a cylindrical body with a conical nose is given in Figure 4.11. In each case the plan area is the same.

At supersonic speeds, the influence of planform shape on wing lift is much less marked. Indeed at higher supersonic speeds, all wing shapes give the almost same lift for a given area. The comparative behaviour of a number of different wings is indicated in Figure 4.12. All the wing shapes shown are at the same incidence; effectively, they are flying directly up the page.

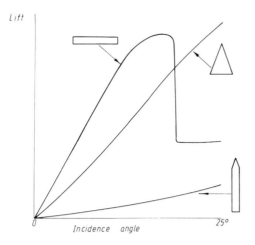

FIG. 4.11a

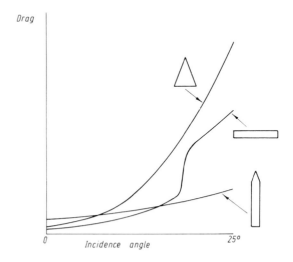

FIG. 4.11b

FIG. 4.11  Lift and drag of wings and bodies

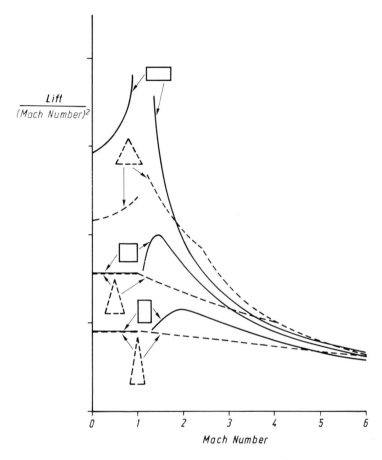

FIG. 4.12 Wing lift at supersonic speeds

## Aerodynamic Drag

### *Types of Drag*

Essentially, there are three separate contributions to the drag force on an object moving through air. These may be summarised as skin friction, the drag due to the pressure forces on the object resolved in the drag direction and the drag associated with the production of lift.

### *Skin Friction*

Viscosity is an intrinsic property of the air. The molecules of air which are immediately adjacent to the surface of an object, stick firmly to that surface.

If the object is put into motion, molecules a little further away from the surface begin to move parallel to it. There is then a layer of fluid close to the surface in which shearing is taking place. This thin layer of air is known as the boundary layer. The air resists this shearing action and therefore a force is needed to move the object against this resistance. The degree to which the air resists the shearing motion is determined by the viscosity of the air. Air is not very viscous and so the shear forces are not very large, except at high speeds. Nevertheless, because of the large surface area over which it acts, skin friction can be a major source of missile drag.

## *Pressure Drag*

Although the viscosity of air is small, it can make a large contribution to the drag of an object because of its effect on the pressure drag of the object. At subsonic speeds, smooth shapes with rounded noses and gently tapering rear sections with sharp trailing edges are required if the pressure drag is to be

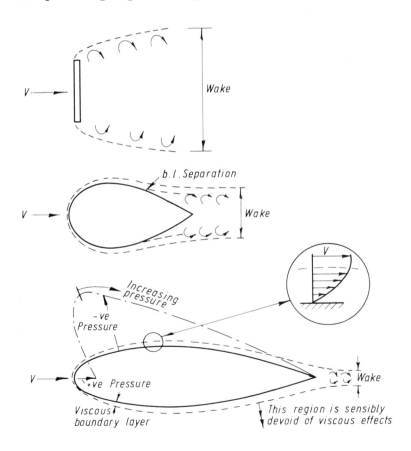

FIG. 4.13 Subsonic flow around bodies

minimised. If sharp corners are present elsewhere on the object or if it changes its cross-sectional shape too quickly, the boundary layer may separate from the surface. Once this has occurred, the flow adjacent to the surface is reversed. The consequence of this is the formation of a region of air behind the object, which tends to move along with it. This region is called the wake. In it the pressure is lower than the average pressure on the forward facing surfaces and a drag force opposing motion is therefore produced. It is in order to reduce this normal pressure drag force that objects are streamlined or faired. Examples of the flow around high drag and low drag objects are given in Figure 4.13.

This figure shows the phenomenon of flow separation which occurs on bluff, ie non-streamlined, bodies at subsonic speeds. The upper sketch is for a flat plate at right angles to its direction of motion. In this case, the flow separates at the sharp edges. Even if the edges are significantly rounded, as for the body in the following diagram, flow separation and hence high drag forces, still occur. It is necessary to use highly streamlined bodies before flow separation is averted. A well-streamlined shape is sketched in the final diagram. Most of the drag on this body comes from skin friction.

At subsonic speeds, viscous drag and pressure drag both increase, to a good approximation, with the square of the speed. They are also proportional to air density at a given speed.

### *Drag Induced by Lift*

Still at subsonic speeds, the final component of drag is that due to lift. The basic lifting mechanism of a wing is to push downwards the air which it influences. It follows that behind a lifting wing, there is a mass of air which is flowing downwards at an angle to the line of flight. The vertical component of this velocity is called downwash. Since the air must be replaced, their is a corresponding upward velocity known as upwash in the region outside the wing tips. This causes an area of rotation close to the wing tips. These are trailing vortices. They can be seen behind any high flying aircraft on a clear day and are popularly known as con-trails or vapour trails. The lifting force produced by the wing is angled midway between the normal to the air direction in front of the wing and to that for air flow behind the wing. There is therefore, a component to the force on the wing which opposes motion – this is the drag due to lift. The situation described above is illustrated in Figure 4.14.

If the wing can influence more air in a given time, then it may turn it through a shallower angle and still obtain the same lift. That component of the total lifting force on the wing which opposes motion (ie the drag due to lift) is therefore made smaller. Hence, it is an advantage to use wings with as large a span as possible, since this will minimise the drag due to lift.

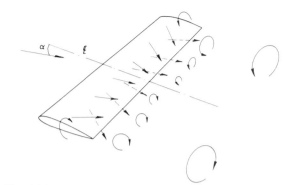

FIG. 4.14a

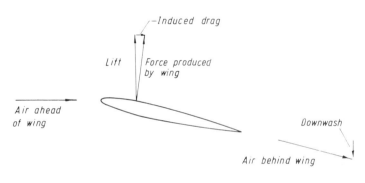

FIG. 4.14b

FIG. 4.14  The generation of induced drag

By the same argument, for a given amount of lift, as the speed of the wing increases, ie as the wing influences more air in a given time, the downwash will be reduced. The force on the wing is therefore tilted back less. It follows that the drag due to lift for a given wing actually reduces as the speed of the wing increases. It may be shown that drag due to lift actually varies inversely with the square of the speed.

## The Cumulative Effect of Drag

When the three components of drag are added together, the result is a curve like that of Figure 4.15. Of particular significance for efficient cruising flight, is that there is a speed at which the drag is a minimum. A cruise missile would be flown close to this speed to obtain maximum range. It may be shown that, at this speed, the components of drag which vary with speed squared ie the viscous and pressure drags, are approximately equal to the drag due to lift.

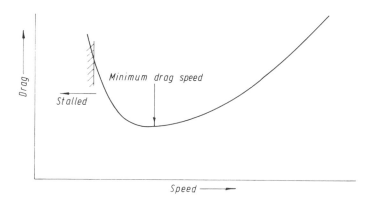

FIG. 4.15 Missile drag at subsonic speeds

At supersonic speeds, the three drag components are still present though, with the exception of skin friction drag, the way in which they are produced changes somewhat. At very high speeds the frictional forces are so intense, that substantial aerodynamic heating of the missile surface can occur. For example, on a missile flying at a Mach number of 4.5 at sea level, the temperature on the surface of the missile skin could be as high as 1000°C.

The pressure drag at supersonic speeds is still the force caused by the pressure distribution around the misile acting in the drag direction. In the case of supersonic flight however, the presence of the shock waves makes this drag component large. Hence, very thin wings and streamlined bodies with pointed noses are necessary. Figure 4.16 shows how the drag due to nose shape alone varies at supersonic speed for different body nose shapes. The drag on the nose at a given height and Mach number is proportional to its frontal area. The drag comparison given in Figure 4.16 is therefore given in terms of the actual drag for a particular nose divided by the product of air density, forward speed squared and frontal area. The resulting quantity has no units and is known as a drag coefficient. It is written in the form $C_D$. The actual drag of the nose may be calculated by multiplying the drag coefficient by one half of the product of air density, forward speed squared and frontal area. For comparison with these values, the total drag coefficient of a typical modern missile, based on the same area, is about 0.5 at a flight Mach number of 2.

For a supersonic wing, the drag associated with the production of lift is almost independent of the planform shape of the wing. This is because it is only the area of the wing which is inside the triangle drawn at the Mach

angle from the leading edge at the wing tip which can receive information
the wing tip is there (see Figure 4.17). The remainder of the wing therefore
produces the same lift and drag, regardless of the tip shape or position.
Because the wing incidence is usually small at supersonic speeds, due to the
high flight speed, the drag due to lift is usually a much smaller proportion of
the total missile drag than at subsonic speed.

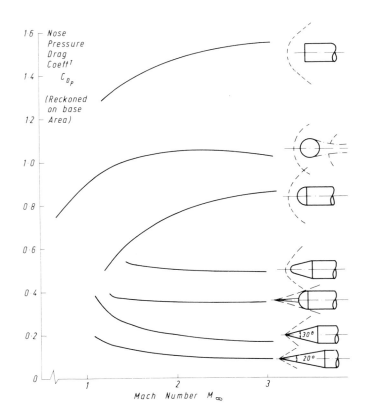

FIG. 4.16. Nose drag at supersonic speeds

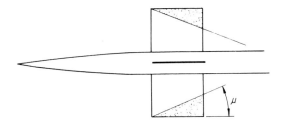

FIG. 4.17. Tip effects at supersonic speeds

## *Moments*

Whilst the manoeuvrability of guided missiles is usually defined in terms of the available lateral acceleration, the ability to manoeuvre and control the missile is intrinsically connected with its moment characteristics.

Consider a wing mounted in a wind tunnel which is free to pivot about its trailing edge. If the wing has an initial small positive incidence, turning the wind on in the wind tunnel will cause the leading edge of the wing to attempt to rise ie a nose-up moment will be generated. The position of the observed lift force, measured along the mean wing surface forward of the trailing edge, which will produce this observed moment is known as the centre of pressure of the wing. For wings in general, it is found experimentally that the position of the centre of pressure varies with the angle of incidence. This makes it a difficult point to use in analysis.

If the pivot point on the wing is now moved forward, it will be found that there is a point, between the leading and trailing edges of the wing, about which the moment does not change with changes of incidence and hence of lift. This point about which there is no change in overturning moment with change in wing lift is known as the aerodynamic centre of the wing. It is convenient therefore, to consider this, for the purposes of analysis, as the point at which the lift acts, though there will usually be a pure couple to be allowed for as well.

There are corresponding points to both of these for a complete missile. The point where the observed total lift acts on the missile to give the observed over-turning moment is the centre of pressure, of the complete missile. In general, it varies with body incidence angle, control deflection angle, and Mach number. The point about which there is no change of moment with change of lift ie the aerodynamic centre of the complete missile, is known as the neutral point. For small incidence angles, the neutral point position depends only on Mach number.

## Stability and Control

### *Static and Dynamic Stability*

The aerodynamic stability of a guided weapon is concerned with its motion following a disturbance from an equilibrium condition. A distinction is usually made between the initial tendency of the missile to return to its starting condition and any subsequent motion. Because the first of these can be analysed without reference to the resulting motion, it is termed static stability. Examination of the motion itself is referred to as dynamic stability analysis.

There are only three classes of static stability which are physically possible. These are:-

▶ Stable – the missile tends to return to its starting (ie equilibrium) condition

▶ Neutrally stable – the missile remains in its disturbed condition.

▶ Unstable – the missile tends to move further away from its starting condition in the same direction as that caused by the disturbance.

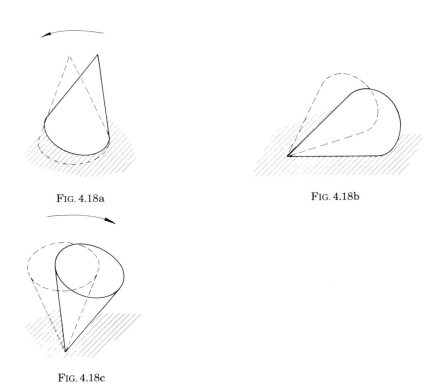

FIG. 4.18a

FIG. 4.18b

FIG. 4.18c

FIG. 4.18 Static stability – principle

These three classes of stability can be illustrated by considering a cone on a horizontal surface as shown in Figure 4.18. In Figure 4.18a, the cone is standing on its base. If the top is displaced sideways and then released, the cone will return to its original, equilibrium position. It is said to be statically stable. When placed on its side, as in Figure 4.18b, a sideways displacement simply produces a change in its rest position. The cone is then neutrally stable. Finally, if the cone is balanced on its point as in Figure 4.18c, any sideways displacement will cause it to tip further away from the equilibrium position. The cone, in this position, is therefore statically unstable.

## Static Stability Considerations

Figure 4.19 depicts a missile in the vertical pitching plane, disturbed in pitch as if by a vertical gust. Because the missile is in free flight, any force which does not pass through the centre of gravity of the missile will cause the missile to rotate. This is therefore the point about which moments must be measured if missile rotations are to be properly predicted. A vertical gust combined with a forward motion of the missile, will produce a change of incidence at the missile. This change of incidence will, in turn, produce an increased lift on the wings, body and control surfaces. Each of these lift forces will, in general, have a moment about the missile centre of gravity. If the sum of these moments is of the right sign to rotate the missile towards the original flight attitude, then the missile is statically stable. If the sum of the moments is zero, then the missile is neutrally stable. If the moment is such as to further disturb the missile, then the missile is statically unstable.

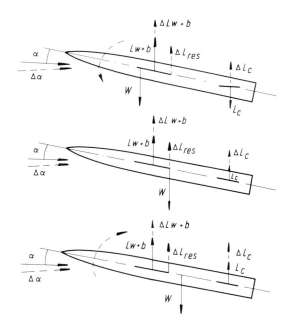

FIG. 4.19 Static stability – application

The moments from both the wing and body and the control surfaces generated by a change in incidence angle can be assumed to act at a fixed point, which has been defined earlier as the neutral point of the missile. The distance of the missile neutral point aft of the centre of gravity is called the static margin. Therefore a missile with a positive static margin will experience a nose down moment if it is subjected to a nose up disturbance ie it will tend to return to its original position. Thus a positive static margin means that the missile will be statically stable. Similarly, a missile with a static margin equal to zero will be neutrally stable, and a missile with a negative static margin will be statically unstable. The actual magnitude of the static margin is therefore a useful measure of the static stability of the missile.

To re-inforce this explanation, let us analyse the situation in Figure 4.19. An increase in missile incidence, caused by a gust, for example, will increase the lift on the wing and body ($L_{w+b}$) by a small amount ($\Delta L_{w+b}$). The force on the horizontal control surface ($L_c$) will also be increased by a small amount ($\Delta_c$). These two incremental forces can now be replaced by a single force ($\Delta L_{res}$) acting at the neutral point of the missile. If this force acts behind the missile centre of gravity, as in Figure 4.19a, then the missile will rotate back towards its original undisturbed state ie it is statically stable. If no restoring moment is produced as in Figure 4.19b, then the missile will stay in its new position ie it is neutrally stable. If, on the other hand, the moment produced tends to overturn the missile ie it tends to increase the effect of the disturbance, then the missile is statically unstable. This is the case for the missile in Figure 4.19c for which the incidence will continue to increase, even if the gust is removed.

It should be noted that, since the missile is initially in equilibrium, the moment about its centre of gravity is zero. This means that, in each of the cases shown, prior to the disturbance, the initial position of the missile centre of pressure and centre of gravity positions are coincident ie centre of pressure and neutral point are not, in general, coincident.

For a given missile, the neutral point position is itself fixed at any constant value of Mach number and missile attitude. The missile centre of gravity is variable in position, however. As the fuel is burnt, there will normally be a significant shift in centre of gravity position. In addition, the point at which the lift acts on a lifting surface moves as the flight Mach number changes. This movement is smaller for slender wings – another reason for the prevalence of these wings in the guided weapon field. It can therefore be seen that the static stability of a missile is likely to vary quite considerably during a typical flight. This has control implications and these are discussed in Chapter 6.


### Aerodynamic Control Considerations

The aerodynamic control surfaces on a guided weapon therefore act to stabilise the vehicle. They are also designed to provide a controllable moment about the missile centre of gravity. This moment should then cause the missile to respond in the appropriate manner. For example, if a change in height is required, movement of the horizontal control surfaces will produce a moment causing the missile incidence to change. The change in incidence causes a change in the lift force acting on the missile and this change, in turn, produces a vertical acceleration on the missile (see Figure 4.20). This vertical acceleration will eventually produce the desired change in height. Controls used in this way are called elevators. The same sort of process can take place in the 'sideways', ie yaw, direction. The controls are then said to be operating as rudders.

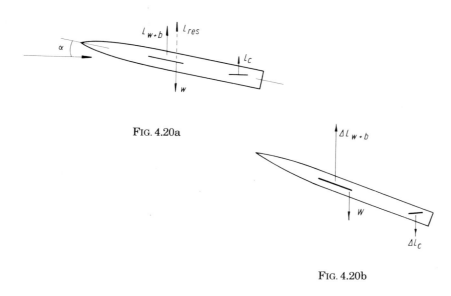

FIG. 4.20a

FIG. 4.20b

FIG. 4.20 The action of elevators

Figure 4.20a shows a missile in steady level flight. In these conditions $L_{res} = W$. Elevator deflection changes the load on the control by an amount $\Delta L_c$ and this rotates the missile. The change in incidence now changes the wing and body lift by an amount $\Delta L_{w+b}$. The result for up elevator is shown in Figure 4.20b. Now, shortly after the application of up elevator, $\Delta L_{w+b}$ is greater than $\Delta L_c$ and the missile consequently accelerates upwards.

The change in incidence which occurs as a direct result of a given control deflection, and hence applied moment, is directly related to the static stability of the missile. If the missile is very stable, it resists all attempts to disturb it, including those from the control surfaces. It is therefore advantageous, from the control point of view, to have a missile which is only slightly stable, or for that matter, even slightly unstable. The difficulty now is that the missile is much more sensitive to extraneous disturbances as well.

### The Choice of Control Surface Configuration

From the viewpoint of static stability, there is little to choose between the canard configuration with the control surface at the nose of the body and the tailed layout with the control surfaces at the rear. An examination of Figure 4.21 will show that the missile can be stabilised in each case; though there will always be a lift acting on the canard control surfaces in steady level flight for a stable vehicle; this produces additional drag and is the one of the reasons why almost all aeroplanes have rear-mounted control surfaces. For both configurations, the resulting force caused by a pitching disturbance acts behind the missile centre of gravity. Therefore a nose down moment is produced and the missile is statically stable.

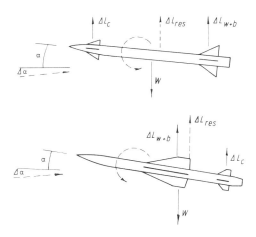

FIG. 4.21  Canard vs tailed configurations 1

If it desired to make the missile highly manoeuvrable, however, there are advantages in the canard configuration. This is mainly due to the sign of the force produced by the control surface, as explained below. Additionally, the canard layout usually provides a longer moment arm for the control surfaces when a real missile is being designed.

The deflection of a set of control surfaces to initiate a manoeuvre, primarily produces a control moment which in turn, rotates the missile. However, the force which initially acts on the missile, before the missile has had time to rotate, is the force produced by the control itself. In the case of canard controls, this initial force is in the direction of the desired motion; for rear-mounted controls it is in the opposite direction to the desired motion.

The initial acceleration of the missile is therefore in the desired direction with canard controls and in the opposite direction with rear controls. The movement in the wrong direction with rear controls is quickly checked because the force on the control surface, acting well behind the missile centre of gravity, produces an increase in missile incidence thereby producing a large lift force from the main lifting surface as shown in Figure 4.20. It is this large force which quickly overcomes the adverse force from the control surface. Nevertheless, this adverse force is still required in order to sustain the manoeuvre, and it makes the total force available in the manoeuvre less than that which could be produced by a comparable canard configuration.

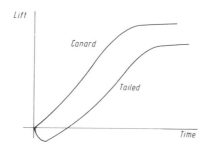

FIG. 4.22  Canard vs tailed configurations 2

Figure 4.22 shows the way in which the lift force builds up with time for missiles having these two configurations. Reference to Figure 4.21 shows that the first out of balance force for the tailed configuration is downwards due to deflection of the elevator.

To summarise therefore, the canard configuration gives improved manoeuvreability for the following reasons:-

▶ The initial force produced by the control surface is in the direction of the required missile movement.

▶ The total force available for manoeuvring is greater.

For roll control, the control surfaces are operated anti-symmetrically. In this mode they are said to be operating as ailerons. Thus, if it is desired to roll the missile, the incidence on one control will be increased whilst on another, diametrically opposed to the first, the incidence will be reduced. The first surface will now develop a positive increment in lift whilst the other will develop a negative lift increment. The net result will be the production of a rolling moment acting on the missile.

A problem can now arise if the missile has a canard configuration. This can be understood if it is remembered that the inevitable accompaniment of lift is a change in the airflow direction behind the lifting surface. Consider a missile, in steady level flight, having canard control surfaces, which it is desired to roll clockwise as viewed from the rear of the missile (see Figure 4.23). The starboard control is given negative incidence to produce a downward force whilst the port control is given a positive incidence to produce an upward force. The two forces are of the same size but opposite in direction so that the result of their action on the missile is the production of a rolling moment in the desired sense.

Behind the starboard control surface the flow is now angled upwards due to the negative lift acting on it. Conversely, behind the port control, the flow is angled downwards. With a canard configuration, the main lifting surfaces are also positioned behind the control surfaces and are subjected to the air flow which has been changed in direction by passage over them. The starboard wing, for example, will now have positive incidence due to the upwash from the deflected control surface ahead of it. It will therefore produce a lift increment in the upward direction. Similarly, the port wing will produce a negative lift increment, of approximately the same size but of opposite sign. The overall result is therefore a rolling moment of opposite sign to that produced by the control surfaces. Since the main lifting surfaces are normally much larger than the control surfaces, the overall result is usually an anti-clockwise rolling moment when viewed from the rear of the missile. This is exactly the opposite result from that required!

To make matters worse, if the missile is set at a larger incidence angle, as might be the case during a manoeuvre for example, the situation is reversed.

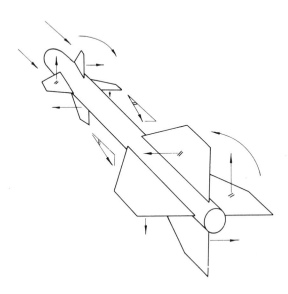

FIG. 4.23 Canard vs tailed configurations 3

This is because the wings are not now immediately behind the control surfaces and they are not therefore affected by the flow behind the control surfaces and so they do not produce an adverse rolling moment. The rolling moment which results from the control deflection is now clock-wise, as expected initially! There will also be an incidence angle, between the two situations described above, for which there will be no resultant rolling moment at all. This is because, at this particular angle of incidence or angle of yaw, the contributions from the control surfaces and the wings will exactly cancel each other.

Much ingenuity has been used on past and present missiles to overcome this inherent difficulty in the use of canard control surfaces as ailerons. Examples are the roll-bearing in Blowpipe and the separate wing-mounted ailerons on Gainful.

# 5.
# Guidance

## The Reason for Guidance

Before discussing the various ways in which missiles may be guided, and the methods of implementation of those guidance systems, it is worth recalling why guided missiles, as opposed to unguided weapons, have assumed so much importance in recent years.

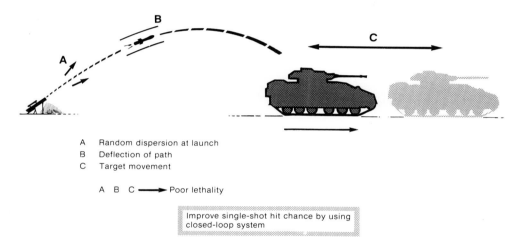

A   Random dispersion at launch
B   Deflection of path
C   Target movement

A  B  C ⟶ Poor lethality

Improve single-shot hit chance by using closed-loop system

FIG. 5.1  Why guide?

It is clear that any weapon should have as high a single shot kill probability (SSKP) as possible. As shown in Figure 5.1 there are three main reasons why unguided weapons may fail in this respect. Excessive miss distance may be caused by incorrect direction of take off when the missile is launched, by perturbation of the missile by wind or weather, or by unpredictable movement of the target after launch of the missile. One way of restoring the SSKP is, of course, to use a larger warhead with a larger lethal area, but this will usually mean a larger missile.

The other method, which is the one adopted in every system discussed in this book, it is to use a closed loop system to reduce the miss distance and thus improve the SSKP.

93

## *The Closed Loop System*

The concept of the closed loop system, which has applications far wider than guided weapon systems, has assumed great importance in the worlds of engineering and science in the last 25 to 30 years. All guidance systems are particular examples of the closed loop concept which in its general form is shown in Figure 5.2.

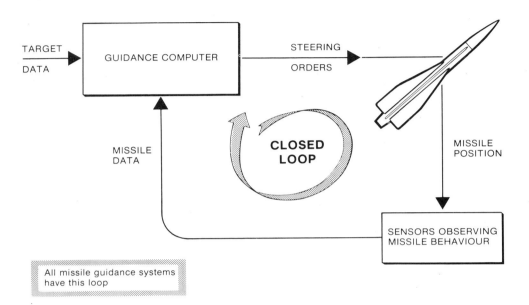

FIG. 5.2 The closed loop

There is some observation instrumentation which measures the behaviour of the missile. Such instrumentation may be actually contained in the missile itself or it may be situated at a ground or mobile platform control centre, such as a ship or aircraft. This missile data is fed to a guidance computer which will also contain information on the desired path of the missile if it is to impact successfully up on the target. The computer is able to determine what manoeuvres the missile should then execute in order to improve its chances of hitting the target. The computer passes steering instructions, such as desired lateral acceleration (latax) in the pitch and yaw planes, to the control system, which motivates the aerodynamic control surfaces of the missile or adjusts the direction of the propulsive thrust.

The resulting adjustments in the motion of the missile are observed by the missile observation instrumentation. The loop is complete. In every guided weapon guidance and control system, and some can be extremely complex, this closed loop concept may be identified.

## Got or Golis

A subdivision of guided weapon systems which has great significance to the type of guidance used, relates to the nature of the observation of the target. In many systems, particularly self defence systems such as surface-to-air missiles (SAM) or tank self protection missiles (TSPM), it is essential to provide a sensor which continually observes the motion of the target during the flight of the missile right up to the time of missile strike upon the target. Such a situation may be termed a target end point guidance or guide onto target (GOT). This situation is depicted in Figure 5.3.

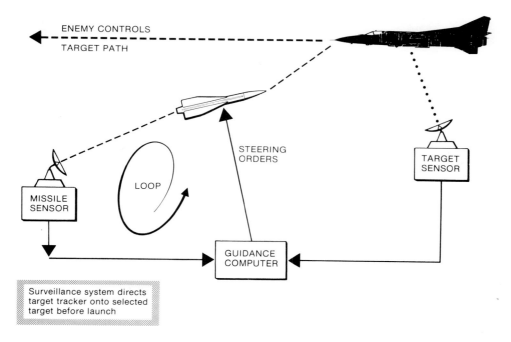

FIG. 5.3    Target end point guidance

On the other hand many GW systems are concerned with the attack of fixed targets which are unlikely to move during the time of flight of the missile. Examples of such systems are strategic surface-to-surface weapons or tactical surface-to-surface weapons called upon to bring fire to bear on short term targets such as stores, dumps, headquarters, or communication centres located by some form of general surveillance system and identified typically by an exact map reference. Such systems may be called 'Fixed Location end point guidance systems' or guide onto location in space (GOLIS).

It is worth noting in passing, that the GOT system tend to be fast response systems with dedicated surveillance equipment and specifications highly dependent on enemy initiative and equipment characteristics. GOLIS systems normally rely upon general surveillance; the time of fire is more likely to be at the choice of the user and the specification largely dependent on the tactical and logistic doctrine of the owner force. Figure 5.4 illustrates this concept.

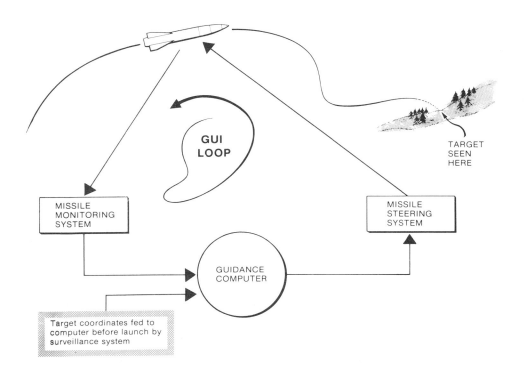

FIG. 5.4  Fixed location end point guidance

## The Desired Path of a Guided Missile

It is necessary now to consider the type of path or trajectory which various types of guided weapon perform from launch point to target. While almost any imaginable trajectory could be employed, by use of the complex guidance and control methods available to the design engineers of today, the majority of the world's guided weapon systems use one or other of the paths described in the following paragraphs.

In summary those which are mainly of interest are, the proportional navigation trajectory, the straight line trajectory, the line of sight (LOS) trajectory, the cruise trajectory and the ballistic or free fall trajectory. Each of these will now be discussed in more detail.

## Proportional Navigation Trajectory

The proportional navigation (PN) trajectory is adopted by nearly all missiles using homing guidance; these are discussed later. The principle of this system may be understood by referring to Figure 5.5. This depicts a motor car and a lorry approaching a crossroads.

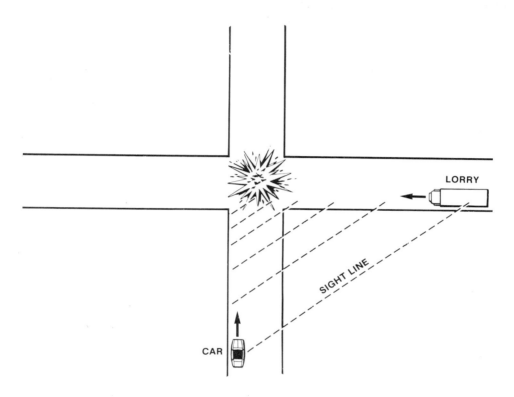

FIG. 5.5 Proportional navigation

The driver of the car will observe the lorry as he approaches the intersection. If the lorry appears to fall back in the line of sight of the car driver, the car will arrive at the crossroads in front of the lorry. If, on the other hand, the sight line to the lorry moves more into the direct ahead region of the car driver's vision then the lorry will cross in front of the car. The dangerous situation will be if the line of sight from car to lorry appears as a set of parallel lines. In such a case the car and lorry will impact at the cross roads.

The homing missile makes use of this concept to achieve impact with the target as shown in Figure 5.4; it is drawn in one plane only for clarity. A target tracket in the nose of the missile is locked onto the target and establishes the sight line from missile to target at all times.

Instruments in the missile measure the rate at which the sight line is swinging in space; usually rate gyroscopes are used to do this. The rate is passed to the missile control system which causes the missile flight path to change at a rate which reflects the rate of turn of sight line. In more exact terms the rate of change of flight path is made proportional to the rate of turn of sight line. If this is continued it will be found that the missile quickly steers on to a constant direction such that the rate of turn of sight line between missile and target is zero – as seen in Figure 5.6.

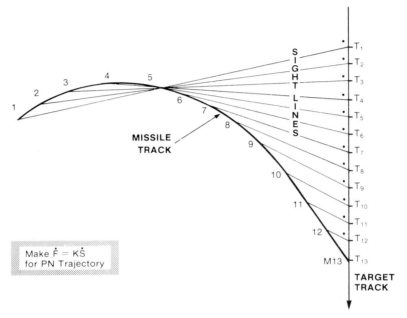

FIG. 5.6 Homing kinematics

The consequence, as has been said, will result in impact between missile and target. This simple form of guidance, called proportional navigation (PN), requires little or no computing effort in the missile although the instruments needed to track the target from the missile may be costly.

### The Straight Line Trajectory

The straight line trajectory does not require much explanation and since it can only be used at short range against stationary or slow moving targets it is not very common in GW systems. The straight line between launch point and impact point is established before launch, as seen in Figure 5.7a.

If the target has a crossing rate a slight aim off may be allowed for. The missile is then launched, usually to supersonic speed along the trajectory, and it is maintained parallel to the original straight line by internal gyroscopic instruments acting through its control system.

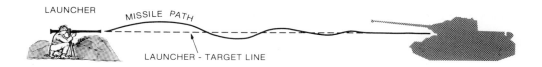

FIG. 5.7a Straight line trajectory

In some cases this technique may be used for the initial flight path of a missile which then follows a ballistic trajectory.

## The Line of Sight (LOS) Trajectory

It is important not to confuse the LOS path with the straight line trajectory which has been discussed above. In that case the missile ideally follows a straight line and requires very little ability to pull lateral acceleration whereas the LOS missile will normally follow a very curved trajectory requiring considerable 'g' capability.

The LOS path is shown in Figure 5.7b, which may be considered as the plan view of the attack paths of attacking Ground Attack Aircraft and of the defensive surface-to-air-missile used to engage them.

At any time the LOS is the line joining the observation point 0, which is also the point from which the missile is launched, to the position of the target at that instant. The Figure shows a number of consecutive positions of the line of sight as the target moves along its path.

The LOS guidance system controls the missile so that it always lies on the LOS between the observation point and the target at any moment. This may be done by Command Guidance or Beam Riding Guidance both of which are discussed later. It will be seen that for the offset target path the LOS trajectory results in a very curved path for the missile. Such a trajectory is commonly used for many of the shorter range and cheaper missile systems. In the special case where the target path passes over the observation point, which is also the launcher location, the missile trajectory looked at in plan becomes a straight line, although there may of course be some curvature in the vertical plane.

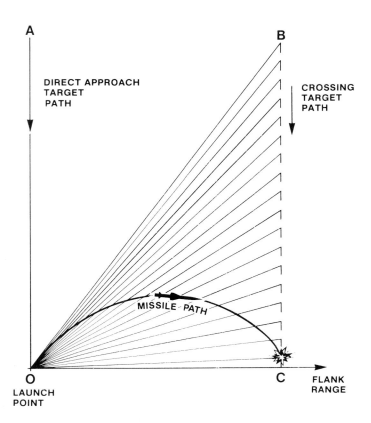

A

B

DIRECT APPROACH
TARGET
PATH

CROSSING
TARGET
PATH

MISSILE PATH

O
LAUNCH
POINT

C

FLANK
RANGE

FIG. 5.7b  Line of sight (LOS) path

## The Cruise Trajectory

A cruise trajectory is one which involves the missile flying at constant speed and constant height for most of its journey from launch to target. In many cases the missile may go through a number of phases involving a change from one height to another and perhaps a change in speed but then each phase will be a segment of cruise trajectory. Weapon systems using this type of path are typical at the moment as both strategic cruise missiles and anti-shipping sea skimming missiles usually adopt this type of trajectory.

## The Ballistic Trajectory

The ballistic trajectory, also called a free fall trajectory, is the path followed by an object or projectile when it is moving without any force acting upon it except the force of gravity.

No missile passing through the atmosphere can adopt this path unaided because it will be subject to air pressure forces brought into play by its aerodynamic shape. However a missile moving outside the atmosphere with no motors running will execute a free fall trajectory. The application of simple ballistic mathematics to such missiles shows that for short range missiles, when the distances are such that the surface of the earth can be regarded as flat and uncurved, the ballistic trajectory is a segment of a parabolic curve. Long range weapons moving over a significant percentage of the earth's surface behave as if they are artificial satellites, as indeed they are, and they have an elliptical trajectory about the earth's centre as a focus.

Guided missiles passing through the atmosphere may be adjusted so that they approximate to a ballistic trajectory by measuring accurately the force acting on them at any instant, other than gravitation, and providing a carefully metered thrust which exactly cancels that force. An example of such a system is the Lance tactical surface-to-surface missile to be found in many NATO armies. Many long range strategic missiles have an approximately ballistic trajectory monitored by Inertial Guidance which is discussed later in this chapter.

## Homing Guidance

### Basic Requirements

A form of guidance which is fast becoming more extensively used for different types of weapon system is Homing Guidance. This is a GOT system which may be defined by the presence inside the missile of a sensor which tracks the target. This sensor, which is nearly always in or near the 'nose' of the missile, maintains the sight line directly from missile to target.

The rate of turn of this sight line may then be used for a PN trajectory with consequent impact with, or a very near miss of, the target. The sensor is called the homing eye or homing head, or seeker in the United States, and tracks the target by detecting energy emitted from, or reflected by the target itself. Three forms of homing have traditionally been defined related to the source of the energy used for tracking the target. Active, passive and semi-active homing guidance are shown in Figure 5.8.

### Active Homing

Active homing uses missile which contains power source and illuminator which beams energy at the target. The energy reflected by the target is detected by the homing head which continues to illuminate and track the target until impact. Such a system tends to demand a relatively heavy and expensive missile albeit one that is totally independent, and referred to as

autonomous, after it has locked onto the target. For this reason, active
homing is usually only employed for the terminal phase of guidance after
some other form of guidance has brought the missile to within a short
distance of the target.

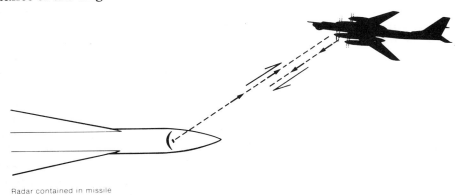

Radar contained in missile

FIG. 5.8a  Active

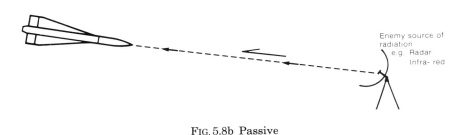

Enemy source of
radiation
e.g. Radar
Infra- red

FIG. 5.8b  Passive

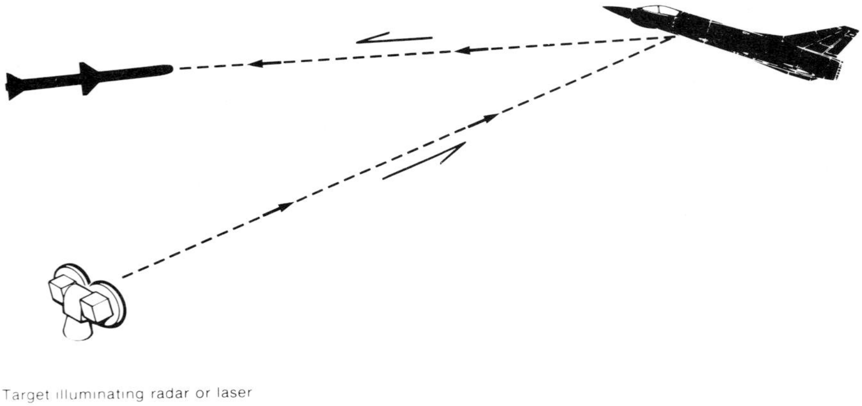

Target illuminating radar or laser

FIG. 5.8c  Semi-active

FIG. 5.8  The three homings

## Passive Homing

Passive homing relies on natural energy which is emitted or reflected from the target. The sensor in the missile makes use of this energy to track the target. There are many examples of weapon systems where passive homing is a relatively cheap and effective method of guidance. Anti-radar missiles home on to the essential transmitted power produced by the radar. A communication satellite would also be an obvious target for a passive homing missile. The tail pipes of jet engines and the smoke stacks of ships are also vulnerable to attack as these are hot spot targets for infra-red passive homing missiles. Recent advances in infra-red detectors such as Staring Focal Plane Arrays, and the use of very light weight signal processing, such as charge coupled devices and microprocessor pattern recognition systems, have made possible the use of imaging sensors which are actually able to single out the image of a tank, or other programmed target, by observation of the infra-red image of the target against its background. Passive homing missiles which lock on before launch (LOBL) and others which lock on after launch (LOAL) are both the subject of current development.

## Semi-Active Homing

Semi-active homing is the name given to the system where the target is illuminated or designated by directing a beam of light, IR or radio energy at it. The purely passive sensor in the missile then tracks the target using the energy reflected from it. In this system the selection of the target is carried out by the target illumination station so that the homing missile has no difficulty in sorting out the target from its background; provided of course the illuminating beam does not 'spill over' onto other objects. In such a semi-active homing system, the illuminating station needs to track the target in order to maintain the energy beam on target so that the system as a whole needs an additional tracker as well as one in each missile. Early examples of semi-active homing GW used radar for the illuminating beam but, more recently, systems using lasers, mainly in the IR part of the spectrum, have entered service for use with small missiles and Precision Guided Munitions (PGM). Radar will, of course, continue to be used for long range systems. The great advantage of semi-active homing is the greatly increased power that can be brought to bear on the target without adding to the weight and size of the missile.

## LOS Guidance

### Classifications

There are two forms of guidance, as seen in Figure 5.9, which may be readily associated with LOS trajectories. Line of Sight Beam Riding (LOSBR) and

Command to Line of Sight (CLOS). CLOS is a very common form of guidance, particularly for small and relatively cheap GW systems. LOSBR was originally used for anti-aircraft missiles riding a radar beam. Modern LOBSR systems are mostly ATGW or low level SAM in which the riding beam is a laser operating in the IR part of the spectrum: they are typically 1.06 micrometre wavelength.

Command - CLOS

Beam Riding - Line-of-sight BR (LOS BR)

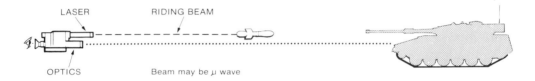

FIG. 5.9 CLOS and BR

## LOSBR

In the case of the LOSBR system target tracking must be performed as before but in this case a laser transmitter, and not a missile tracker, is laid parallel to the LOS: in large systems a radar beam may be used in place of a laser. The laser beam thus shines along the LOS and will illuminate the target.

The laser beam is constrained to perform a very precise scanning pattern in the space immediately around the LOS. The shape of this pattern is such that a rearward looking laser receiver in the missile can locate the position of the missile relative to the LOS which forms the central spine of the scan pattern. Thus the beam riding missile, again with the help of a gyro carried in the missile, navigates to the line of sight which is in the centre of the scan pattern. Beam riding is therefore a special form of navigational guidance (NG).

It will be noted that the target may be altered that it is under attack if it detects the laser beam. With LOSBR it is a simple matter to ride several missiles up the one riding beam whereas with CLOS different commands would be required for each missile launched at a single target. It is generally considered also that LOSBR systems are more difficult to jam than CLOS systems. It should be noted that the clear distinction made here between CLOS and LOSBR is not universally agreed. Some writers on GW regard beam riding as a special form of command guidance even though the guidance computer in a beam rider is in the missile while that for a command system is at base.

## CLOS

The CLOS form of guidance requires a target tracker and a missile tracker situated at the base or the aiming point from which the system is operational, and which, in most cases, is the point from which the missile is launched. The zero axis of the missile tracker is laid parallel to the zero axis of the target tracker which is kept on the target by the target tracking process. The missile is then launched towards the target and, with the help of a flare or beacon shining backwards from the missile, the missile tracker detects any displacement of the missile from the LOS. A simple computer, also located at base, calculates the lateral acceleration required of the missile to bring its flight path back onto the LOS. This is translated into a coded signal which is transmitted to the missile over a suitable command link (CL). This command link may be a pair of wires, an optical fibre, a laser communication link or a radio link.

On receipt in the missile, the signal must be decoded and the lateral thrust applied, either by the correctly positioned aerodynamic fins or by a sideways directed propulsive jet. A position gyro in the missile will usually be required to provide the reference direction for this process. It will be noticed that if both target and missile trackers operate passively there is no power directed towards the target which may give the alarm that it is under attack unless the CL does so. Both target and missile must be tracked until impact occurs.

Because CLOS is a form of guidance which has been used extensively for small missiles from the very beginning of GW technology, CLOS systems are usually subdivided into three main sub groups. Manual command to line of sight (MCLOS) semi-automatic CLOS (SACLOS) and automatic CLOS (ACLOS). These distinctions relate to the type of tracking used for the missile.

Figure 5.10 shows the essential elements of the CLOS system and the lower picture shows how they are provided in an MCLOS system.

## MCLOS

In this type of system the human eye is used (with or without help from any optical system) to observe the relative direction of both target and missile and the brain of the operator, acting as the guidance computer, estimates what adjustment is required to bring the missile onto the LOS. The operator is provided with a missile steering control, usually in the form of a small joy stick or thumb pressure switch, and thus with the missile under his direct control he superimposes the missile between his eye and the target until impact occurs. The command link in MCLOS systems is very often a wire spooled out by the missile as it flies. A flare is usually provided at the rear of the missile to make it more visible.

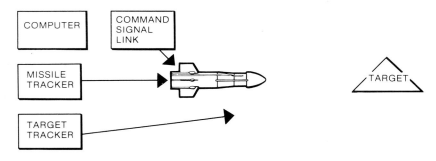

Command Guidance Elements

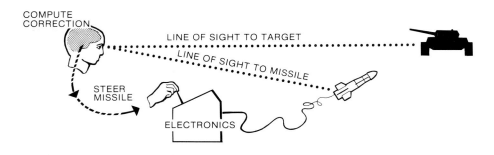

Manual Command to
Line of Sight (MCLOS)

FIG. 5.10 Command guidance elements and MCLOS

MCLOS GW are simple, cheap, and have good resistance to electronic counter measures (ECM) but the highly skilled operator needs expensive and continuous training. For this last reason few, if any, MCLOS systems are likely to enter service in the future.

## SACLOS

As shown in Figure 5.11 SACLOS guidance uses a human eye, usually assisted by a magnifying optic with a cross wire, to track the target throughout the engagement. An automatic missile tracking system, called a goniometer, is either rigidly aligned with the bore sight of the target tracker or is slaved to it by some form of servo system. In this arrangement the missile tracker is looking along the line of sight to the target. When the missile is launched, as nearly as possible along the LOS, the automatic missile tracker detects any departure of the missile from the LOS. This error is passed to guidance analogue or digital guidance computer which is built into the tracking system.

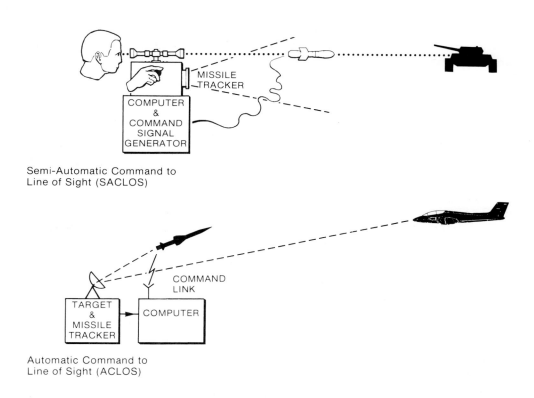

Semi-Automatic Command to
Line of Sight (SACLOS)

Automatic Command to
Line of Sight (ACLOS)

FIG. 5.11 SACLOS and ACLOS

The computer determines the correct coded command to be sent to the missile and this is passed to the missile over the command link.

A beacon or flare on the back of the missile provides a good signal-to-noise ratio for the missile tracker. Ideally, in order to avoid possible confusion of the operator, whose sole task is to track the target, this beacon should not be visible to the eye.

SACLOS guidance demands far less operator skill than MCLOS but the missile tracker may be seduced by decoys which simulate the beacon on the missile. Beacons which have a unique code that can be selected before launch are thus a useful electronic counter counter measure (ECCM).

A form of CLOS guidance which is very unusual has been used in which the target is tracked automatically, for example by radar, but the missile is maintained on the line of sight indexed by a cross wire in an optical system or on a television (TV) monitor by an operator steering the missile by a joy stick. This type of guidance has no widely agreed name but might reasonably be called a semimanual CLOS or SMCLOS.

In both SACLOS and SMCLOS it is essential to provide checks to ensure that the target and missile tracker boresights are maintained absolutely parallel or collimated.

## ACLOS

Figure 5.11 also shows the arrangement for an ACLOS system. In this form of guidance the human operator is not involved in the tracking of either target or missile, both of which are observed automatically. The position data on both target and missile are passed to the guidance computer by the respective trackers and the calculated and coded commands are sent automatically to the missile over the command link. In some systems target tracker and missile tracker may operate quite separately; for example there may be a target radar tracker and missile IR tracker. In such a case careful collimation between the two must be maintained.

In other systems a single tracker, perhaps a differential tracking radar, may track both, using a single antenna or lens system. In this case there must be some signal processing technique in the circuits of the tracker to recognise the target signal and the missile signal separately. Typically, range gating or doppler shift filtering of approach velocity may be used for this purpose.

### *Geneal Characteristics of CLOS Systems*

CLOS GW systems are widely used particularly for short range ATGW, out to about 5 Km, and for low level SAGW systems. The missile is relatively cheap and simple and contains only a beacon and a command link receiving terminal as guidance equipment. This allows the shape and packing of the missile to be optimised to suit the payload, propulsion, and air frame.

On the other hand, the missile must be guided all the way to impact and the system may suffer degradation or total failure if there is obscuration of the LOS for whatever reason. In SAM systems where the LOS swinging rate may be high, the simple calculation of latax derived from missile departure from the LOS must be replaced by much more complex computer modelling of the changing geometric situation. CLOS GW are not suited to long range systems as any angular error of tracking, which cannot be entirely eliminated even with large antennas or lens systems, will result in a miss distance at the target directly proportional to impact range.

For this reason, long range GOT missiles use, almost without exception, homing guidance; that is at least in the terminal phase.

Longer kill range may be obtained with CLOS guidance, or three point guidance, as it is known in the Soviet Union, by carrying a larger warhead. But this demands a larger missile and, in turn, larger launch point equipment.

### Command Off the Line of Sight (COLOS) Guidance

A form of guidance which was one of the first to enter service and is still used, mainly for high altitude SAM, is the Command Off the Line of Sight System (COLOS) system of guidance: it is illustrated in Figure 5.12. Unlike the CLOS system the target tracker ad the missile tracker are capable of looking in totally different directions. In such a system the trajectory of the missile is not confined to the LOS and the missile may be controlled onto the most efficient path to impact the target.

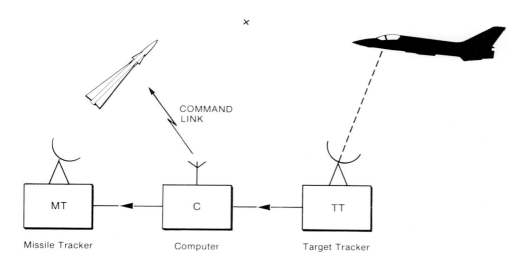

FIG. 5.12 COLOS

The missile carries a beacon which gives a larger signal to the missile tracker. In some systems the missile radar tracking transmitter itself may be used to convey the steering commands from the computer to the missile. The computer requires to know the direction and range of both target and missile and for this reason noise jamming by the target can easily confuse the system. Such jamming may, however, be overcome by various devices such as the use of additional radars to obtain range, by using optical rather than radar tracking and by falling back to CLOS guidance.

## Navigational Guidance (NG)

### *Elements of Navigational Guidance*

The basic characteristic of navigational guidance is that the missile carries the guidance computer and that information concerning missile position is obtained from instruments or sensors which are also carried in the missile. In most systems GOLIS rather than GOT is involved although, as has been seen in the case of beam riding, there are examples where moving targets may be engaged by navigational guidance. It is also frequently used in conjunction with a terminal homing phase of guidance. The most common type of NG is Inertial Navigation (IN) usually found in missiles following a near ballistic or a cruise trajectory. The two main sub types of IN are stable table IN and strap down IN.

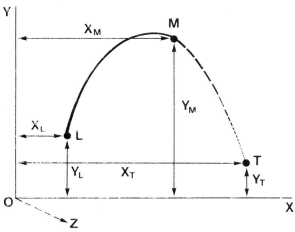

Coordinates of L and T, also
prescribed TRAJ, fed to computer before launch.

$X_M$ $Y_M$ and $Z_M$ measured by accelerometers

FIG 5.13 Inertial navigation

A typical IN trajectory which represents a missile moving in the plane of the page is shown in Figure 5.13. Before launch, the positions of the launch point L and the target T (or desired point of impact) are known.

These locations are fed into a guidance computer on board the missile, probably in the form of co-ordinates $X_L$, and $X_T Y_T$. After the missile is launched, it is the task of the inertial navigator to measure the distance moved by the missile parallel to the reference axis OX and parallel to axis OY. If these measurements are made and fed to the guidance computer it will then have all the information needed to correct any error in the missile position by passing steering instructions to the control system. The measurement of missile displacement in space is carried out by measuring the acceleration in three mutually perpendicular directions. In Figure 4.13 only two dimensions are concerned but, in general, there will be three: in the diagram this would be OZ, directly out of the page. With the acceleration in the X, Y and Z directions known at every instant in time, the computer can calculate first the missile speed in the three directions at every instant and then the distance moved in the three directions. In mathematical terms this is called double integration with respect to time.

Three accelerometers are required in both the stable table and in the strap down systems but the arrangement differs as explained below. The accelerometer consists essentially of a small weight sliding along a straight rail and held back by a spring. When the instrument is accelerated, the weight moves against the pull of the spring and the distance it moves measures the acceleration. The spring balance type of kitchen scales works on exactly the same principle.

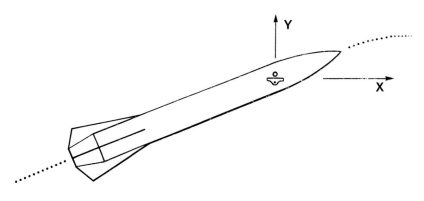

1  Table maintained in X Y Z
   space axes by gyros and servos
2  Accelerometers along X Y and Z measure $\ddot{X}$, $\ddot{Y}$, $\ddot{Z}$
3  Derive velocities and displacements
4  Guidance computer has total geometry

FIG. 5.14 Stable table IN system

### The Stable Table Inertial Navigator

A stable table inertial navigator is shown in Figure 5.14. Inside the missile there is a metal table or platform located by high quality gimbals. As the missile pitches and yaws, a system of gyroscopes and servo controls maintains the stable table in exactly its original orientation in space. The three accelerometers mounted on the table with their measurement directions mutually perpendicular are then always pointing in the same direction in space regardless of the movements of the missile. Such a system can produce accurate guidance but the instruments, bearings and gimbals must be engineered with a very high order of precision which can be provided by few manufacturers throughout the world. Such systems are costly, particularly for long range missiles, where drift of the instrumentation must be kept to a minimum.

### Strap Down Inertial Navigation

A potentially cheaper way of achieving the same result may be engineered with the help of microcomputing techniques. In this system the accelerometers and gyroscopes are fixed directly to, or are strapped down to, the missile airframe so that the actual accelerations measured are those along the axis of the missile and along the pitch and the yaw axes. With the help of gyroscopes, also strapped down the rates of turn of the missile about the three axes are also continuously monitored.

As seen in Figure 5.15 all this information is fed into a microprocessor which continuously computes the value of the acceleration along the three space axes, X, Y and Z. This information may now be handled within the computer as if it had been provided by accelerometers mounted on a stable table.

Existing systems use normal mechanical gyroscopes to measure rates of turn but some projected systems may use the all solid state ring laser gyros which are now becoming available.

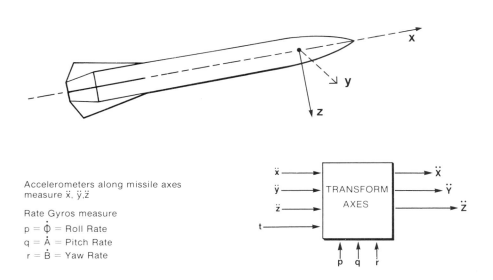

Accelerometers along missile axes
measure $\ddot{x}$, $\ddot{y}$, $\ddot{z}$

Rate Gyros measure
$p = \dot{\phi}$ = Roll Rate
$q = \dot{A}$ = Pitch Rate
$r = \dot{B}$ = Yaw Rate

FIG. 5.15 Strap down IN system

## Other Forms of Navigational Guidance

IN is by far the most usual form of NG but several other systems have been proposed or tried from time to time. These include the use of artificial radio fields, such as the Decca Navigator, the earth's magnetic field and an automatic form of the traditional technique of 'shooting the Pole Star'. There is an important new concept which has not yet been brought into use but which is planned to become available during the next few years. A system under development in the United States is called the Global Positioning System (GPS), while a planned Soviet system has been given the English language Acronym GLONASS (Global Navigation Satellite System).

## The GPS Navigational Guidance System

The GPS system is based on the concept of placing a number of earth satellites in such orbits that at least four of them may be seen from any point on the surface of the earth at any time. The satellites emit coded signals. These carefully time-synchronised, may be received and analysed by a suitable receiver carried by any ship, aircraft or missile. By noting the time of arrival of the signals from the various transmitters, the computer carried by the receiving vehicle can calculate its own position on the earth's surface to an error of a few metres. Such a navigational guidance system could be used as a single stage guidance package for a GOLIS missile, or for the midcourse guidance of a two stage missile with some form of terminal homing guidance. The Soviet system, though different in detail and in the number of satellites planned, is similar in concept.

It should be noted that this form of navigational guidance, as with IN, does not involve the use of transmitters on the missile itself and as a result does not alert an enemy of its approach.

## Compound Systems

Homing guidance is the best system for obtaining small miss distance at the target. However, for longer range systems, homing all the way from launch demands a large diameter missile so that the radar or IR homing eye can gather sufficient energy to provide a large signal at or before launch. Also such a lock before launch (LOBL) system requires a line of sight between launch point and target. This may imply undesirable operational constraints on the system.

To an increasing extent new systems are being designed in which the missile locks on after launch (LAOL) when it is near to the target. Such systems, which are known as compound or two stage systems, use some other form of guidance, usually navigational or command guidance to bring the missile into a funnel over the target within which the homing phase can begin. This funnel is known in the United States as the Basket.

In many cases such systems use a carrier missile, or bus, which deploys a number of mini missiles or terminally guided submunitions (TGSM) into the funnel over the target or array of targets. Considerable ingenuity is brought to bear on the problem of preventing more than one TGSM attacking a given target which is in the field of view, or Area of Authority (AOA) of more than one missile deployed from the bus.

There is also much research being mounted to investigate the relative merits of various forms of terminal homing. Semi-active laser homing, active and passive IR are all under test against various forms of target. There have been examples of compound guidance systems using three stages of different homing phase, but such systems are rare.

## Guidance Sensors and Data Links, The Future

### Scope

Mention has been made in the preceding pages of various sensors and communication links used in the physical realisation of the guidance techniques that have been described. It is beyond the scope of this book to enter into a detailed discussion of the various systems that may be used. For further detail the reader is referred to other Volumes of this series. However, a few words here must be devoted to the rapidly changing technology appearing in new guided weapon systems.

### Improved IR Sensors

The development of mature IR sensors has greatly improved the capability of small homing weapons. However IR sensors cannot easily detect targets through cloud, fog or dust.

### Millimetric Radar

For this reason, much effort and research funds are being expended on the development of millimetric radar and passive radiometers. The resolution ability of sensors working at these wavelengths, while not as good as that of IR systems, is better by far than that which could be provided by centrimetric radar. The propagation of millimetric waves through adverse battlefield conditions is considerably better than that of IR. In terms of equipment size they lie between microwave and IR. When components are more fully developed, millimetric sensors are likely to be extensively used. The main interest at the present time is in equipment operating at 94 GHz. It is hoped that cheaper components and more output power may become available shortly.

## Optical Fibres

The rapid progress being made in the use of optical fibres as a means of transmitting data will certainly make considerable impact on guidance systems. It may even be possible to transmit television pictures from a homing head to a ground observer by means of an optical fibre unwound from the missile. Such a link, could, of course, also carry commands to the missile.

## Computer Improvments

Substantial reduction in the size of computers and signal processing elements has already given rise to missiles which have a much greater capability than their predecessors. This trend is likely to continue, particularly as a result of intense research into very high speed integrated circuits (VHSIC) and also the probable use of light pulses rather than electronics in future computing elements. With the ability to design greater computing power into a smaller space, it may be expected that LOAL homing missiles with the ability to find and recognise given targets will become available at reasonable cost.

## Gun Launched Guided projectiles

There is a growing interest in the possible development of Guided Weapons using conventional guns to project missiles which have no propulsion system of their own but which are guided onto their targets.

Such systems present a particularly interesting technical problem since the guns themselves are designed to perform some other task, usually employing a spin stabilized shell, although smooth bore guns may also be involved. In many cases, the guns may be rapid fire systems using fast automatic feed of the projectiles, in which case the guided round must have much the same size, shape, and weight as the normal shell.

The internal instrumentation of such projectiles must withstand the high acceleration within the bore of the gun. If the gun is rifled to impart spin to its usual shells, the guided projectile must almost certainly be designed to avoid such rapid rotation by 'de-spin' driving bands.

The resulting guided projectile will need aerodynamic stabilisation by the deployment of fletching surfaces as soon as it leaves the muzzle and its rotation rate must be reduced to a few tens of revolutions per second if bonker control is to be used. For conventional aerodynamic control roll position stabilisation is likely.

Bonker control is achieved by providing a ring of dense metal slugs round the circumference of the missile body, usually near the centre of gravity of the missile, one of which may be ejected radially by firing a small explosive charge – one behind each slug. Provided that the slug is ejected at exactly the correct roll position of the missile, a change of missile heading will result in the direction opposite to that of the slug path. The number of individual course corrections available is equal to the number of slugs in the ring.

The guidance of such a projectile must determine the direction of the correction to the heading required to impact the target and providing a firing pulse to the charge behind the slug at exactly the right roll position of the missile. If a relatively expensive missile is acceptable, a homing head may be provided, such as laser semi-active homer. In this case conventional aerodynamic control, applied through an autopilot with the usual instruments and actuators (made rugged to withstand the launch forces), is probably used. The Copperhead System uses this type of technology.

If the requirement is for a cheap missile, perhaps fired in a salvo of several rounds against a single target, then the missile-borne guidance equipment must be kept to a minimum. In such a case some form of command or beam riding system is most probable. The missile equipment could then be confined to rugged solid state electronics providing a firing pulse to the bonker.

In such a missile it is highly desirable to avoid the use of such instruments as gyroscopes which are both costly and difficult to harden against launch forces. The roll position of the missile can be obtained by external information – particularly if laser beam guidance is employed. Significant advances in this type of missile may be expected shortly.

## The Changing Relationship Between Guidance and Control

The relationship between guidance and control for missile systems now in service is shown in Figure 5.16.

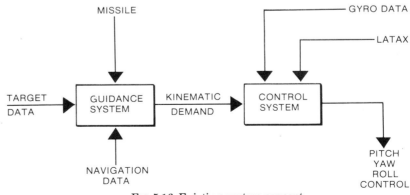

FIG. 5.16 Existing system concept

As discussed in the chapter on control system, with the help of attitude and acceleration sensors, establishes the airframe of the missile in stable flight by adjustment of pitch, yaw and roll position. One or other of the guidance systems given in this chapter passes demands for trajectory adjustment to the control system which effects the correction required.

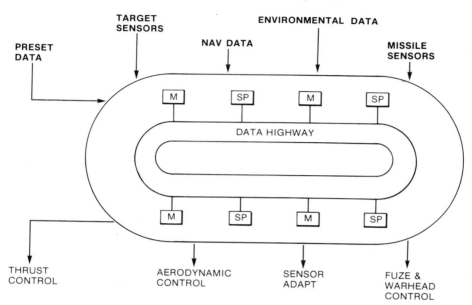

FIG. 5.17  Guidance and control – emerging concept

This concept is changing, a little at a time, to the situation shown in Figure 4.17. In this case the guidance, the control, and perhaps the fusing and warhead also, are all under the supervision of a set of interacting signal processing elements or microcomputers. They are linked by a common data highway or data bus channel which may be a bundle of optical fibres.

All the sensors available feed information into this common brain whose elements are shown in Figure 5.17 as memory elements, M, and signal processing elements, SP.

The functions of guidance, control, safety and arming fusing, and the adaption of sensor parameters are carried out making use of the total data base available in the system. Propulsion and aerodynamic adaption may also call on the full data available.

The rapid development in guided missile technology, evident for many years, shows no sign of abating.

# 6.
# Control

## The Role of the Control System

### The Basics

We have seen in the previous chapter that the guidance system is the brains of the whole missile system and provides two signals (steering commands) usually in the form of an up-down command and a left-right command. This type of control is called Cartesian control. The two steering signals could be presented in Polar form, as R and ø, for a 'Twist and Steer' missile, as we will see later. It is the task of the missile control system to execute these steering commands efficiently and consistently. The efficiency of the missile reflects the skill of the airframe designer and can be measured in terms of lift-to-drag ratio. The consistency of the missile flight performance is the task of the missile control engineer. Let us now consider some aspects of the requirement for consistency.

A very common form of guidance is 'three point guidance', that is line of sight (LOS) guidance, where the target tracker is not in the missile, but is separately situated and is usually on the ground. The three points are the target, the tracker and the missile. The method of obtaining a hit is to constrain the missile as nearly as possible to the line of sight, the line joining the tracker and the target. Consider a target flying straight and at approxi-

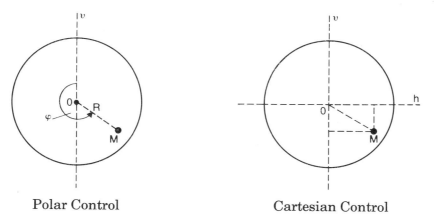

Polar Control       Cartesian Control

FIG. 6.1 Steering signals

119

mately constant speed, and a missile flying at a different speed having been launched, from close to tracker at 0, when the target occupies a position $T_0$, see Figure 6.2. We can show this two-dimensionally, whether the target is directly overhead, or in the horizontal plane, or in any intermediate position, since the direction of motion of the target and the tracker together define a plane. At intervals of time 1, 2, 3, etc seconds after launch, the LOS is shown as $OT_1$, $OT_2$ $OT_3$, etc. Since the missile ideally always lies on these lines, the flight path will be a curved one and, for an approaching target, the curvature becomes increasingly severe towards the end of the engagement. This means that the missile must be manoeuvring throughout the entire engagement, even though the target may be flying straight; moreover the lateral acceleration of the missile or, 'g' required will not be constant. An exception to this is the unique case of the target flying directly towards the tracker.

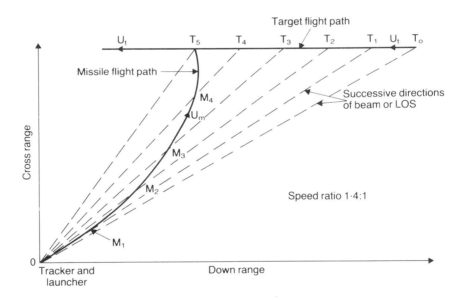

FIG. 6.2 Intercept geometry

The missile 'g' requirements are a function of the product of the target speed and the missile speed and inversely proportional to the range of the target. The missile 'g' is also much greater for angles of $\theta$ in the range $50^0 - 90^0$ than for small angles. For example, if we consider a typical surface-to-air engagement with a target speed of 240 m/s (about Mach number (0.7), a missile speed of 545 m/s (about Mach number 1.6) and impact occurs when $\theta$ = 90⁰ at a range of 1 km, the missile will have to pull, at impact, nearly 27g to keep in the LOS. If however we can hit the same target at a range of 4 km, when $\theta$ is about 15⁰, this requirement is reduced to 2.4g. If we now consider a situation more typical of an anti-tank engagement, and we are attempting to hit a tank crossing directly in front, when $\theta$ is 90⁰, at 10 m/s with a subsonic missile whose speed is 250 m/s we find that the 'g' requirement at impact is only 1g. The 'g' requirements for homing missiles tend to be rather less, but here again, fast targets, fast missiles and short ranges are the factors which result in large missile 'g'.

## The Effects of the Missile Role

How then do these considerations affect the requirement for a consistent missile response to a given demand for a manoeuvre? We have already seen in Chapter 4 that the manoeuvrability of a missile for a given control surface movement is, other things being equal, inversely proportional to the size of the static margin. In the case of an anti-tank or anti-ship missile the 'g' requirements are very small so we can afford to have a reasonable large positive static margin, say 5-10% of the missile length. If, in addition, we can place the propellant approximately symmetrically about the missile centre of gravity, fly more or less at sea level, with a constant air density, and fly at constant speed, then the missile will not be exercised through a large range of incidence. Hence the position of both the neutral point and the centre of gravity will change very little and therefore the percentage change in the static margin will be small. Conversely, to produce a very manoeuvrable missile we must have a small static margin and then a small change in the neutral point position will result in a large percentage change in static margin. As has already been explained, the point at which the lift acts on the lifting surface of the missile moves as the flight Mach number changes and therefore the static margin will change. This will effect the consistency of response of the missile.

If, in addition, the missile is required to operate over a range of heights (eg surface-to-air and air-to-air) and the propulsion system is of the boost-coast type, resulting in large speed changes, the response of the missile to a given control surface deflection will be extremely variable. In such a case the missile will have a rather more complicated control system called an auto-pilot which is considered later.

## Missile Control Configurations

### Aerodynamic Cartesian Control

Many missiles are steered using aerodynamic control. For aerodynamic control you must have, 'aero', ie air to push against, and 'dynamics', ie sufficient speed.

Some early missiles were steered using moving wings. In Figure 6.3 we consider a moving wing configuration. By this we mean that the main lifting surfaces themselves are moved in order to manoeuvre the missile; there are fixed stabilising surfaces at the rear. In this figure, and also Figures 6.5, N refers to the normal force due to the incidence of the body, wings and control surfaces, the latter being regarded as in being in the central position. $N_c$ is the extra force due to the deflection of the control surfaces, $\xi$ is the rudder deflection, $\beta$ is the incidence, and $U_m$ is the missile velocity.

Consider an extreme case in which the aerodynamic centre of the wings coincides with the centre of gravity of the missile. A movement of this wing will produce a normal force which will alter the flight path of the missile but it will exert no moment on the body. Hence there is no body incidence, so we get no lift at all from the body or stabilising surfaces. This would be very inefficient as the airframe's potential is not being utilised.

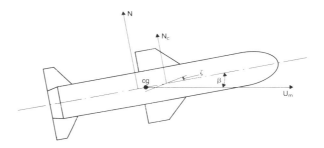

FIG. 6.3 Moving wings

Consider Figure 6.4 which shows a view of the medium range semi-active homing missile BLOODHOUND. The general configuration was conceived in the early nineteen fifties and two ramjets mounted externally were to form the sustaining propulsion system. These air-breathing engines can easily go out unless there is a free unimpeded airflow to the air intake so a constraint of a maximum of a few degrees of body incidence was imposed. This missile has moving wings slightly forward of the centre of gravity so that some lift from the body is generated as a result of a wing deflection. It should also be pointed out that to move large control surfaces needed large heavy actuators. Also, if these wings had been fixed, they would have been supported structurally along the whole of the root chord. If they are moving they are supported by a shaft only and this means that the centre section has to be much thicker. Hence they are heavier and the drag is significantly increased. Seadart, designed later, also uses ramjet propulsion and has the engine integral with the body with the intake at the front of the missile. However, this missile has flown with a body incidence of $18^0$ without the intake choking so that this is now not so much a problem to demand the use of moving wings and it is steered by using rear controls.

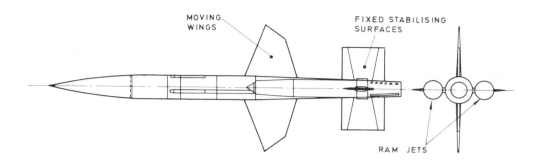

FIG. 6.4 The Bloodhound missile

Many modern missiles are steered by aerodynamic controls using fixed lifting surfaces, and small control surfaces. These control surfaces, or fins, are placed either forward of the lifting surfaces (and called 'canards') or placed at the rear of the missile.

Some of the arguments for and against canard controls and rear controls have already been considered in Chapter 4. Figure 6.5 shows some typical plan views of different configurations. Refer to Figure 6.5a and consider a steady turn where there is no resultant moment on the missile, otherwise there would be an angular acceleration. If the neutral point, that is the position through which N acts, is at a distance from the centre of gravity equal to 5% of the missile length and the distance of the control surface from the c.g. is 40% of the length then, in this case $N = 8 N_c$ and since the senses of these two factors are in opposition, the total normal force available for manoeuvring is $7 N_c$. If there is a small change in the position of the neutral point or centre of gravity so that the static margin is 10% of the missile length then $N = 4 N_c$ and the total effective normal force is $3 N_c$.

Rear controls are very common because of the comparative ease of obtaining control in roll, as already mentioned. Also, since it is desirable to obtain as large a moment as possible, it follows that canards may not be the best choice for a homing missile. For example, the homing head must be at the front of the missile and this would result in a shorter lever arm if canards were used. Similarly a shaped-charge armour-piercing warhead is efficient when placed at the front of the missile. The use of such a warhead usually rules out the use of canards.

Figure 6.5b shows a type of configuration that has been used for a subsonic anti-tank missile. In subsonic flow, a flap immediately behind a lifting surface will affect the airflow all round that surface, whereas in supersonic

flow, a control surface can never affect the airflow ahead of itself. A
disadvantage of this arrangement is that the servos controlling the control
surfaces have to be more powerful to overcome the considerable aerodynamic
hinge movement. In the conventional arrangement the aerodynamic centre
of the control surface, as far as possible, lies on the axis of rotation.

Figure 6.5c shows a typical arrangement with canard controls. Of course, if
one moves the control surfaces to the front, the overall neutral point moves
forward in order to retain a stable missile, the main lifting surfaces are
moved aft somewhat.

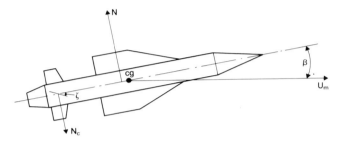

FIG. 6.5a  Rear control surfaces supersonic

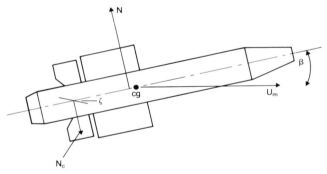

FIG. 6.5b  Rear control surfaces subsonic

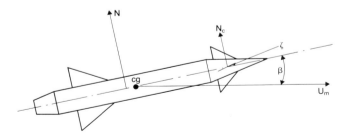

FIG. 6.5c  Canard controls

FIG. 6.5  Types of missile configuration

If one assumes a static margin of 10% of the length and a control surface level arm of 40% of the length then the total normal force is $N_c + N = N_c = 5 N_c$. This compares with $3 N_c$ for the missile shown in Figure 6.5a with the same static margin. If the static margin is 5% the missile length in both configurations, the total normal force with canards is $N_c + 8 N_c = 9 N_c$ and this compares with $7 N_c$ for the missile with rear controls. In addition, it has already been pointed out in Chapter 4 that with rear controls the initial lateral acceleration is in the opposite sense to that intended. It is very difficult to be specific concerning these effects on system efficiency and accuracy in this short and rather general treatment but it is the author's opinion that, provided the static margin can be kept down to about 5% or so of the missile length, both rear controls and canards can be efficient methods of manoeuvring a missile; the advantages of canards can easily be exaggerated.

Before leaving the topic of canards, consider once again a typical long thin missile as shown in Figure 6.5c. This shape reduces the drag and the airframe designer will, in general, aim for the smallest body diameter he can. Sometimes a homing missile requires a large diameter homing head; sometimes a certain type of warhead requires a minimum diameter to be effective. In the absence of such constraints there is this strong argument for a long thin missile. If now the propulsion motor is situated roughly in the middle of the missile, a blast pipe has to be used to carry the hot gas to the expansion nozzle at the rear. This will leave very little room for the servo designer to work in. If rear controls are used, the body diameter may have to be increased. Several missiles, both supersonic and subsonic, use the whole of the rear half or so of the body for the propulsion motor (or motors, if there are separate boost sustainer motors). As the propellant burns, the overall centre of gravity moves forward, but often only to the extent of about 10% of the body length. Such missiles are generally designed with a small negative static margin in the full condition. If the boost motor is at the back and burns very rapidly, the missile becomes stable with a positive static margin before it can seriously deviate from the desired flight path. Such a strategy is feasible only if the propellant weight is not a large proportion of the total missile weight. In more difficult cases, we can design in a rather larger initial negative static margin and employ autopilot to assist in overall stability. The object of all this is to make the propulsion system designer's task simpler and more efficient. It is a packaging consideration. We need canard controls to do this.

### Aerodynamic Polar Control

We have one more aspect of missile control to consider. The reader will have noticed that BLOODHOUND (Figure 6.4) can have only one set of wings because the ramjets are in the way of the other pair. Let it be said at once that this is an unusual arrangement and the great majority of missiles have a cruciform cross-section with two pairs of wings and two pairs of control surfaces; they manoeuvre equally well up-down as left-right. Indeed, the guidance system issues two commands, one up-down and the other left-right and these two commands are fed to the elevators and rudders respectively. If there is only one set of control surfaces and wings, the commands have to be issued, not in cartesian form, but in polar form. If the missile has to manoeuvre to the right, and we call this command x, and up, which we call y, then in polar form the commands are R and ø such that:

$$R = \sqrt{x^2 + y^2} \qquad \text{and} \tan ø = {}^x/_y$$

The missile now has to roll through an angle ø and manoeuvre outwards in this correct roll orientation. The control surfaces must be able to function as aileron and elevators. With two surfaces only how can this be done? Suppose the "R" command needs $4^0$ of elevator and we need a small adjustment in roll angle, say $1^0$ of aileron. The method is to demand $5^0$ from one control surface which is $4^0$ of elevator plus $1^0$ of aileron, and $3^0$ from the other. When the roll orientation is correct the ailerons cease to function and the control surface deflections return each to $4^0$. The addition or subtraction of demands is done very easily electrically.

The obvious question is then, why not always use polar control, or 'twist and steer' as it is often called? After all, this is how an aeroplane manoeuvres, except that a civil aircraft is said to bank rather than roll. Using two wings and control surfaces instead of four leads to a reduction in weight and drag. Such a shape is far more convenient to carry under the wings of an aircraft and will take up less space when carried in the very limited space between decks of a ship. The answer is not very clear-cut. First, if one attempts to implement the 'R' and 'ø' commands simultaneously, the resulting manoeuvre is complex and impure. It is much more difficult to model and predict the system behaviour with this type of guidance-control philosophy. If one delays the execution of the 'R' command until the 'ø' command is implemented there is, by definition a delay; the system is less responsive. But this may not matter much when the target is stationary or slow moving. Also the missile must have some on board device for giving a space reference from which to measure ø. The fact remains however, that, at the present time, there are very few twist and steer guidance-control systems. Nevertheless, these days the aerodynamicists are suggesting some novel shapes of missiles for increased aerodynamic efficiency and these require polar control; we might well see more systems using this form of control in the future.

### Thrust Vector Control

Thrust vector control (TVC) is a form of rear control. One alters the direction of thrust to steer the missile. If the magnitude of the thrust is T and its direction is defected by an angle ø then the axial or trust force is T cos ø and the force perpendicular to the body in T sin ø. It is the latter force which applies a moment to the missile.

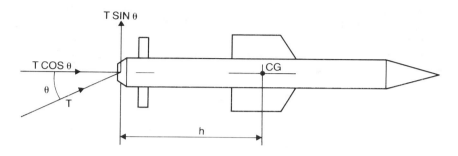

FIG. 6.6 Forces on a missile due to a thrust deflection of $\theta$

In what circumstances, then, is thrust vector control likely to be used? The simple answer is, when you cannot use aerodynamic control; i.e. when there is no 'aero', and, or no 'dynamics', speed. Firstly, all very long range missiles have to be launched gently to avoid destroying the airframe the weight of which has to be cut to an absolute minimum. They also have to be launched vertically. It is impossible in practice to ensure that the motor thrust line passes precisely through the centre of gravity; a small offset will cause the missile to turn. Gyroscopes are used to detect any deviation from the vertical, but it would be useless to try and correct this in the early stages by moving aero-dynamic surfaces. Hence all long range missiles use thrust vector control to maintain the correct trajectory.

Secondly, a number of short range air-to-air missiles use thrust vector control. Such missiles need extremely high manoeuvrability to be able to hit fast targets at short ranges, especially if the target is crossing. It is not a practical proposition to fit trainable launchers under the wings of aircraft, and, initially, the missile may even be pointing behind the target. One just cannot wait for the missile to attain full speed before full manoeuvrability is obtained.

The thoughtful reader may now see an apparent flaw in the argument. Have we not said that the object of both rear and canard controls is to apply a moment to the missile in order to obtain some incidence so that some normal aerodynamic force may be generated by the whole airframe? If the missile velocity is low, are we not still ineffective? If aerodynamic forces are the only forces acting on the missile the answer is 'yes'. When a missile is being boosted longitudinally at say 5 or 10g and the thrust is defected by a few degrees, the missile body can be turned through a large angle say 45° or more, in a fraction of a second. If however there are negligible aerodynamic forces and the body is not turned, the boost motor will propel the missile directly ahead. If the body is turned through say 45° or whatever the boost motor will direct the missile in this new direction. Indeed, at all times when the thrust is greater than the drag, one can achieve some manoeuvrability from the propulsion system. Put in another way, if we are boosting at 10g and the body is turned through 45⁰, and since the cosine and sine of 45⁰ are both equal to 0.7 approximately, then the combined effect is equivalent to boosting in the original launch direction at 7g with a normal acceleration of 7g also. Any aerodynamic normal force can now be regarded as a bonus. Many short range air-to-air missiles use thrust vector control together with an augmented boost motor so that the missile can literally be pointed almost anywhere.

Another example of the use of thrust vector control is the British anti-tank missile SWINGFIRE. This system allows the operator to control the missile when the launcher is situated up to 100 metres away and hidden or camouflaged. The system uses line-of-sight guidance. The use of aerodynamic controls would mean that it would take a long time to bring the missile into the operator's field of view and hence result in an unacceptably long minimum operating range. And finally, the concept of vertical launch even for short range missiles is being actively pursued by many countries, especially for ship-borne missiles; in such a case, they can be stored and fired from below deck with an increased rate of fire and without the necessity of heavy trainable launchers. Thrust vector control makes it possible for the missile to be turned through any angle efficiently and quickly.

We now consider some of the methods commonly used. All very long range missiles use liquid propellants which are fed under pressure to a combustion chamber through flexible pipes. The combustion chamber is mounted on a set of gimbals and rotated by servos. Figure 6.7a indicates the general method.

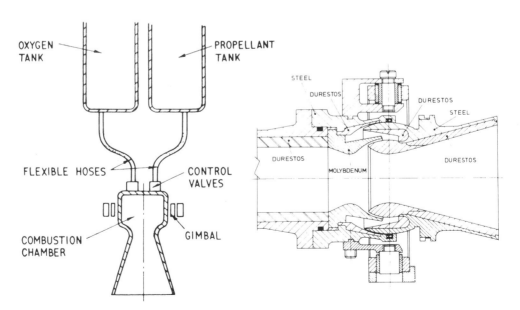

FIG. 6.7a  Gimballed motor                    FIG. 6.7b  Ball and socket nozzle

However the great majority of missiles use solid propellant and this cannot be fed through a flexible pipe! Now, to maintain the propulsive efficiency of a convergent-divergent nozzle, the smooth internal outline must be maintained, otherwise shock waves are set up with an increase in pressure and a loss of efflux momentum. Hence there is no problem with a gimballed combustion chamber, but with solid propellants things are not so simple. The ball and socket nozzle shown in Figure 6.7b maintains a shock-free gas flow over a deflection angle of about ± 15°. The disadvantage of this method is that a rather heavy nozzle, plus the friction of the seals requires fairly powerful servos. Figure 6.7c shows end view of a spoiler system. In the undeflected state all four spoilers lie outside the gas flow. Movement of one or more of the spoilers will deflect the direction of the thrust at the expense of setting up shock waves and reducing the thrust by about 1% per degree of thrust deflection. Despite this disadvantage, the method has small moving parts and therefore small servos.

If one wishes to control the roll motion of the missile as well, a more complicated system is required. One of the many types of thrust vector control package jointly developed by IMI Summerfield and Sperry Gyroscope is shown in Figure 6.7d. It was developed for a motor developing 20,000 Newtons thrust and uses twin nozzles which can be independently moved in two planes, giving control in roll pitch and yaw. In general it has been found that ± 15° nozzle deflection, coupled with a separation distance of approximately one third the missile diameter, is sufficient to cater for all roll movement from a high pressure helium bottle. The reader will have realised that TVC is inoperative after motor burn-out. In this arrangement, the servos are sufficiently powerful to enable aero-dynamic control surfaces also to be direct-coupled during any coasting phase.

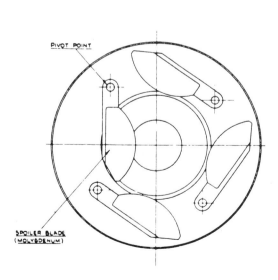

FIG. 6.7c Semaphore spoilers

FIG. 6.7d Twin nozzles

### Missile Actuators

To move the control surfaces, jetavators or spoilers of a missile, some type of actuator is required. These actuators may need to produce considerable amounts of power to move the fin or missile when it is flying supersonically. Actuators can either be linear or rotary, depending on the application and the space available within the missile, and, currently, can be electrical, hydraulic or pneumatic.

Hydraulic motors, or Rams, use the energy stored in pressurised oil which is controlled by a spool valve, the movement of which is determined by the error signal in the fin control system. Hydraulic actuators have the fastest response, (highest bandwidth), of the actuator as the oil is incompressable, and also the largest power to weight ratio. They also tend to be the most expensive.

Pneumatic actuators use the energy stored in either cold gas, (pressurised air), or hot gas, usually from burning some form of Cordite charge. Cold gas has the disadvantage of having to carry within the missile the heavy container in which the air is stored. In general hot gas takes up less space, as the gas is burnt in the missile when it is needed. It does however tend to burn up the actuator and therefore can only be used once, and for short time of flight missiles, and procludes full testing. Unlike hydraulics, hot and cold gases are compressible and this may cause stability problems in the fin movement and they are not as fast as hydraulics.

Electric actuators, either ac or dc, are more likely to be used in the future for small fin actuators, with the development and use of rare earth magnetic materials. These motors develop greater power for a given size of motor than the conventional electric motors of the last generation. They also have the advantage that they can easily be tested in the missile.

## Missile Autopilots

### Roll Autopilots

Every system engineer has to make the decision either to roll position control the missile, that is stop it rolling, or to allow it to roll freely. However, there is no choice if polar control is used, as in this case, we have to demand a certain roll position and then change this position from time to time as the engagement proceeds. As has been indicated in Chapter 4, the great majority of missiles have a symmetrical cruciform configuration so that they can manoeuvre quickly and accurately in any direction. There is no strongly stable position in roll as with aircraft which are designed with dihedral.

Hence, even at subsonic speeds, there is a tendency to roll, due to small unavoidable airframe misalignments and fin biases. In supersonic flight there can be appreciable asymmetric pressures on lifting surfaces if the incidences in pitch and yaw are not equal; this can result in large induced rolling moments.

In a homing missile there is apparently no problem. Imagine the homing head senses the target too high and as a result it sends an up command to the elevators. If the target is still high and the missile now rolls clockwise through 90⁰ say it will see the target to the left, so it will send a command to the rudders; but the rudders also have rolled with the missile and the homing head and are now really elevators. So with a homing missile a change in roll position does not create a language problem as to what is 'up' and what is 'across'. However, there are dangers.

A homing missile tends to head off the target by establishing a lead angle, so the homing head, although pointing at the target, is at an angle to the missile body. Any sudden missile roll may disturb the homing head to such an extend that it may lose sight of the target. Hence in practice the majority of homing missiles are roll position stabilised. Although the homing head servos are designed to keep the head pointing at the target, it is difficult to fit really powerful fast acting actuators when nearly all the space is taken up by the homing head itself.

In line-of-sight systems with the missile and target trackers accurately levelled and on the ground, there is a problem if the missile is allowed to rotate about the fore and aft axis. The guidance system is in no doubt about the meaning of up-down and left-right. If the missile does not roll at all, all we have to do is to ensure that the missile is launched with its elevators in the horizontal plane and that up-down commands are routed to the elevator servos and left-right commands to the rudder servos. We use a roll-control autopilot to maintain this orientation.

Now all autopilots are examples of 'closed loop systems' or 'negative feedback systems' or 'automatic control systems'. All these expressions mean the same. So perhaps it would help if the general purpose and the structure of such systems is explained. The object is to make the response of a system to a command much more predictable in the presence of external disturbances, loads and biases, changes in the environment and variability in the object being controlled (often called the plant).

In order to control accurately we have to measure accurately. If we wish to control temperature we have to measure temperature, to control position we measure position, to control acceleration we measure acceleration. For example, in a simple system the demand goes to a controlling device, such as an electric motor, to control the speed of a machine. But we know that the speed of the machine will vary with the nature of the load and perhaps other factors. With closed loop control we make three fundamental changes in approach. First we employ an instrument or transducer to measure the actual achieved output. Secondly we compare this output with the input, often called the demand; this implies that the quantity fed back must be negative. And thirdly, we amplify this difference and feed this amplified signal, or 'error', to the controller. The general idea is shown in Figure 6.8.

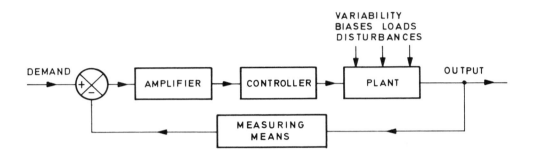

FIG. 6.8 General arrangement of a negative feedback system

The negative sign in the circle is a universal symbol indicating a negative feed-back system. All we need appreciate is that with high amplification the difference between the input demand and the measured output must always tend to be small. Indeed if the amplifier gain tends to infinity this difference would tend to zero. In practice there is a limit to the amount of amplification or 'gain' that can be built into a closed loop system on account of system stability.

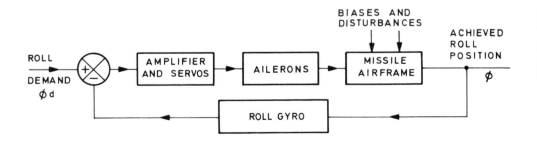

FIG. 6.9 Roll position autopilot

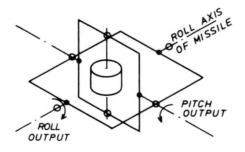

ROLL AND PITCH GYRO
(VERTICAL GYRO)

Fig. 6.10a

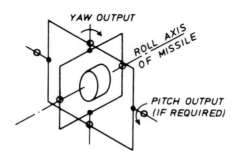

YAW AND PITCH GYRO

Fig. 6.10b

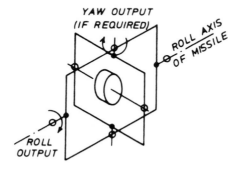

ALTERNATIVE ROLL (AND
YAW) GYRO

Fig 6.10c

Fig. 6.10 Alternative gyro arrangements

A roll control autopilot therefore is of the form shown in Figure 6.9. In the case of a twist and steer missile we require a roll position demand $\phi_d$, but with a roll position stabilisation autopilot this demand is always zero, as we require the missile to have zero roll. The missile roll attitude is measured by a roll position gyro.

Figure 6.10 shows alternative arrangements for measuring the attitude of a missile. In Figure 6.10a the gyro wheel is spinning about a vertical axis and holds the inner framework or gimbal in a vertical plane. A simple angular potentiometer placed between the missile framework and the outer gimbal can be made to give a positive or negative signal according to the direction of roll. If, incidentally, one wishes to measure the pitch attitude of the missile, one can do this with a potentiometer operating between the inner and outer gimbals. It will be noted that in each one of the possible arrangements, one can measure two missile orientations; movement around the gyro spinning axis cannot be measured. However, if the gyro wheel drifts in attitude due to imperfections in manufacture, the roll position of the missile will drift by the same amount also, or in the case of the roll position demand autopilot, the achieved position will be in error by the amount of the gyro drift. What extra then is involved in the design of a roll autopilot? We need a roll gyro of course, but as we shall see we need one of these on the missile in all line-of-sight systems. The extra complication is that we need more than two fin servos. If elevators and rudders only are used, one servo can drive both elevators by means of a simple mechanical connection: likewise the rudders. If ailerons are required as well, at least one more servo is required driving quite separate ailerons. In the great majority of cases though, we use the original pairs of elevators and rudders as before but with four servos driving each surface independently. Aileron demands are added algebraically to the elevator and rudder demands, as already discussed.

### Freely Rolling Missiles

The alternative is to allow the missile to roll freely. In the case of a line-of-sight system we need a roll gyro as before, but instead of an extra servo or servos we use a resolver. This resolver is really a variable transformer with two primary windings and two secondary windings. One set of windings is prevented from rolling with the missile by being attached to a gimbal of the roll gyro. As the missile rolls the electromagnetic coupling between the two sets of windings varies in an orderly and cyclical manner. If the guidance commands are fed to the primary windings and the output of the secondary windings is fed to the respective servos the correct combination of elevator and rudder movement will be achieved for any missile orientation. The overall arrangement is rather simpler than that which calls for roll position stabilisation. When, therefore, does the system engineer call for roll position stabilisation?

## Arguments for Roll Control

First, there is a danger, even with line-of-sight systems, which have no homing head, if the roll rate builds up temporarily to a high rate, say 5-10 revs/second or more. Imagine a constant 'up' demand and a rotating missile. The two servos will be in constant motion. The elevators will have to be in the 'up' position when the missile is in the original roll position, in the mid-position when it has rotated through $180^0$. Similarly the rudders will have to be elevators in the $90^0$ roll position etc. Now, due to the inertia of the control surfaces, the servos will lag behind these ever changing demands and, at an given time, will never be quite in the correct position. The faster the roll rate, the greater the lag and this will result in guidance inaccuracy and even total system instability. Nevertheless, if one can measure the roll rate, one can advance the timing or phasing of the servos, rather like advancing the ignition of a car to allow for the time taken to burn the fuel and build up pressure. So the situation is not really dissimilar to that with homing missiles; it is a high unpredictable roll rate which is the danger. Nowadays the mechanism of large induced rolling moments is well understood by the missile aerodynamicist who can make small changes in the overall configuration to mitigate this effect. For example, the supersonic surface-to-air missile RAPIER has a symmetrical cruciform configuration and it is allowed to roll freely. As far as the author is aware, a roll rate in excess of 2 revs/second has never been observed.

Nevertheless, there could be other considerations which lead the systems engineer to call for a roll-position-stabilised missile with line-of-sight guidance. For instance, if a beam-riding missile is designed to fly low over the sea, a vertically polarised aerial, which is maintained in the vertical position, and a vertically polarised beam, will help the receiver in the missile to discriminate against spurious reflections from the sea. Or with a sea-skimming missile, using an altimeter to measure the height above the sea, we will want the altimeter to be pointing downwards plus or minus a few degrees. If certain types of warhead are used with directional characteristics, we may require the warhead to point in a given direction, eg if we intend to overfly a target and point the warhead downwards. Again, in the case of a vertical launch followed by a rapid turnover, it is much easier for a homing missile to search for a target if it is not rolling. Finally, it is the author's opinion that, if extreme accuracy is required, such as in an anti-tank-missile, it is possible to obtain slightly more accurate guidance control if the missile is roll-position-stabilised.

## Lateral 'g' Autopilots

Lateral 'g' autopilots are designed to enable a missile to achieve a high and consistent 'g' response to a command. They are particularly relevant to surface-to-air and air-to-air missiles. We have already seen that a very small static margin is essential if high manoeuvrability is required and even small changes in the static margin plus many other contributory factors can result in a highly variable response from the missile. There are normally two lateral autopilots, one to control the pitch or up-down motion and another to control the yaw motion. They are usually identical, so we need consider one only, say the yaw autopilot associated with rudder servos. Consider Figure 6.11. We place a small accelerometer in the missile so that it will sense the sideways acceleration of the missile; the accelerometer produces a voltage proportional to linear acceleration. We compare the measured acceleration with the demanded acceleration. It is an example of the closed loop system. The reader will note the absence of an amplifier in this figure.

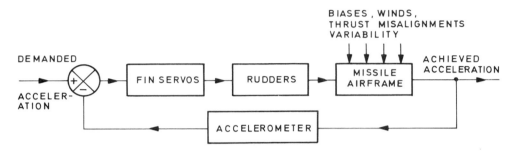

FIG. 6.11 Lateral 'g' autopilot

The reason is that if a very small static margin is designed in, the airframe response to rudder movement is so large that further amplification is usually unnecessary. Let us examine some typical numerical values. If the rudder servos deflect $4^0$/volt in the steady state, the airframe generates 40 metres/second$^2$, or about 4g, per degree of rudder deflection and the accelerometer produces 0.1 volt/metre/second$^2$ then, in the steady state, if the demand is 17 volts, the reader will see that if the output is 160 metres/second$^2$, the feedback voltage is 16 volts, leaving a nett input to the servos of 1 volt. The reader may wish to check that if the airframe gain, or response, is doubled, because the static margin has halved the system response is NOT doubled, but, for the same demand, the output increases from 160 to 165 metres/second$^2$. Likewise, if the airframe gain decreases to one half of the original value, the system response drops to 151 metres/second$^2$. In each case we see that the error, which is the difference between the demanded acceleration and the actual achieved acceleration, is small. In practice there is usually some additional feedback from a rate gyro to provide overall stability. Further details on this can be obtained from P. Garnell's book *'Guided Weapon Control Systems', 2nd Edition.* (See Bibliography.)

The reader may find the following additional explanation helpful. If the airframe for any reason becomes less responsive there will be less output for a given input. But if there is less output there is less negative feedback and therefore the nett input to the servos is increased. Hence the rudder deflection is increased. A closed loop system automatically regulates the controller output; the controller works hard when the plant is unresponsive but is automatically restrained when the plant is working at high efficiency. It can be shown that this sort of autopilot can cope with an airframe that is actually unstable (negative static margin). Hence many really manoeuvrable missiles using this sort of autopilot are often designed with an average static margin around zero. Another useful characteristic of lateral autopilots is that they assist a line-of-sight missile in the gathering phase. If the launcher is 50-100 metres away from the tracker, the missile has to fly for some time with no guidance signals until it enters the narrow guidance beam. During this period, the propulsion motor will be boosting and any small thrust misalignment will tend to turn the missile. Side winds and any fin biases will also tend to deflect it. Any sideways acceleration of the missile will be sensed by the accelerometer and the negative nature of the feedback will try to resist this. Moreover, if the missile body turns, the rate gyro will sense this and, again, the negative feedback will tend to restore the status quo.

## *Directional Autopilots*

There are many examples of guided missile systems where guidance proper does not begin until the last few kilometres of the engagement. The most obvious example is that of a sea skimmer which flies 4 to 5 metres above the sea to be below the enemy's radar horizon. It follows that if the target cannot see the missile, the missile cannot see the target. When the target comes into view the missile can use its homing head to provide guidance signals, but until then how do we ensure that the missile arrives in approximately the right place?

Let us launch a missile in a given direction without an autopilot and sustain it at a speed of 250 metres/second. Suppose, due to very accurate manufacture, we can reduce the effects of body, wing and fin misalignments so that the missile has a very low lateral acceleration bias of about 0.2g say 2 metres/second$^2$. It is easily shown that this missile has a radius of turn of 30km, so the missile is soon not only a considerable distance off line but is not even looking at the target, and we have ignored the effects of cross winds and thrust misalignments. To keep the missile on line we design a directional autopilot similar in principle to one designed to keep a ship on course. We use an azimuth gyro to measure direction and compare its output with the demanded direction; it is convenient to express both these quantities as voltages. The general form of such an autopilot is shown in Figure 6.12.

How accurate is such a system? First the gyro direction drifts slowly. Now there are gyros in existence that drift less than 0.01°/hour but they are expensive. Taking a more realistic figure for a cheaper gyro of 1°/minute we would expect the missile to gradually change direction at the rate of 1°/minute, such an autopilot will resist any tendency of the body to change direction due to thrust misalignments and randon wind gusts, it will not in any way, affect the tendency to drift down-wind due to a steady cross-wind. Any ship or aircraft navigator knows this, the former having to make due allowances for tides. The reason why the azimuth gyro knows nothing of this is that it senses, that is it measures, the direction in which the body is pointing; it does not measure the precise direction in which the body is moving. If say, we keep a ship, aircraft or missile pointing north but there is a westerly tide or wind we will not only move towards the north but will move towards the east also. In fact if the wind is from the west and its strength is 4 metres/second we will find that, independent of our forward speed, we will have an easterly component equal to 4 metres/second. This means that after a flight time of say 100 seconds the missile will have drifted about 400 metres down-wind, but it will still be pointing in the same direction.

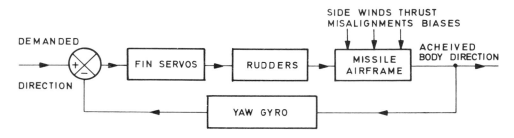

FIG. 6.12 Directional autopilot

The only way this state of affairs can be improved upon is to employ an inertial navigator using high quality accelerometers and some on-board computing. The argument here is that it is not possible to change position without a velocity and a velocity change requires an acceleration over a period of time. This is a rapidly expanding technology especially as the computing effort involved can be done so cheaply in almost zero space. The reader is referred to C.S. Edwards *The Story of Strapdown Inertial Systems* for further reading. (See Bibliography).

So far we have talked of direction in the horizontal plane only. Suppose now we wish to keep a missile flying at a certain height over a long distance. First, on all guided weapon systems we insert a permanent 1g bias in the vertical plane. If this is not done and we consider a case where guidance signals are available say in a line-of-sight system, the missile will start to drop due to gravity but the guidance will sense this and will send a signal to the missile saying you are too low. The result will be that the missile will eventually stop accelerating downwards but will always sit low in the beam. Such a contribution to inaccuracy is quite unnecessary, so a permanent 1g bias command is built into the system. But to implement this perfectly is not possible. The bias will consist of a given voltage bias into the elevator servos; but the missile will not respond absolutely consistently to this bias. So we cannot expect a missile to fly on a precisely level flight say at 4 metres above the sea without some further complication. The method used is to use a closed loop system and to measure the actual height above the sea by means of a radio or laser altimeter. The accuracy of measurement these days is within a fraction of a metre. The difference between the demanded height and the measured height is the actual signal fed to the elevator servos. If, however, a minimum height of about three hundred feet or more is satisfactory then the feedback from a simple barometric device or a peizo-electric pressure transducer can be used. Really accurate control requires really accurate measurement; the good guided missile systems engineer selects those methods which are only just good enough as these are nearly always the cheapest.

# 7.
# Electroic Warfare Applied to GW

**Introduction**

Electronic warfare (EW) is the exploitation by each side in a conflict of their opponent's use of electromagnetic (EM) waves. The parts of the EM spectrum used are:

*Ultraviolet* – very little used   *Millimetre Waves (MMW)*

*Optical Systems*                   *Microwaves* (metric and centimetric radar)

*Infra-red (IR) Systems*            *Radio* at all wave lengths

It is useful to note that the Soviets call EW Radio Electronic Combat (REC).

Figure 7.1 lists the wavelengths with their main uses in GW systems: 1 micrometre ($1\mu$m) is one millionth part of a metre or $10^{-6}$m. 1 centimetre (cm) is $10^{-2}$m.

The frequency of EM waves and their wavelength are related by the formula.

Frequency of Wave in Hz = $\dfrac{\text{Velocity of Light}}{\text{Wavelength in Metres}}$

$$\text{or} \quad f = \frac{3 \times 10^8}{\lambda}$$

E.g. Radar wave with wavelength 3cm = 0.03m

$$\text{has a frequency} = \frac{3 \times 10^8}{0.03} = 10^{10}\text{Hz} = 10\text{GHz}$$

Lasers are high power transmitters providing a very narrow beam of radiation. They can operate at either optical wavelength or IR wavelengths. Both $1.06\mu$m and 10.6 are commonly used. The use of super powerful damage lasers is not considered in this chapter. Although they are closely related, the use of damage lasers is not usually considered to be part of EW.

## MAIN SENSORS USED FOR BATTLEFIELD GW

| SENSOR | WAVE LENGTH | USE |
|---|---|---|
| ULTRA VIOLET SAGW | <0.4$\mu$m | ONLY FOR VERY SHORT RANGE FUZING OR GUIDANCE |
| VISIBLE SAGW AND ATGW | 0.4 – 0.7$\mu$m | TARGET AND MISSILE TRACKING IN FAIR WEATHER EYEBALL SURVEILLANCE |
| NEAR IR SAGW | 0.7 – 1.5$\mu$ | TAIL CHASING IR HOMING MISSILES |
| MID IR SAGW | 3– 5$\mu$m | FORWARD HITTING IR HOMING MISSILES |
| FAR IR ATGW AND SAGW | 8 – 14$\mu$m | IMAGING HOMING HEADS TI SURVEILLANCE PASSIVE DETECTION OF AIRCRAFT |
| MMW ATGW | 1 – 10mm | ACTIVE AND PASSIVE HOMING MMW TRACKERS AND BEAM RIDING SHORT RANGE SURVEILLANCE |
| CENTRIMETRIC RADAR SAGW | 1 – 10cm | TARGET AND MISSILE TRACKERS HOMING HEADS FOR LARGE MISSILES MEDIUM RANGE SURVEILLANCE |
| LONG WAVE RADAR | >10cm | GETTING TOO BIG FOR TACTICAL BATTLE |
| LASERS ATGW AND SAGW | <15$\mu$m | NARROW BEAM TRANSMITTERS IN IR OR OPTICAL REGION FUZING. TRACKING. BEAM RIDING. |

FIG. 7.1  Which wavelength?

This chapter is only concerned with the application of EW to battlefield weapons and does not discuss the important subject of Communication EW. EW in naval and air operations has been of growing importance since the early years of the 20th century and is highly developed. In many respects the impact of EW on land wafare has yet to be realised. Much of this chapter relates to likely future developments rather than established practice. EW applied to SAGW is, however, already fully considered both in operations and in equipment design and there is an extensive literature on this aspect of the subject.

There are three main areas of activity in EW. Electronic Support Measures (ESM), or REC Collection, is the process of obtaining information on enemy tactical activity and equipment by listening to his transmitters. Electronic Countermeasures (ECM), or REC neutralisation and deception, is the frustration of enemy receiving systems by jamming, physical destruction of his equipment operators, providing screens to block his transmission, or the use of decoys or false targets. Some authorities exclude physical attack from the definition of ECM. Jamming is the process of beaming strong signals at enemy receivers to either drown out his own signals (confusion or noise jamming) or to inject false data into his system (deception or repeater jamming).

## EW Applied to ATGW

The conflict between the Main Battle Tank (MBT) and ATGW becomes progressively more technically sophisticated as new types of armour and new and varied forms of ATGW enter service. The following sections consider in turn the main types of existing and future ATGW together with the appropriate ESM, ECM and ECCM for each system. It must be said again that EW of this type is still in its infancy.

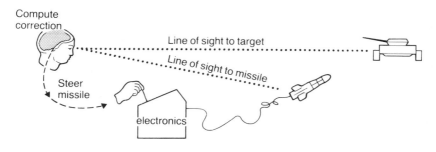

FIG. 7.2 MCLOS EW

## ESM

Tank detects missile launch and approximate direction by IR detection of boost motor.

## ECM — Defeat the Target Tracker

1    Tank attacks missile controller with main armament or MG.

2    Tank projects smoke onto line of sight (LOS)

3    Tank breaks LOS by moving into dead ground or behind cover.

4    Tank shines powerful lamp along LOS to dazzle controller.

## ECCM

1    Missile designed with low launch signature.

2    High speed missile reduces time of flight (TOF).

3    Use of thermal imager (TI) to reduce effect of smoke.

4    Launch missile from behind cover, using separated sight to avoid launch
     signature.

The MCLOS system is falling out of favour mainly because of its demands on
highly trained controllers but from an EW viewpoint it is a good system because
of the ability of the trained operator to avoid decoys and other ECM tricks.

The wire command link and, in the future perhaps, an optical fibre link, is
virtually impossible to jam but where radio command links are used these
can be jammed. The truly jam proof radio link has yet to be derived.

## SACLOS Electronic Warfare

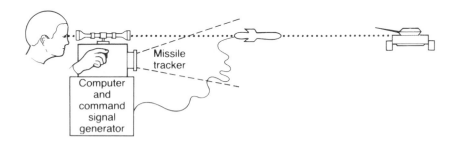

FIG. 7.3 SACLOS EW

The ESM and ECM against the tracker is as for MCLOS.

## Additional ECM Against Missile Tracker

1   Tank uses decoy flares to seduce tracker.

2   Tank shines IR lamp to paralyse tracker.

3   Tank transmits IR signals copying missile tracker chopping disc (reticle) frequency to confuse tracker.

4   Tank projects IR smoke bombs behind missile to blind missile tracker.

## ECCM

1   Use coded becaon on missile (flash tube).

2   Make missile tracker field of view (FOV) as small as possible.

3   Use missile tracker technique avoiding reticle (static split tracker).

The SACLOS System is more vulnerable to ECM than the MCLOS missile. If a coded beacon is adopted the system should include the facility to select one of several available codes (typically flashing frequency) to make the design of a decoy more difficult. It would be possible to design a SACLOS system with a separated sight to conceal the launch signature but this is not usual practice.

## EW for Line of Sight Beam Riding ATGW

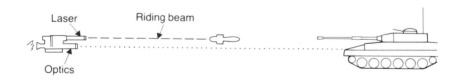

FIG. 7.4  EW for line of sight beam rider

The ESM and target tracker ECM is as for MCLOS.

*Additional ESM*   Laser will be detected by laser receiver (LWR) on tank.

*ECM*   Project smoke bombs making laser smoke screen behind missile.

*ECCM*   High speed missile.

It is almost impossible to jam the laser receiver in the rear of the missile.

For certain types of terrain it might be possible for the tank to use its gun to create a dust cloud behind the missile which would interrupt the beam. Specially designed smoke shells would be more universally effective however.

### EW for Mortar Bomb with Terminal IR Homing.

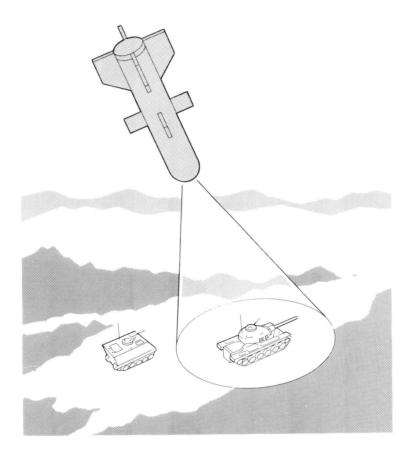

FIG. 7.5  IR Homer EW

### ESM

1   Not available.

2   Use weapon locating radar to locate mortar position.

3   Missile is passive and cannot be detected without radar.

4   Launcher is hidden from tank.

## ECM

1   Destroy mortar.

2   Reduce IR signature of tank.

3   Deploy IR smoke above tank.

4   Eject IR decoys.

5   Jam IR reticle in homing head.

## ECCM

1   Use static split tracker in missile. A Static Split tracker is one which has no moving reticle or chopping disc. It is much more difficult to jam.

It is probable that this system will be controlled by a forward observer, in which case the communication link back to the mortar might be susceptible to jamming. ECM against this system is made very difficult because there is nothing to alert the tank of the pending attack. Consequently it may be necessary to equip future MBT with self protection radar but this would have a major impact on tank design.

## EW for Mortar Bomb with Active MMW Homing Head

## ESM

1   Locate mortar as for IR homer.

2   Use MMW ESM receiver on tank to detect and locate bomb.

## ECM

3   Jam MMW homing head.

4   Eject MMW decoys.

## ECCM

1   Home on jam

2   Use combined MMW and IR homing head.

3   The tank could jam with random noise or a deformed copy of the missile transmission (noise jam or repeater jam).

4   The actual form of jamming would depend on the method of angle tracking used by the MMW homing tracker.

MMW jammers might well need to have a library of possible amming transmissions. The correct response for a particular missile would be chosen automatically as a result of the ESM receivers analysis of the missile transmission.

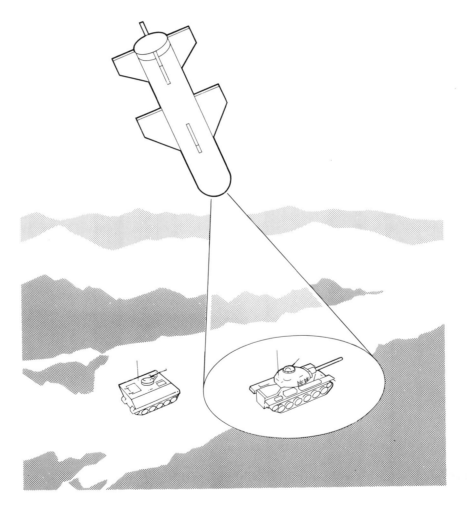

FIG. 7.6 MMW Homer EW

# EW for a Semi Active ATGW using Laser Designator

## ESM

1 Detection of missile launch.

2 Laser warning receiver (LWR) detects and locates laser designator

3 Communication link between laser and launch platform may be detected.

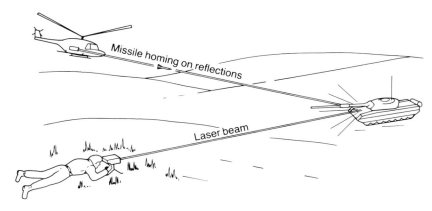

FIG. 7.7 Semi active Homer EW

## ECM

1 Destroy laser

2 Jam laser/launcher link

3 Retro-lamp to dazzle laser operator

4 Project smoke onto missile path or laser or both

5 Use laser repeater jammer

## ECCM

1 Rigid drill and timing

2 Use jam resistant laser/launcher link

3 If possible launch missile on a mortar type trajectory from behind cover.

This system is highly vulnerable to ECM unless the launch can be concealed and the laser turned on a few seconds only before impact. The laser may be directed from the launch helicopter, a second helicopter, or from a tank or other vehicle. If the time of flight of the missile is long the attack of moving targets is uncertain.

## EW for IR Homing Missile which Locks on Before Launch (LOBL)

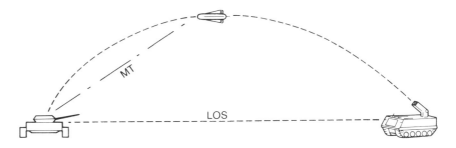

FIG. 7.8  LOBL IR Homer EW

### ESM

1   Detect and locate missile launch

### ECM

1   Make smoke above tank to block the path MT

2   Eject IR decoys

3   If simple IR homing head, IR jammer may be possible.

### ECCM

1   Use complex signal processing in missile to reject decoys.

Given that the tank can detect the launch of the missile, this system is very vulnerable to smoke and decoys but, in the fog of battle, this may not always be the case. The LOS between tank and launcher is unfortunately essential for a LOBL missile.

## EW for Heli-Launched ATGW

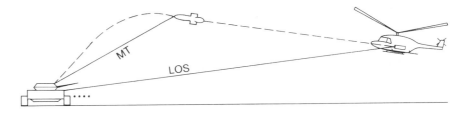

FIG. 7.9  Helicopter launch ATGW EW

## ESM

Acoustic, visual, IR or radar detection of helicopter may help alarm.

### Other ESM

As for ground launched system with same guidance.

### ECM AND ECCM

As for ground launched systems with the same guidance.

In the case of those systems in which the helicopter must continue to track or designate the target after missile launch, destruction of the helicopter before missile strike would provide an effective counter measure. Such a counter attack might be achieved by the use of a guided projectile from the gun of the MBT.

This will lead to ECM equipment being fitted into the helicopter.

### EW for a Long Range ATGW

Where the attack of tanks is undertaken by long range (e.g. 15Km) missiles, which may be ground-launched or air-launched, missiles may either be dispersed from a bus missile or they may be directed independently. The widely discussed MLRS Phase 3 is an example of the former, while several suggestions for 155mm Gun Launched projectiles exemplify the latter approach. In both systems final guidance is achieved by IR or MMW Homing in most cases. The remote launch system would only be observed by general surveillance systems so that no ESM on launch would be available to the target or targets. The EW situation is therefore very similar to the mortar launched ATGW and the same arguments would apply to the passive and active systems respectively.

Another possibility could be for the bus missile to deploy unguided but so called 'smart missiles' falling slowly on parachutes until their IR or MMW fuzes detect a tank. A pre-formed fragment warhead then attacks the top armour. The EW situation with such fuzes would be very like that discussed for IR or MMW Homing.

### EW for LOAL Fibre Optic Track Via Missile ATGW

### ESM

None. The missile is passive and the launcher is concealed.

## ECM

Use radar to detect approach or missile. Deploy smoke above tank. Possibly optical decoys.

FIG. 7.10 Long range ATGW EW

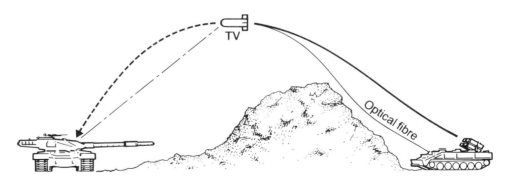

FIG. 7.11 Fibre optic ATGW EW

**ECCM**

Use twin band TV camera.

This system would be inherently highly resistant to ECM. The human operator, looking at the TV monitor if adequately trained, would be difficult to deceive by decoys.

Vertical launch might improve the system, but it would also mean that the missiles would be more expensive.

## Land Based Medium/High SAM Electric Warfare

Although land forces are greatly concerned about attack from low and very low aircraft, medium level and even high level attack cannot be neglected. It becomes progressively more important as the effectiveness of low level SAM is improved and as air launched stand off surface attack weapons become an increasing threat.

EW in this context has been developed over many years and an extensive literature is available. Only a short summary of the more important aspects will be attempted here. The need for all-weather operation and long range impact requirement results in radar being used to the virtual exclusion of IR and optical subsystems. Ground attack from medium level and above is unlikely to be attempted by single aircraft. A co-ordinated attack involving airborne comand and control aircraft, specialised jamming and ESM platforms, and attack diversity in both time and approach must be expected.

The general picture is one of a true tactical battle in which ESM, ECM and ECCM on both sides are of paramount importance. The ability of airforces to achieve rapid and intense concentration of force in both space and time puts the SAM defense at an initial disadvantage. The air attack must not be allowed the advantage of surprise as well so that highly efficient surveillance in the first priority for SAM. If possible many SAM sites should work in close cooperation including high capacity communication links between them.

### Surveillance Radar (SR) EW

The opposing airforce will use ESM aircraft or RPV to determine frequency of transmission and location of the SAM radars. This may be done by reconnaissance, including the use of feint attacks. There is little point in an aircraft flying into the coverage of an SR applying ECM carried by itself. This will only herald its approach to the SR.

**Stand Off Jammer (SOJ) Circus**

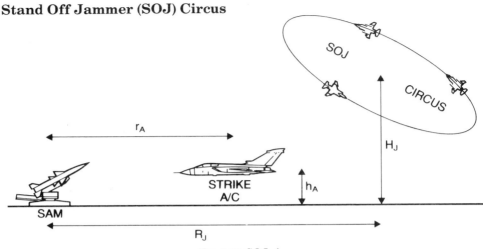

FIG. 7.12 SOJ circus

However the use of a stand off jammer (SOJ) circus as shown in Figure 7.12 can be highly effective in hiding the approach of a fighter ground attack aircraft (FGA) which will be invisible to the SR against the blinding background of noise jamming.

The SOJ are themselves beyond the range of attack and the circus may be maintained for any length of time as individual aircraft refuel and return to their station.

The number of SOJ in the circus may be increased to defeat any known SR but it is, of course, very expensive in terms of resources.

The SR is likely to remain the most susceptible component of the Medium SAM in spite of modern methods of antenna design (three dimensional phased arrays with adaptive beam shape control), spread spectrum transmission (carrier frequency jumping from pulse to pulse) and pulse compression techniques (inspired by the sonar of the bat). This latter development permits improved resolution of targets without reduction of transmitted power and consequent degradation of signal to jamming signal ratio.

### Guidance System EW

All modern Medium/High SAM systems use either semi-active homing all the way from launch to target – or, more probably, COLOS flyout with terminal homing, usually semi-active radar homing. Older systems may use COLOS only. The target is alerted by its radar warning receiver (RWR) and, since its location is known to the enemy, it is free to start active jamming. This jamming will be designed to 'break the lock' of the target tracker (or homing head). Such jamming is usually deceptive repeater jamming which throws back the identical signal to that transmitted by the radar and then introduces a subtle change such as a time delay (Range gate pull off) or frequency shift (Velocity gate pull off).

Injection of false angular data may also be present in the form of artificial glint i.e. jamming transmissions which make the target echo jump about in the vicinity of the target. This produces tracking jitter in the missile's homing head leading to large miss distances.

The track-via-missile facility, as used in the Patriot SAM system, allows an accurate assessment of the jamming environment, as seen by the missile homing head, to be made by computer with operator assistance, on the ground. The down link and up link can be made highly resistant to jamming.

When a homing missile switches to 'home on jam', the target needs to turn off its jammer. A game of on-off hide and seek follows. Another form of jamming difficult to counter is when two aircraft fly side by side at a fixed spacing and employ 'Box and Cox' jamming, one turning on while the other turns off.

In set piece attacks on a given area by an opposing airforce, the actual attack may be preceded by the distribution of chaff to conceal aircraft and cause false data in the SAM radars. Chaff consists of strips of metallised plastic of such a length (about one half wave length) that a strong reflected signal is received by the radar. The chaff is scattered in bundles which break up to produce large clouds of chaff which appear as a false target. 'Black chaff' is optimised to reduce the strength of the radar signal passing through the chaff cloud. It may be said to be radar smoke.

Clearly there are many ways of employing chaff in a tactical battle between aircraft and SAM systems. Chaff may be dispersed from manned aircraft, UMA, bus missiles, shells, bombs, free flight rockets or guided missiles. The settling or fall rate of chaff depends greatly on many factors of design, altitude and wind conditions but is of the order of one foot per sec (0.3 m/s).

## Land Based Low Level SAM Electronic Warfare

Low level and very low level SAM may use optical, IR or radar sensors though, in nearly every system, a SR is used for surveillance or target acquisition. In the first generation low level SAM, design against ECM was given low priority. The situation is now very different as the increased cost of manned aircraft and the progressively improving SSKP of later versions of SAM have made it cost effective for aircraft to devote part of their payload to airborne self protection jammers (ASPJ) and expendable decoys such as IR flares or chaff rockets.

The art of tactical employment of UMA and dump jammers to paralyse the ground defence for the short duration of a ground strike has also advanced greatly.

Ground based SAM deployment is dominated by the effect of terrain on the unmask and remask window. This is the distance or time (at aircraft flying speed) between the point at which the aircraft becomes visible from the SAM site and the point at which it disappears from view. An aircraft flying at say 300 m/s would fly through a window of 3000m in 10 sec, a window of 6000m in 20 sec and so on. The SR must clearly have a high data rate (one revolution per second is typical) to detect the aircraft as soon as it unmasks.

For a known SAM site location, the aircraft can afford to eject expendable decoys throughout the time it is in the danger window. The length of the danger window can be increased for most directions of attack by careful selection of the position of the SAM site in relation to buildings, hills, and other features which may mask approaching targets. As the surveillance range of the SAM is almost certain to be fixed by the unmask range, target-borne jamming will not provide the SAM weapon with enhanced detection range although it may assist high level airborne surveillance systems such as (AWACS).

In addition to the use of decoys and chaff, ECM against low level, SAM sites may include anti radar missiles (ARM) and jamming from the target aircraft (ASPJ). Jamming from separately controlled remotely piloted vehicles (RPV) or autonomous UMA may also be encountered. The actual jamming techniques are in this chapter. However, where the distance between jammer and victim receiver is small, the power of the jammer required is much smaller for a given level of radar or IR signal. Thus a stand-in jammer (SIJ) requires a smaller carrying platform than a SOJ.

Paradoxically the ASPJ has to increase its power by a factor of four each time the radar-target range is halved. This is because the radar signal increases more rapidly than the jamming signal in the radar receiver as range is reduced. IR self protection jammers however remain effective at a constant level as range changes.

## Tactical use of ECM Against Low Level SAM

The following examples give a few methods employed for the attack of ground targets protected by low level SAM sites.

Figure 7.13 shows an attack under the control of an RPV in contact with an airborne command aircraft (e.g. an AWACS) or a ground based command station. The manned FGA is preceded by a small UMA which deploys expendable SIJS.

Control RPV

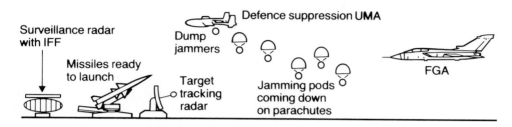

FIG. 7.13 Tactical use of ECM against low level SAM

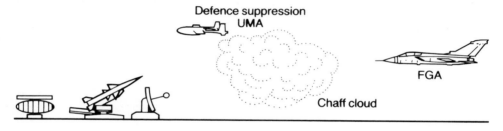

FIG. 7.14 Concept of ECM using RPV

Figure 7.14 depicts a similar attack but, in this case, the defence suppression UMA scatters a chaff cloud through which the FGA makes its attack.

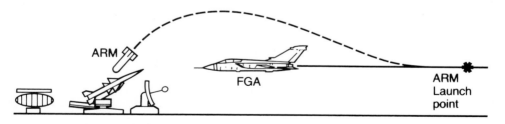

FIG. 7.15 Use of ARM against radars

Figure 7.15 an ARM is launched to destroy the radars of the SAM system just before the arrival of the FGA. The ARM may be launched by the FGA itself or by some other platform. If the radars protect themselves by switching off they will be unable to guide the SAM missiles.

The above techniques, and several others, may be used in various combinations to maintain the element of surprise.

The ECCM which may be used by the ground base missile systems are difficult to devise in advance particularly in view of the flexibility and numerous options open to the attacking airforce. However intensive crew training must have high priority. If possible, a carefully concealed and totally silent additional SAM weapon site, which is only brought into use at the last moment, may also prove effective.

## Future Battlefield EW

The technical and tactical aspects of EW will almost certainly continue to evolve at a rapid pace, as they have done since the early days of EW. Each new conflict involving sophisticated weapons seems to result in a sudden acceleration in EW development. A much greater involvement of EW in the land battle seems inevitable. The most important factor in EW remains the same. This is the ability to react quickly and effectively to new and unforeseen enemy initiative.

# 8.
# Warheads

## Introduction

The object of the design of any missile is simply to deliver a warhead to a designated target. No book on Guided Weapons is complete without some comment on warheads. The missile is just a transporting vehicle. Even the most accurate guidance and propulsion systems are of limited value if the warhead cannot produce a sufficiently lethal effect at the right moment to disable or destroy the target. It is essential that the warhead is considered from the first conception of the GW system since missile performance can be seriously degraded if there is any mismatch of its components.

The term warhead is generally accepted as meaning the destructive or damaging element of the missile, but it is likely to be located in positions which are not in the head of the missile as shown in Figure 8.1.

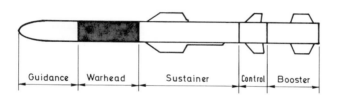

FIG. 8.1 Typical guided weapon component layout

Early guided weapons used modified aircraft 'iron' bombs as the explosive payload with some form of guidance and propulsion system encased in a suitable airframe. They were heavy, and not initially matched to the target's requirement. However, constant research and experimentation in warhead design now enables designers to obtain an optimised effect against a wide range of targets.

Warhead selection depends on the characteristics of the target and the effect required. Targets may be classified as aerial, surface or underwater targets, and these classifications can be further subdivided according to height, in case of aerial targets, degree of dispersion or concentration and the amount of protection that needs to be defeated. Using this as a basis, and knowing the standard error of guidance and warhead weight, it is possible to arrive at a list of warhead designs that might suit the requirement.

159

If we could guarantee hitting a target rather than achieving a near miss, the kinetic energy of the missile could be sufficient to destroy many targets, particularly aircraft. However, there are occasions when the protection afforded to the target is so great that some form of active warhead is needed. The weapon's designer is also faced with the dilemma of whether to increase the ability of missile to hit the target by improving the guidance, which may be expensive, or to use an explosive warhead to achieve a kill at a given miss distance.

### Warhead Components

The warhead essentially consists of a payload, a fuze and a safety and arming mechanism. it may be varied by changing any or all three of these basic components, and they may not be necessarily physically separate items. The fuze and safety and arming mechanism are often combined.

It is the payload that directly causes damage to the enemy, and achieves the aim of the weapon. Although damage is usually destructive, it does not have to be. Illuminating effects that expose the enemy, propaganda leaflets which affect his morale, and, of course, electronic warfare, chemical, biological or radiological effects should not be ignored.

The payload, in most conventional warheads, relies for its effect on a bursting explosive charge. For safety reasons it is normal to use an insensitive main charge. An explosive train, which is an arrangement of a series of explosives, is used to initiate the bursting charge. A small quantity of sensitive explosive, an initiator or detonator, sets up the initial detonation wave, a booster picks up this weak detonating wave which results in sufficient energy to set off the main charge. The arrangement is shown in Figure 8.2.

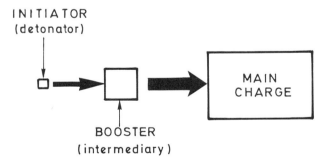

FIG. 8.2 High explosive train

The initiator (detonator) and booster (intermediary) are often integral parts of the fuze and/or safety and arming mechanism, and these warhead components are discussed later in the chapter.

## Target Effects

The warhead is the primary element of the weapon, and it is designed to achieve effective damage to the intended target. This will depend upon the warhead's ability to transfer its destructive energy to the target, and is known as energy coupling. The energy includes thermal, kinetic and chemical energy, and in addition, pressure (shock waves) produced as by-products of blast.

If a series of identical missiles were fired at a target and the miss distances, plotted, the result would be a normal distribution, as shown in Figure 8.3.

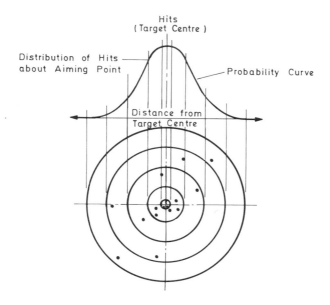

FIG. 8.3 Dispersion

Dispersion will occur whether the missile is guided or not. If the target is taking evasive action then the resulting dispersion is likely to be less for a guided missile than for the unguided projectile when fired under the same conditions. If a direct hit on a small target is needed a large number of missiles must be fired. There is a choice: improve guidance to decrease dispersion, or improve lethality of the warhead to ensure the critical damage level is achieved despite the miss distance.

Although the warhead is the centre of the destructive power, there exists, in addition, an envelope of destructive capability that follows the missile's trajectory or flight path. The volume enclosed by this envelope is known as the damage volume. It is shown diagrammatically in Figure 8.4. The radius of the damage volume is dependent upon the warhead energy and the vulnerability of the target.

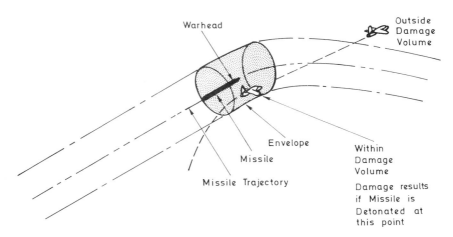

FIG. 8.4 Damage volume

The kinetic energy missile will have a maximum damage volume determined by the diameter of the projectile alone. A missile that has a large damage volume, may affect the target even though it misses. The damage volume is only a potential effect until the warhead is initiated. If the warhead is initiated too late or too early no effective damage may result. It is the fuze that determines the moment to achieve the real effect.

As blast and fragments radiate from the point of detonation, their destructive power is reduced the further they travel. This loss of power is known as attenuation. The environmental conditions, such as air density, water pressure and temperature will all have an effect on the velocity and, possibly, the direction of the blast wave and fragments. The actual distance to which the damage volume extends will be a function of attenuation, target protection and explosive efficiency.

The manner in which energy and material travel through the environment on detonation is known as propagation. If it is uniform in all directions, it is known as isotropic propagation, but a payload may be designed to release more energy in a particular direction. Such a reaction is known as non-isotropic propagation. If a non-isotropic payload is used in a weapon then specific target information on location and direction must be available to the fuze to ensure optimum lethality, whereas with the isotropic payload, only distance from the target is needed.

## Types of Warhead

There are many types of warhead available, and some of the more important will now be examined.

### *Blast Warheads*

A blast warhead is one in which the payload is designed to achieve its effect and damage level primarily from blast. The payload of this type is high explosive. On detonation this produces a centre of high pressure which propagates isotropically. In reality, the pure blast weapon does not exist, since the explosive has to be contained, and fragmentation from the container will inevitably be produced on detonation. These fragments are a secondary effect.

When the high explosive filling detonates, some of the energy is absorbed in expanding the charge casing, the remainder is imparted to the surrounding medium and a shock wave is produced by the rapidly expanding gases. The shock wave moves out radially from the centre of detonation, rather like a sound wave.

Preceding the shock wave is an extremely sharp front, called a shock front, which is a zone of rapid change of density, pressure and temperature. During the positive phase, the pressure rises steeply from ambient to peak pressure and falls gradually to ambient. Then, in the negative phase, it falls below ambient, as shown in Figure 8.5. This negative phase is less intense, but lasts 4-5 times longer than the positive phase. Primary damage secondary damage will be caused by the fragmenting warhead case and debris resulting from the blast waves.

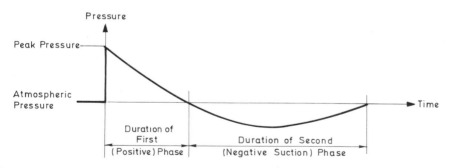

FIG. 8.5 Pressure/time relationship of a blast wave

Essentially, blast warheads are containers filled with high explosive which is initiated by a fuzing mechanism. They may be used against air, surface and underwater targets, and each may be further subdivided into two types, internal and external.

An internal blast warhead is designed to cause damage by detonating on target impact or very shortly after penetration. Since an internal blast warhead must hit the target to cause damage, the guidance system must ensure a strike for the warhead to be effective. It is possible to use internal blast warheads as sub-missiles in cluster warheads, in which case the guidance system does not have to be so precise, provided that it takes the warhead to the vicinity of the target before the main carrier warhead functions. The external blast warhead is designed to inflict damage when detonated near the target, consequently it can be used in less accurately guided weapons, and proximity fuzes are normally used.

The design of the casing will depend upon whether the warhead is intended to detonate outside the target or after it has penetrated. Figure 8.6 shows the essential differences in design.

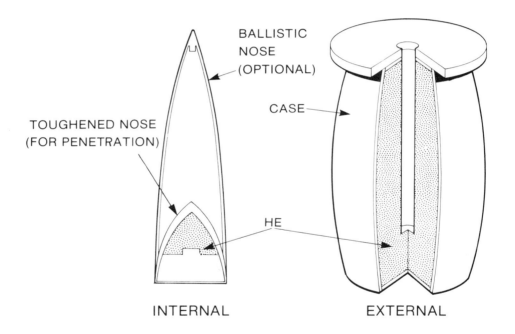

FIG. 8.6 Typical blast warheads

The density of the medium greatly affects the performance of the blast warhead. At altitude, the blast warhead is less effective due to the reduction in air density, and it is best used at heights of less than 7000 metres. On the other hand, a blast warhead has greater effect underwater due to the increased density of the water medium. Figure 8.7 shows the increase in explosive quantity required to achieve a given damage level at altitude.

## Fragmentation Warheads

Fragmentation warheads consist of an explosive charge surrounded by a casing, or wall of pre-formed or pre-scored metal. On detonation, the fragments are propelled outwards at velocities of 2000 to 4000 metres per second. They also create a blast effect, but this is secondary. The damage inflicted is slower acting compared to the blast warhead.

They are effective against both air and surface targets. Against aerial targets they are more potent at high altitude than blast warheads due to the lower air density. Against surface targets, fragmenting warheads are particularly efficient for attacking dispersed, lightly armoured targets and personnel. They are capable of damaging lightly armoured surface vessels, and, more recently, have proved to be a useful weapon against the surface skimming, anti-ship missile.

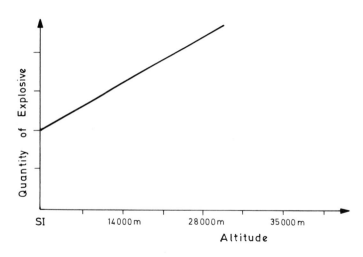

FIG. 8.7  Increase of explosive to achieve same damage level with
altitude increase

Fragmentation warheads are usually designed to be detonated near, rather than to hit, the target. Proximity fuzing is normally used and the guidance system need not produce a hit to ensure lethality. the lethal distance is chiefly dependent upon the target, fragment size and velocity of strike (the kinetic energy delivered to the target). The strike velocity is the vector sum of the fragment velocity and the target velocity.

The initial fragment velocity is primarily dependent upon the charge-to-mass ratio and the characteristics of the explosive filling, particularly its brisance (shattering effect) and its power. As a fragment travels through the air, it is slowed by air resistance so that the strike on a stationary target will be lower than the initial velocity at detonation. The drag velocities acting upon the fragment depend on its shape and air density. Fragments that are aerodynamically more stable will have a higher velocity than randomly produced fragments formed from natural case break-up and are preferred in modern fragmentation warheads found in GW.

Fragment weight depends on the required effect at the target, and can range from a few gains to about 6 grams. The optimum size for attacking aircraft is about 4 grams.

The fragments can be produced in one of three ways. First, and least efficient, by natural fragmentation in which a solid metal container filled with explosive is detonated causing case break-up and the formation of random fragment shapes. Such a system produces some fragments of the optimum lethal size, but also many either too small or too large. Up to 50% of available explosive energy may be consumed in expanding and breaking the casing.

Second, the fragment size can be controlled by causing stress in the case to encourage the formation of fragments of the required size. Such case fragments are known as fire-formed fragments. There are various ways of achieving this. Frequently, grooves on the inside face are used to control fragmentation, and the cheapest way to do this is to use a wound, notched wire coil brazed together in a spiral shape. Alternatively, grooves may be cut into the explosive filling at the case/explosive interface as shown in Figure 8.8.

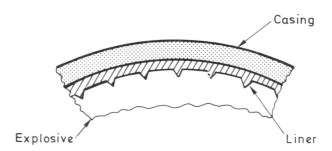

FIG. 8.8 Cutting to control fragment size

The other method used to control fragment size is to place triangular shaped inserts in the explosive at the charge/case interface as shown in Figure 8.9.

Finally, and arguably the most efficient is the use of preformed fragments. By using appropriately shaped and sized fragments, such as cubes, balls, cylinders, and packing them in resin or a weaker material like aluminium to form a warhead casing the correct size of fragment can be guaranteed. Examples of the three types of fragmenting warheads are shown in Figure 8.10.

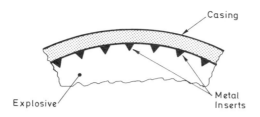

FIG. 8.9 Metal inserts in explosive

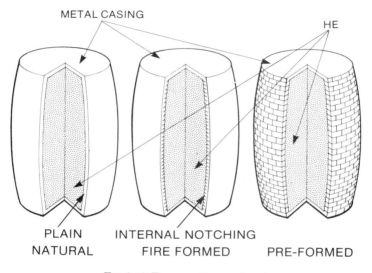

FIG. 8.10 Fragmenting warheads

The pattern that the fragments form as a group on detonation is largely dependent upon their orientation around the charge before detonation. Figure 8.11 shows the effect of changing the explosive shape on fragment pattern.

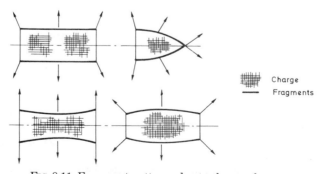

FIG. 8.11 Fragment patterns due to charge shape

### Continuous Rod Warheads

Small fragments are not necessarily the complete answer to defeat aircraft, and, ideally, fragments which can slice through major assemblies and structures are likely to be more effective. By surrounding an explosive with long metal rods, which are propelled outwards in a broadside manner on detonation of the explosive, a higher damage potential may be assured. This forerunner of the Continuous Rod Warhead was known as the Discrete Rod Warhead. Unfortunately, long rods have a tendency to topple, lose velocity and sometimes to present arrow-like effects on the target making them little better than normal fragments, except at very high altitudes.

The shortcomings of the Discrete Rod Warhead prompted designers to join together the rods at alternate ends to form a continuous rod or hoop which was found to be more effective. The rods are similar in length and thickness and are matched to the warhead size. The cross-section profile of the rods may be circular, square or trapezoidal, and about 5 mm$^2$ is found to be effective at strike velocities of around 1000 m/sec.

The maximum hoop radius is largely a function of the summation of all the lengths of rod used in the warhead construction. In practice it is about 80% of the theoretical maximum. Figure 8.12 shows a section of a rod bundle and its accordion-like appearance as the section begins to expand.

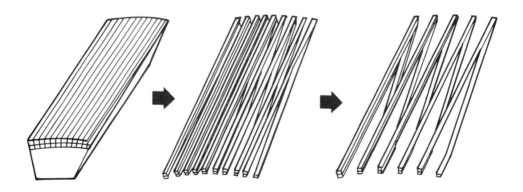

FIG. 8.12 Section of continuous rod bundle

The welding together of the rods is particularly important to ensure correct formation of the hoop, and it is necessary to control the explosive detonation speed to the rods by wave shaping. On detonation, the explosive forces expand the rods outwards into a hoop. Once the rods break up into individual rods, which tend to tumble and lose direction, the warhead rapidly becomes less efficient. An example of the operation of this type of warhead is given in Figure 8.13.

### Shaped Charge Warheads

This warhead consists of a thin case, filled with explosive, with a symmetrically placed lined cavity at the front with initiation at the rear of the charge. Figure 8.14 shows the arrangement diagrammatically and a typical warhead design. Other names for this type of warhead are hollow charge of High Explosive Anti-tank (HEAT).

The liner is normally cone shaped, but other shapes such as trumpet shaped and bell shaped may be encountered. As the detonation wave reaches the liner (usually copper, but steel and aluminium are among commonly used materials) the liner collapses extremely rapidly to form a high speed gaseous metallic jet at very high pressure. Concentrated on the target plate, it overcomes the plate which moves radially away from the point of concentration and the plate is penetrated by the jet. The jet velocity may be of the order 6-8000 m/sec at the tip while the rear, forming a slug, moves at about 1000 m/sec. The shaped charge warhead is excellent at penetrating armoured targets, capable of defeating 3-4 cone diameters of plate dependent on stand-off. Stand-off is required to allow the jet to develop and is optimised at about 4 cone diameters from the cone base.

The table below gives a comparison of basic effects and requirements of shaped charges against armoured and air targets.

| Parameter | Armoured Target | Air Target |
|---|---|---|
| Cone Angle | $40^0$ - $60^0$ | $90^0$ + |
| Cone Diameter (mm) | 125 mm | 200 mm |
| Cone Material | Copper | Aluminium |
| Liner Thickness (mm) | 2 mm | 12 mm |
| Type of Jet | Long + Thin | Short + Fat |

The reasons for the different values in the above table is that aircraft targets are usually engaged at long stand-off distances, and the short fat jet, that the large angle produces, travels better over these large distances. The aircraft skin is much thinner than an armoured target, and is easily penetrated by this type of jet. The use of aluminium for the liner increases the incendiary effect on air targets, but is less effective as a penetrator for armoured targets.

Against high speed, low flying aircraft it is very difficult to ensure a hit and shaped charge warheads are seldom used., However multi-shaped charge warheads may be encountered which improve hit probability.

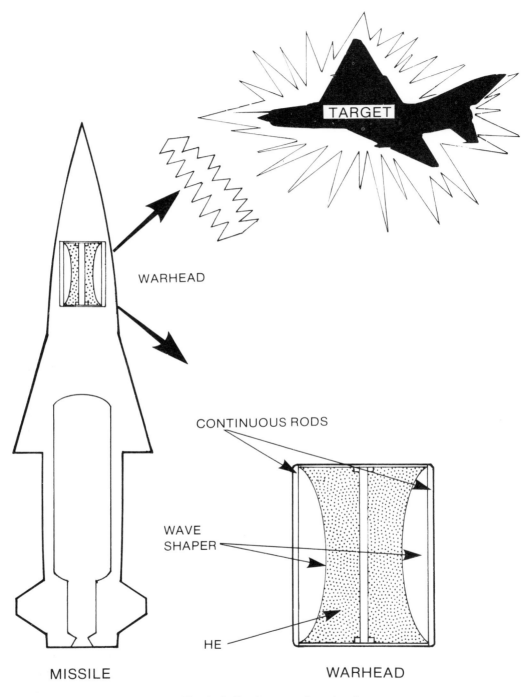

MISSILE                  WARHEAD

FIG. 8.13 Continuous rod warhead

As a means of attacking armour the shaped-charge warhead has many advantages. High velocity is not required, indeed it can be detrimental to its function as it quickly reduces stand-off, and the low launch velocity and acceleration forces make it ideally suitable for short range lightweight shoulder launched weapon systems that the infantryman can use against enemy armour.

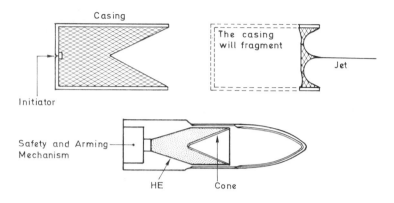

FIG. 8.14 Shaped charge warhead

Against modern armours, such as Explosive Reactive Armour (ERA), designed to disrupt the jet formation of shaped charges, tandem cone warheads may show an advantage. The first shaped charge is used to cause the ERA to react and the second shaped charge, fired fractionally later, punches through the exposed armour. Figure 8.15 shows a possible layout of a tandem shaped-charge warhead.

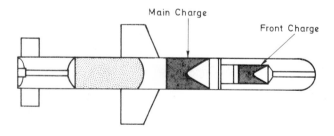

FIG. 8.15 Tandem shaped-charge warhead

Another means of defeating the armoured target is to choose to attack the less well protected areas, typically the top or the belly armour. Therefore warheads that overfly the target and have an angled-down shaped charge have been designed to attack the thinner top armour. Figure 8.16 shows the arrangement.

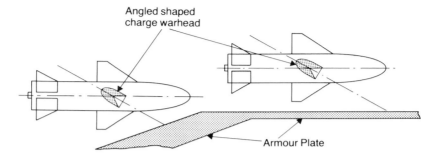

FIG. 8.16 Top attack shaped-charge warhead

## *High Explosive Squash Head (HESH)*

Although early anti-armour missiles used HESH as a means of defeating targets there are few, if any, still designed with this type of warhead for guided missiles. It is heavy for a guided weapon and modern armour plate, such as spaced armour, composite armours and ERA all provide effective defence against this type of attack. It is included to complete the family of warheads that might be considered by the warhead designer.

The HESH warhead is a relatively thin walled container filled with high explosive and fitted with a base fuze. On impact the warhead squashes or collapses and the rear fuze initiates a shock wave which passes through the armour plate and detaches a large scab from the plate due to the reversal of the shock wave at the armour/air interface on the inside of the vehicle. The effect is shown in Figure 8.17, and the reader is directed to the Ammunition Volume in this series for further information on this principle of attacking armour.

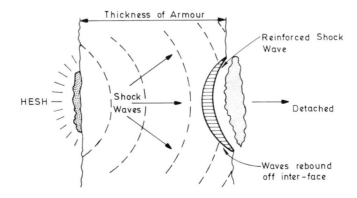

FIG. 8.17 The HESH effect

## Cluster Warheads

A cluster warhead consists of a large cased warhead containing sub-munitions (in bomblets) that can be ejected or dispensed to cause maximum effect at a moment decided by a fuzing mechanism. The missile delivers the main warhead to the target area where the outer skin may be removed explosively or by aerodynamic forces before the sub-munitions are released. In some designs, the bomlets may be forcefully ejected through the outer skin of the warhead casing. The sub-munitions may be released at random by aerodynamic and gravitational forces or they may be ejected by gas and propelled at some force in a given pattern. They may be used against air or ground targets.

The individual bomblets may be sub-projectiles which after release or ejection carry their own propulsion, guidance and control systems. They may also be simple shapes falling under gravity or aerodynamically stable designed to glide to a target area. Retractable fins or drag stability systems are frequently employed.

The sub-munition may be blast, fragmenting shaped-charge or filled with chemical, biological or incendiary material. It is a system that can be used to remotely deliver mines. Figure 8.18 shows typical stabilised bomblet designs that may be encountered, whereas Figure 8.19 shows concepts that are to be found in sub-missile warheads designed to eject the sub-missiles from the carrier warhead.

## Explosives used in Warheads

Properties of explosives can be utilised to give the desired effects in warheads from efficient initiation through to optimum target effect. The significant properties are sensitivity, power and velocity of detonation.

Complete explosive trains are required to ensure reliable and consistant performance, together with safety devices to ensure safety throughout the logistic system, during launch and up until the time of functioning at or near the target.

Future explosive fillings may well include the use of plastic bonded explosives, reduce the chances of premature detonation should the missile be struck by a fragment or small-arms bullet.

## Fuzes, Safety and Arming Mechanisms

### General Requirements

The fuze is the part of the warhead which initiates the payload at the right moment. In a guided misile the fuze must detect the target and initiate at the

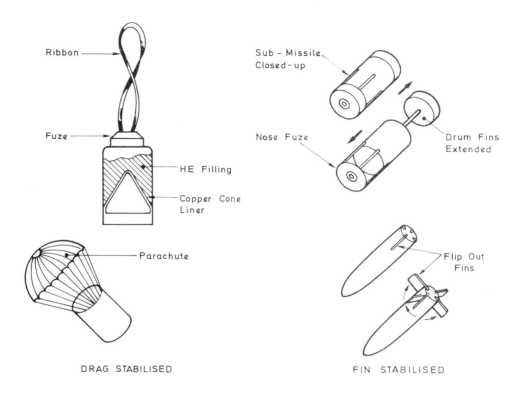

FIG. 8.18 Typical stabilised bomblet designs

time when the payload will hve the greatest effect. Some method is needed to determine this optimum time and some method of acquiring the data for this to happen. The data may be gathered from self-generated energy or target-emitted energy. The fuze may vary from the simplest impact device to a complex proximity system.

The safety and arming mechanism has two prime functions. First, the prevention of accidental detonation of the warhead – usually by interrupting the path between the fuze and the payload. Secondly, it provides the detonation path between the fuze and payload by removing the interrupting device. In addition, it may also provide a delayed arming system to protect friendly forces during initial flight and a self destruct device to destroy the missile should it not engage the target correctly.

The forces available to assist in the operation of safety and arming mechanisms include set-back at launch, creep forward when flight is steady, but each is of a much lower order than those experienced in a gun launched projectile. It is likely, due to little or no spin, that centrifugal force is insufficient to cause arming or to remove safety devices. In this circumstance there are other sources of energy to drive various mechanisms: it can be stored in gas pressure, springs and batteries; it can be generated from pneumatic, electrical and hydraulic systems; or it can be produced by bleeding off some of the rocket motor gases. In modern systems there is a steady move from mechanical devices to the use of transducers and electronic control.

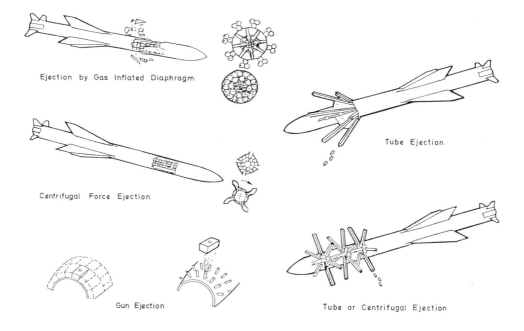

Ejection by Gas Inflated Diaphragm

Centrifugal Force Ejection

Tube Ejection

Gun Ejection

Tube or Centrifugal Ejection

FIG. 8.19 Sub-missile warhead ejection systems

## Safety Requirements

Explosive systems in missiles in the United Kingdom should comply with the Ordnance Board design safety principles and safety and arming mechanisms form an important safety function in the system. Some of the basic principles are fail-safe, visual indications of arm/nonarm state, compatibility and no possibility of mal-assembly. Often, duplicate systems are provided to improve reliability and safety.

## Summary

Most types of warheads have been described in this chapter, but there are others and variations on the basic designs mentioned. Designers are continuing to warhead performance by the introduction of new materials, methods and techniques and no doubt will continue to do so in the future.

The development of the high velocity missile (HVM) may make it possible to introduce high velocity kinetic energy penetrators to attack armoured targets. The probability is that hybrid warheads, combining different methods of attack, say kinetic energy and directed energy (shaped charge), will be designed to defeat future targets. Further development of the tandem-shaped charge warheads is inevitable, as will be warheads designed to attack the more vulnerable parts of the armoured target. Fragmentation will continue to play an important role in the defeat of the Anti-Ship Missile (ASM) and aircraft. The use of blast and directed energy warheads to defeat underwater targets will develop further and it is even likely that kinetic energy penetrators could be developed as a means of defeating the highly protected submarine target. However, the dramatic improvement seen in the electronics field, that has revolutionised guidance and control, is unlikely to be seen in warhead designs which are much slower to change in basic design.

# 9.
# Anti-tank Guided Weapons and Light, Unguided Anti-tank Weapons

## Scope

The last three chapters of this book are concerned with the military application of guided weapons. In this chapter on Anti-Tank Guided Weapons (ATGW) it is necessary to look first at the weapon characteristics, then at the operational requirements and, finally, to determine the best method of meeting those requirements, bearing in mind the design restraints which have been mentioned in previous chapters.

To provide a complete study of anti-armour weapons in this series of books, there is a section at the beginning of this chapter on unguided, short range, shoulder launched anti-armour weapons, which are normally referred to as Light Anti-Armour Weapons (LAW). Anti-tank guns are covered in other Volumes. It is not intended to write any more about them in this volume, other than to remind readers that anti-tank guns, LAWs and ATGWs are complementary. They combine into a system to make up the battlefield commander's defence against tanks, with overlapping ranges and responsibility.

## Limitation on LAWs

Any weapon which is designed to be carried by and fired from the shoulder of a soldier, who has many other roles to fulfil, must be light in weight and easy to use and must include a single sighting system. LAWs have a very important place in the anti-armour battle, but they are limited in lethality and short on range. For longer ranges, guidance is required.

## The Need for ATGW and LAW

Direct fire anti-tank guns are not easily portable and their accuracy falls off beyond 2,000m. During the 1939-45 war, they increased progressively in size and weight as larger tanks with improved armour protection were produced.

By the end of that war, anti-tank guns weighing approximately six tons were being designed. They were quite obviously too large to be moved about and concealed in forward positions

Guns have the advantage that they can fire kinetic energy, HESH and HEAT forms of warhead. They also have a rapid rate of engagement. For this reason they are retained on main battle tanks and several forms of tank destroyer, which, like the West German *Jagdpanzer*, mount a gun on a tracked chassis. But they are costly and few countries can afford to buy and maintain tank destroyers and tanks, so they concentrate on the latter.

Recoilless guns such as the United States 106mm and the British 120mm Wombat, shown in Figure 9.1 have been developed. They are much lighter than conventional guns but they are still too large to manoeuvre and conceal easily in forward positions. Like all guns, at long ranges their accuracy is limited by the need for precise range estimation, errors in laying the gun, lack of ammunition consistency, the effects of wind speed and the necessity to determine accurately the target's crossing speed. Recoilless guns are less accurate and have a shorter range than other guns.

FIG. 9.1 The British 120mm recoilless anti-tank weapon

The weight and accuracy limitations of guns led to a search for alternative anti-armour weapons. The LAW for short ranges and ATGW for longer ranges were the result.

## Characteristics of LAW

### Lethality

Like all weapons, a LAW must have effective lethality. In the search for light weight, the warhead weight is the controlling factor. The user must first decide, therefore, whether he needs to go through the front armour of a tank and accept that the warhead will be large and the whole weapon heavy, like the 10kg British LAW 80 in Figure 9.2, or if he is willing to compromise by accepting that his LAW will not penetrate the front. A considerable saving in weight can be made if the second option is accepted: the Swedish AT4 weighs 6kg, but it entails tactical limitations and risks. Much of the decision on the weight depends on what option is adopted and on the definition of manportability.

### Manportability

Many LAWs have been considered to be two man crew weapons; indeed it is difficult to see how a shoulder launched weapon which is loaded at the rear can be operated by one man. The modern trend is towards a one-man-throwaway LAW; but, although it may be lighter, it will have less range and/or less lethality. Probably the ideal is a LAW which can be carried and fired by any soldier. This has implications for training.

### Ease of Training

If a LAW is to be made so that it can indeed be fired by any soldier, it must be very simple to use. Its operation must entail little more than the movement of a safety switch, the pulling of a trigger or its equivalent and the use of a simple sighting system. It is a difficult requirement to meet, and a simple sighting system is particularly difficult because an armoured target is often moving. The United States M72, which is a 66mm short range anti-armour rocket, has gone a long way to meeting the requirement, but it has a short range and a limited lethality. The Swedish 84mm AT4, which can be seen in Figure 9.3 is larger, has a greater range of 300m and a higher lethality.

Until recently, most LAWs have remained two man weapons demanding some degree of specialist training. Two examples are the Swedish 84mm Carl Gustav and the French STRIM pictured in Figure 9.4. Specialist training can allow the use of more complex sighting on such weapons. One result can be increased range.

FIG. 9.2 The British LAW 80 *(Huntington Engineering Ltd)*

### *Range*

The level of lethality required, the weight limitation, the accuracy and the level of training which can be attained, all affect the effective range of the weapon. A high degree of lethality demands a large warhead: any increases in warhead weight result in a dramatic increase in the overall weapon weight. A requirement for extra range demands more propellant and more weight. The sighting problem has already been discussed.

Without guidance and a firm mounting, it is difficult to envisage an effective fighting range of more than 400m or 500m. To date these have been the practical limits of two-man crewed LAWs.

### Propulsion for Laws

### *Options*

The two main propulsion methods for shoulder launched LAWs have been based on the rocket and the recoilless principle. There are advantages and disadvantages for both.

## Rocket Propulsion

The United States Bazooka was perhaps the most famous early rocket launcher: it was the fore-runner of the 3.5 inch rocket launcher which was used widely in Western Block armies. The launcher tube has two main purposes. It guides the projectile on to the correct line and it protects the firer. A rocket must all be burnt before it emerges from its tube: its efflux will burn the firer if it is not. This necessitates long, often unwieldy tubes. To improve their portability, they have been hinged or separated into two parts which could then be interlocked for use.

Fortunately a rocket in an open ended tube does not build up such a high pressure as a recoilless weapon. Consequently there is no need for it to be strong and heavy. The resultant light weight tube has given birth to one shot disposable launchers; unfortunately the rocket cannot also be light weight.

FIG. 9.3 The Swedish AT4 *(FFV)*

When a rocket is launched, the rocket and its casing must be accelerated away in addition to the warhead. If a high muzzle velocity were demanded then the launcher would be very long and the rocket would be large and heavy. On the whole, as a consequence, rocket launchers tend to have a low muzzle velocity and a restricted effective range. In the case of the 3.5 in rocket launcher, the effective fighting range was some 150m. Modern systems such as the British LAW 80, pictured in Figure 9.2, have improved on this: battle ranges for rocket launched LAW will probably be 300m to 400m in the future, using a two stage rocket.

### Recoilless Propulsion

Increased range can be achieved by the use of a recoilless LAW. The principle is identical to that explained in Volume I. In this case the propellant provides its thrust in one short blast as in a normal gun. There is no danger for the firer from the efflux at the muzzle and only the mass of the warhead need be accelerated away. There is a gain, not only of range, but also because the launcher tube can be shorter. Figure 9.4 compares the length of the 3.5 inch rocket launcher and the Swedish 84mm Carl Gustav recoilless LAW (Figure 9.4).

The modern Carl Gustav M3 has a weight of 9kg compared with the 5.5kg of the rocket launcher. Its effective range is 400m or more and this has been extended to 700m by the incorporation of small rocket motors which give extra in-flight thrust. However, at such ranges the sighting becomes complicated for a shoulder launched weapon and guidance becomes desirable.

### Adaptations of Propulsive Methods

Two interesting approaches have been made to decrease the weight of LAWs whilst retaining lethality and range. The Russian RPG7, pictured in Figure 9.5, has a small calibre launcher which takes an oversized warhead.

The propellant, which is composed of two parts, fits into the launcher. An initial charge launches the rocket clear of the launcher and firer before a rocket ignites and provides the remainder of the thrust. This design results in a light launcher whilst maintaining a large and lethal warhead. On the other hand the accuracy is suspect because the rocket may well ignite whilst the projectile is yawing and it will then be driven off line.

The French STRIM, shown in Figure 9.6, has a launcher tube, on to the rear of which fits the projectile in its container: it doubles as a disposable extension to the launcher. The container takes the majority of the force of the propellant. The main tube takes only a little of it and, although it is light weight, can withstand one hundred launchings. This system has the advantage of a good propulsive thrust combined with a light launcher.

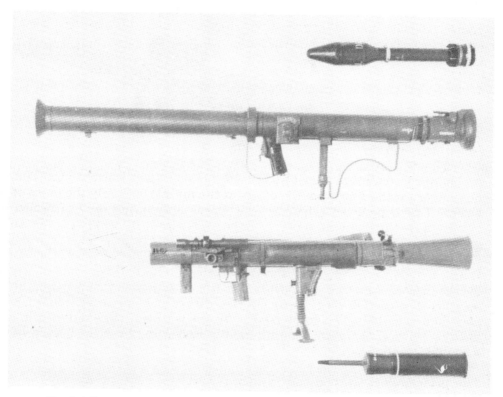

FIG. 9.4 Comparative lengths of a rocket launched and recoilless LAW

FIG. 9.5 Russian RPG7 showing oversized warhead

FIG. 9.6 The French STRIM light anti-armour weapon *(Luchaire SA)*

## Warheads for LAWS

It has already been indicated that the weight of a LAW is determined largely by the size of its warhead. A large warhead demands a large amount of propellant to accelerate it away. It also demands a large projectile casing and launcher tube. The tight restriction on warhead size and weight has always limited them to the inherently light weight HEAT method of defeating armour.

The performance of a HEAT warhead is largely determined by its cone diameter. Although the lethality of the design is gradually being improved, it is difficult to envisage a major break-through even if tandem warheads are used. On the other hand there has already been a break-through in tank armour. Modern compound armours and explosive reactive armours (ERA) have considerably degraded the lethality of HEAT warheads. As tanks will optimise their protection on their fronts, it will become even more difficult for LAWs to defeat frontal armours. The current swing of the pendulum appears to be in favour of the tank, consequently LAWs may be confined to attacking the sides and top for a time. However, a LAW capable of defeating the side of a tank is also able to defeat the armour protection of APCs and MICVs.

## LAW Sighting

There is a dichotomy in the sighting requirements for a LAW. Ideally it should be simple enough to be used by any soldier and, if attached to a disposable launcher, cheap enough to be thrown away. On the other hand it must be capable of coping with a moving target and this indicates a degree of complexity. From this it can be deduced that the whole question of whether a weapon should be disposable or not rests, to a large degree, on the sighting system. If a very short range, in the region of 100m to 150m is acceptable, a disposable sight which can be used by all soldiers is feasible. Longer ranges create problems.

A novel sighting system is used by the British LAW 80. It is a cheap disposable spotting rifle. The spotting rifle is a well proven method used on tanks and anti-tank guns and has proved to be a good way of achieving a good range with a minimum of user training.

## Backblast Elimination

LAWs and many ATGWs have backblasts. In any position this demands careful siting, but the problem is greatest in built-up areas. The short ranges met in urban warfare do not suit ATGW which often have minimum ranges of 200m to 300m, so LAWs are particularly important in such a scenario. The most severe restrictions occur when firing from buildings in which there are few rooms sufficiently large to accommodate the backblast.

At least two attempts have been made to overcome this problem. The West German Armburst and the French AC300 have both used the concept illustrated in Figure 9.7.

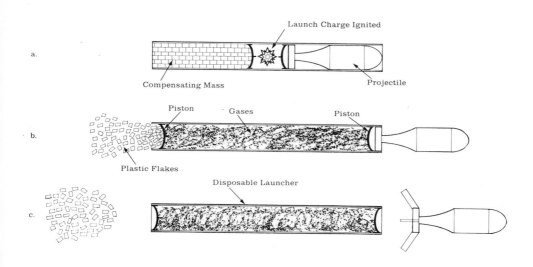

FIG. 9.7 A method of overcoming backblast

In both cases the weapons were disposable, so they were delivered as a complete round. When the propellant is ignited in the centre of the tube (Figure 9.7a), two pistons are forced outwards. That which moves forwards

propels the missile and the other moving rearwards pushes out a compensating mass (see Figure 9.7b). The mass consists of plastic strips or flakes
which are individually light and have few aerodynamic properties; so they
fall rapidly and harmlessly behind the weapon. The movement of the
pistons, meanwhile, is arrested by annular stops at the end of the launcher
tube (Figure 9.7c).

This design offers a solution to the tactical limitations imposed by backblast.
One penalty is a short range, unless a two stage rocket is used as in the
French AC300, because only a restricted amount of propellant can be used;
but in an urban short range setting, such a limitation could well be
acceptable. Another is that extra weight is added both by the compensating
mass and to the container which must be stronger than an open ended
launcher because it must contain the explosion.

## The Approach to ATGW

Much of what has been written earlier in the chapter about LAW is
applicable to ATGW, but ATGW are medium and long range anti-tank
weapons, even out-ranging anti-tank guns: consequently they are more
complex. The earlier chapters of this book have dealt with the method of
operation and the options for the components of all military missiles. This
chapter will deal with ATGW characteristics using the knowledge already
gained. It will then look at the operational requirements, see how they can be
met and indicate the compromise which must be made between conflicting
requirements. It will not attempt to give priorities to the requirements,
because they will alter with the threat and the level of technology.

## ATGW Warheads

The first missile characteristic to be considered must be the warhead: the
missile only exists to carry it to its target. The warhead size, just as in the
case of LAW, will have the major influence on the total missile size: in
ATGW it is generally considered that the missile must be three or four times
the weight of the warhead.

Until the 1970s, before the advent of compound armours, it was assumed
that ATGW would be designed to penetrate the frontal armour of tanks. It is
not conceivable that such expensive weapons as ATGW could ever be subject
to such limitations as only attacking from defilade positions, so warheads
must be designed to defeat a tank from whichever angle it is launched.

With few exceptions, such as the early Malkara, ATGW have taken
advantage of the light weight HEAT warheads. Until recently warheads
with a cone diameter of approximately 100mm could be expected to be
sufficient. In future either the warhead will need to be larger to penetrate

frontal armour, or a type of warhead will be required which can fire sideways as it passes over or to the side of the target to defeat non frontal armour: this is the method used by the Swedish BILL missile (Figure 9.8). The warhead technology should not be too difficult: HEAT warheads facing outwards could be used. The difficulty will be with the fusing and sensing components. However pattern recognition is a rapidly advancing technology and this may indicate the way forward.

FIG. 9.8 The Swedish BILL ATGW. It can fire its warhead as it passes over or along the side *(Bofors Ordnance)*

Warheads vary considerably in size. According to the manufacture, the French Eryx, which can be fired and carried by one man, has a missile diameter of 160mm and a warhead weight of 3.6kg: its overall weight of 15.8kg is so small because its range is restricted to 600m. The two man Franco-German Milan has a diameter of 116mm and a warhead weight of 3kg, but the MkII version improves on this: the system weighs 15.6kg. The vehicle mounted British Swingfire has a diameter of 175mm and a warhead weight of 7kg. In each case the HEAT warhead cone diameter will be a few millimetres less than the overall missile diameter. The penetration of a modern HEAT warhead, allowing for sufficient behind armour effect, is approximately five times the cone diameter if the correct stand-off distance can be achieved when the warhead is initiated.

FIG. 9.9 Milan ATGW with thermal imaging *(British Aerospace)*

## ATGW Propulsion

In Chapter 2 the subject of propulsion was dealt with in detail. ATGW tend to be unexciting and currently they use single solid propellant motors. They often perform both the function of boosting the missiles to their aerodynamic velocity and sustaining them at that velocity to their maximum range.

As in the case of a LAW, care must be taken to protect the firer when the missile is launched from its container. Separation provides any necessary protection as does firing from inside a vehicle; but protection by itself is not a sufficient reason for separation. In many cases the necessary protection safety is provided by ejecting the missile to a distance from the firer before the main motor is properly ignited: Milan, pictured in Figure 9.9, uses this method. Behind the missile is a piston. Behind the piston is a gas generator which, when initiated, pushes the piston and the missile forward. The missile is ejected with a velocity of 75m/s. The recoil force of this operation is used to eject the spent launcher tube backward from its mounting. The motor, which has a double base powder propellant, is then ignited by gas from the generator and boosts the missile to 125m/s in 1.31 seconds. The sustain phase of the propellant burns for 11 seconds which is sufficient to take the missile to a range of 2,000m at which time it is travelling at 200m/s.

## ATGW Guidance

### Requirements

When designing a guidance system for ATGW, the factors which control its design are first an accuracy of $\frac{1}{4}$ mil at the launcher; second it must be able to withstand ECM; third there must be no mutual interference with other equipments; fourth, a modern ATGW must have a day, night and all weather capability; finally comes the ever present, but difficult to achieve combination of light weight, small size, low cost and simplicity.

### Types of Guidance

It is possible to have a laser beam riding ATGW, but it would be costly and complex. It is more probable that a semi-active homing system would be used, with a laser as a target designator. Although this could be suitable, especially for a helicopter launched missile, it would still be costly and complex. The laser itself would demand a high specification with a beam width of approximately $\frac{1}{4}$ mil: a wider beam would overspill the tank target and cause confusing return signals.

As a generalisation, first generation ATGW such as Sagger, Swingfire (pictured in Figure 9.10), and SS11 all used manual command to line of sight (MCLOS), which is accurate, technically simple and demands considerable training; but second generation missiles like Eryx, Milan and Tow use semi-active command to line of sight (SACLOS) which, though technically more complex, is more simple to operate and has a shorter minimum range. Apart from its simplicity, MCLOS still retains some advantages in relation to SACLOS. MCLOS is more accurate because the operator tracks both target and missile, whereas in the SACLOS system great reliance must be placed on the collimation of the tracker to within 0.1 mil: this consideration becomes more important as the range increases. In addition it is possible to imagine that SACLOS missiles, which use infra-red flares for tracking, can be decoyed by IR flares, a common ECM tactic used against SAGW.

A wire command link is normal for ATGW. Its overwhelming advantages are its immunity to ECM and the simplicity of both the launcher and the missile. On the other hand wire is heavy: the wire for a missile with a range of 4,000m will be 3kg or more. Wire also restricts the speed of a missile: there is

FIG. 9.10 Swingfire, a MCLOS missile *(British Aerospace)*

a limit to the speed at which the wire can be unwound. Radio links are quite feasible and some press reports indicate that the Russian Spiral ATGW fitted to the Hind E helicopter has a radio link. Other possible systems in the future could use laser or IR guidance links, but complexity and susceptibility to ECM would be a problem.

## Control

ATGW can be controlled by a variety of aerodynamic controls or Thrust Vector Control (TVC). Both are used: Swingfire and Sagger use TVC; Hot and Milan use deflectors in the sustainer motor efflux; Tow, Mamba and Swatter all use aerodynamic surfaces. In all ATGW with wire command links, the wire is used for passing the control signals.

## Poor Visibility Operation

Most modern ATGW are being fitted with night sights. Image Intensifiers do not provide a sufficient range of visibility to match the range of ATGW, nor do they have much capability to see through poor weather visibility or battlefield smog. Consequently ATGW night sights are most likely to be thermal imagers in the foreseeable future, similar to that shown on Milan in Figure 9.9.

## Operational Requirements for ATGW

There is now a sufficient background in the book to allow us to look at an army's operational requirements for ATGW. We can consider how they can be met and what compromises are necessary. What the soldier looks for is:

Good mobility
High first round kill probability
Long maximum range
High rate of fire
Short minimum range
Good angular coverage
Separated firing capability
Simple operation
Simple logistic support
Low cost

The order of priority in which these characteristics should be placed is debatable. The order used in this chapter is chosen for ease of discussion.

## Mobility

### Types of Mobility

Mobility is relative and can cover vehicle-borne missiles or those which are manportable. Vehicle-borne ATGW, in terms of weight, can be compared with anti-tank guns, in which case they compare very favourably: they can be carried by and fired from the smallest vehicle. In Figure 9.11, Swingfire, which is a large ATGW, is shown fitted on to a jeep. The type of vehicle hinges on whether or not the tactical situation will demand an armoured vehicle as shown in Figure 9.10.

### Manportability

Manportability has a tendency to mean portable and operable by a two man crew. We have seen that there are one man portable missiles. Eryx, pictured in Figure 9.12, is an example. The system weighs 15.8kg, but it has a restricted maximum range of 600m. The limit on ATGW, which can be truly carried and operated by two, appears to be 2,000m. As an example, the Milan has a missile which in its launch tube weighs 11.5kg, a launcher which weighs 15kg and a tripod of 3.7kg. Any soldier who has carried his normal equipment for any distance will realise from this that a launcher, tripod and two missiles will be near the reasonable maximum load for two men. Missiles with larger warheads or larger motors to give greater range will tend to be too heavy for two men.

### Trends

It will be realised that the requirement to defeat modern compound armours, which fitted to new tanks demands larger warheads, which in their turn will cause manportability difficulties. Another solution, which does not cause the same increase in weight is described at the end of this chapter.

## High First Round Kill Probability

### Definition

A high first round kill probability ($P_K$) is a function of the lethality of the warhead ($P_L$), the hit chance of the system ($P_H$) and its reliability ($P_R$):

$$P_K = P_L \times P_H \times P_R$$

FIG. 9.11 Swingfire mounted on a jeep *(British Aerospace)*

## Lethality

Warheads have already been discussed earlier in the chapter. It is difficult to forecast what size of warhead will be necessary to defeat the frontal armour of future tanks. If more efficient warheads are not devised, it will be necessary to accept less range, less mobility or to devise an ATGW which can attack the top or side armour of a tank, no matter from which angle it is fired.

## Hit Chance

The guidance system and the ease of control are the main factors to affect the chance of a hit. SACLOS systems make control easier, but MCLOS systems offer better accuracy at long ranges. A full comparison has not been made under battle stress, but the easier to use SACLOS method would almost certainly have the advantage.

*Reliability*

The improvements in electronics, reliability and experience gained in the development and manufacture of ATGW will improve on the present level of overall system reliability. Currently, a system reliability of approximately 90% should be achieved.

## Long Maximum Range

*Factors*

The factors which affect the distance that an ATGW will travel are the weight of the warhead, the amount of propellant, the time of flight and the predicted visibility. We have already discussed warhead weight.

*Amount of Propellant*

It must be obvious that longer ranges can be achieved by having more propellant. It is affected, however, by the time of flight also: a high velocity also requires more propellant. So it may be, if overall weight is a restraint, that there must be a trade-off between increasing the range and decreasing the time of flight.

*Time of flight*

The first consideration to affect the time of flight is the probable exposure time of the target. It is unlikely that a tank with a well trained crew will remain exposed for more than 30 seconds at a time and it will frequently be much less than that. To achieve a short time of flight requires a powerful boost motor; but a review of missile times of flight indicates that there is, at first sight, little problem. The Eryx can reach its 600m maximum range in 3.6 secs, Milan goes to 2,000m in 12.5 secs, Tow reaches 3,000m in 15 secs and Hot achieves its 4,000m in 17 secs. These timings are reasonable for one engagement, the problem arises when there are many targets to be engaged.

There are some objections to faster missiles. If they are wire guided, they are limited by the speed at which the wire can be dispensed: it is difficult, at present to conceive a system which will dispense at more than Mach 1. At very high speeds, too, any small error or noise in the control system may cause the missile to go off line and ground before it can be corrected. A high speed missile also entails a large motor. However, the use of very high speed ATGW, which may reach speeds of Mach 3 or 4, is being considered. The British Starstreak is an example.

FIG. 9.12 The French Eryx, which can be operated by one man
*(Aerospatiale)*

## High Rate of Fire

## MCLOS and SACLOS Limitation

If a force equipped with ATGW is to face a mass armoured attack, as is probable, a high rate of fire is necessary. We have already seen that MCLOS or SACLOS weapons involve the firer until the missile hits. This time could only be shortened marginally by the use of more powerful rocket motors.

## Homing Missiles

A homing missile would be the ideal answer and it can be envisaged technically as well as tactically. It would reduce the time of engagement and increase the rate of fire dramatically. Practically it is a costly solution and would result in a complex missile. A simpler solution would be a terminally homing missile. In such a case, the firer would guide it until it locked on to the target with its homing system. It would still be quite complex.

## Semi-Active Homing Missile

The cheapest solution will be a semi-active homing system using a laser target indicator. Figure 9.13 illustrates its operation.

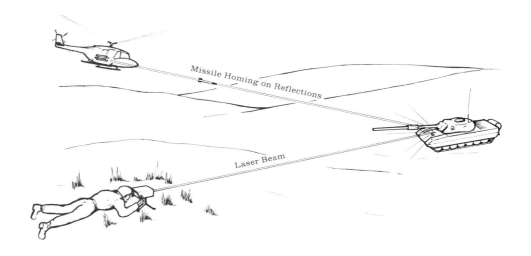

FIG. 9.13 Semi-active homing missile with laser designator

When the firer has launched the missile, he can switch immediately to another target, leaving the laser operator to complete the engagement. Although this is illustrated using a helicopter as a launching platform and the laser being operated from the ground, other combinations could be used.

As would be expected, there are technical and tactical penalties. Technically, the missile would be more costly and complex than the present missiles. Tactically, the operation of the system would demand a high degree of co-operation and training, together with highly reliable communications between the firer and the designator operator.

## Short Minimum Range

It takes time to gather a missile into the field of view of the guidance system when it has been launched. The time, and consequently the range, are affected by whether or not the launcher operates from a fixed line or can be turned; if it can be turned on to line with the target, it will gather its missile more quickly. A missile which is boosted quickly to a high velocity will reach a greater distance before it can be gathered. Wind direction and speed can vary the speed of gathering from engagement to engagement. A SACLOS system gathers its missile more quickly than a firer using MCLOS.

The need for a short minimum range is most apparent when fighting in close country or in urban areas. Although it is possible to use an ATGW in an unguided mode at very close ranges, it soon becomes necessary to guide it. The minimum distance after which guidance will become possible is normally in the region of 200m to 300m. Much shorter distances, of tens of metres, for minimum range are often quoted, but these are the arming distance of the warhead.

Two factors, not yet mentioned, which may well increase the minimum range are the angular coverage of a fixed line launcher and the capability to fire from a separated position.

### *Good Angular Coverage*

If a launcher can be turned, as in the case of Milan on its tripod, the angular coverage is infinite. If it is fixed for line, a good angular coverage is tactically necessary. Figure 9.14 demonstrates how the angle off line can affect the minimum range.

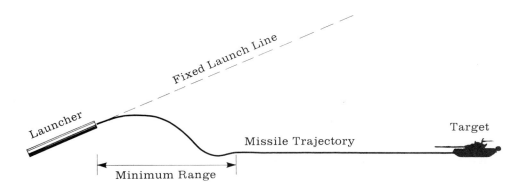

FIG. 9.14  How angle affects minimum range

## Separated Fire Capability

There are considerable tactical advantages to be gained if a firer can be separated laterally and vertically from the launcher. Unencumbered, the operator is able to choose a good position observation, perhaps in a high building or on high ground. Meanwhile the launcher can be concealed in dead ground. In the case of Swingfire, the firer can be separated from his launcher by some 100m. The tactical advantages are a little offset by extra complexity, cost, the extra time taken to come into and out of action and finally the increase in minimum range which is illustrated in Figure 9.15.

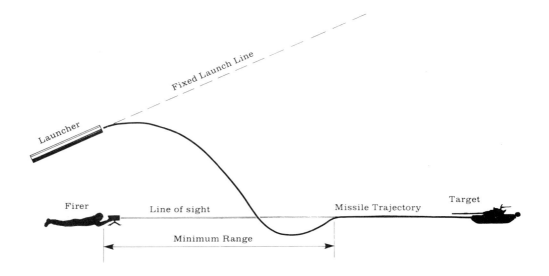

FIG. 9.15 Effect of separation on minimum range

## Simple Operation

It is easy to confuse simplicity of the missile system with simplicity of operation. In practice they tend to be in opposition. A missile which is designed to be more simple to operate will almost certainly be more complex in design and so may not be so reliable, because the less the operator does the more the missile must do. The order of complexity of ATGW from the most simple is MCLOS, SACLOS, Semi-active Homing, Homing. The simplicity of operation improves in the same order!

Ideally, armies would like an ATGW to be so simple that any solider with a minimum of training could use it. The design complexity this would entail has not, as yet, allowed it.

## Simple Logistic Support

ATGW provide a good example of simple logistic support. The normal ATGW leaves the factory in a container from which it emerges only when fired; no interim maintenance is required. There remain the launching and guidance systems and the training equipment: some trained craftsman with test equipment are required to look after them.

## Low Cost

It is apparent from a study of missile characteristics that the cost of ATGW is affected in part by its size but most by the complexity of its guidance and control systems. It may not be so immediately apparent that a complex missile which is simple to operate may require much less operator training with consequent savings in training equipment and time. If a missile could be designed for operation by a smaller crew, manpower savings would accrue and may affect the overall cost of a more complex missile system.

It is most important that costs for the whole life of the missile be considered, rather than just the production costs.

## Future

There are two identifiable main pressures which may well cause changes in ATGW. The first is the desire for simplicity of operation and, as has been highlighted already, the penalty will be a more complex, costly system: it may be worthwhile. The second is the improvement in protection afforded to tanks by compound armour. This may force the development of warheads which work on a new principle. It is already providing ATGW systems designed to attck the sides or top of tank, rather than the front as in the Swedish Bill (RBS56). Its concept is illustrated in Figure 9.16.

FIG. 9.16 Concept used by Swedish Bill (RBS56) *(Bofors Ordnance)*

Such a design will demand a warhead which fires sideways and a sensing system, which may well incorporate a pattern sensing capability, to initiate the warhead. On the one hand the advance in micro-electronics may make this more feasible; on the other hand it is certain to increase cost.

# 10.
# Surface-to-Air Guided Weapons

## Complexity

The role of battlefield SAGW systems is to prevent an enemy from interfering with the conduct of ground operations from the air. This can involve the detection and destruction of aircraft flying at speeds well in excess of Mach 1 at heights of well over 15,000m or of slow moving helicopters and Remotely Piloted Vehicles (RPVs) which may be flying very close to the ground.

Technologically, SAGW systems are the most complex systems on the modern battlefield. Although SAGW missiles and their systems are costly, they earn their keep by knocking down very expensive aircraft carrying very dangerous payloads. Their failure could result in devastating blows delivered against their own battlefield forces, so a high investment in air defence can be cost effective.

## Height Bands

In NATO there are agreed names for various height bands covered by SAGW. They are useful for describing system capabilities:

| | |
|---|---|
| Very low level | Below 150m |
| Low level | 150 - 600m |
| Medium level | 600 - 7,500m |
| High level | 7,500 - 15,000m |
| Very High level | Above 15,000m |

The very low level weapons are only self defence. At this height even small arms may be brought into use. Although statistical studies show that there is very little chance of shooting down a low flying Fighter Ground Attack aircraft (FGA) with small arms fire, it sometimes happens. It can be a deterrent to pilots and is good for the morale of the troops being attacked.

## Guns and Missiles

Cannon can reach into the medium level band, but, if they do not have a fire control system, their chance of shooting down a FGA is poor. Helicopters on the other hand, are somewhat more vulnerable. To be effective, guns need a good fire control system and a very high rate of fire.

In the Yom Kippur war many Israeli aircraft were shot down by the Russian ZSU23-4: they were used when the Israelis tried to fly under the cover given by the Egyptian manned SAGW cover. The ZSU23-4 has four 23mm guns, which can produce a rate of fire of 4,000 rounds a minute between them. With an optical sight, it can engage aircraft at 2,500m and its radar direction increases this to 3,000m. The West German Gepard, pictured in Figure 10.1, has two 35mm guns and it, too has radar and optical fire control systems.

FIG. 10.1 West German Gepard air defence vehicle
*(Krauss-Maffei Aktiengessellschaft)*

The lessons learned from the development of these two air defence gun systems is that the fire control system is very costly and complex, although the guns may be cheap.

Operationally, air defence guns, as a complement to SAGW systems, have proved to be very effective in the hands of the Egyptians and were obviously missed by the Royal Navy in the Falklands in 1982. In both cases they were needed because the SAGW forced the attacking aircraft to fly low. They have a better multi-target capability than missiles and are effective when defending point targets against approaching aircraft at close ranges.

Later in this chapter, we will note that the Israeli airforce learned from the Yom Kippur war and developed Electronic Warfare (EW) methods of dealing with SAGW. In this way, they avoided being forced down into the fire of the waiting guns.

There is no doubt that, even at low levels, missiles have a much higher kill probability against aircraft. Ideally, to cover all eventualities, any army would like both, but costs may prevent it.

## Elements of an Air Defence System

The air defence of a battlefield army demands a system in which there are a number of elements under centralised control. A modern aircraft, if allowed, can roam over a whole continental battlefield area in a few minutes. Defence against them must be co-ordinated and controlled at a very high level. In NATO in Europe, the medium, high and very high level systems are co-ordinated and controlled by the NATO Integrated Air Defence System (NATINADS).

The components of any air defence system are similar, but the capability and complexity vary greatly. The main elements are a detection system, followed by an acquisition system which leads to the launching of a SAGW, then its guidance and control to destroy the target. All this is shown diagrammatically in Figure 10.2.

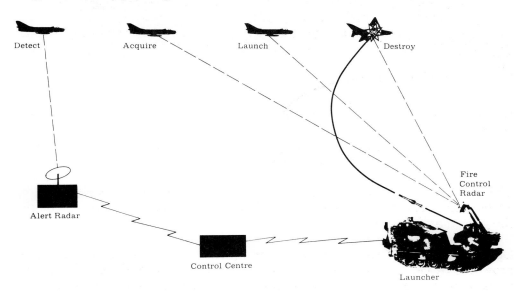

FIG. 10.2 Elements of an air defence system

# Detection

## *Alerting*

The first element to come into operation is some form of alerting system. Failure to alert the air defence in sufficient time for it to react could prove decisive.

In the case of shoulder launched SAGW, such as the British Javelin, pictured in Figure 10.3, the alerting system could be men with binoculars and a radio link to the fire unit. It is becoming apparent, however, that some better method is required. At the other extreme it can be as extensive and remarkable as the Ballistic Missile Early Warning System (BMEWS) with a range of 5,000km enhanced by an Airborne Warning And Control System (AWACS).

In the European theatre, NATO has a very comprehensive alerting system provided by a number of radar chains. They include radars of the NATO Air Defence Ground Environment (NADGE) radars which are very high powered. They also include a line of mobile radars on the border between Western Germany and her Eastern Block neighbours. They are normally referred to as Tactical Control (TC) radars. The Swedish Giraffe shown in Figure 10.4 is an example.

The high powered surveillance radars, until recent years, have had large rotating antennas. They are now being replaced by more powerful and flexible electronic scanning versions like that shown in Figure 10.5. In all cases, they must be capable of detecting small and fast targets in a large area despite the problems caused, particularly at low levels, by clutter. It is quite possible too, that IR devices will be used to detect approaching aircraft.

## *Identification Friend or Foe (IFF)*

Having achieved an initial detection, an identification is required. Although hostile acts would indicate that an aircraft is hostile and visual identification may play a part, they normally occur too late to result in the effective alerting of an air defence. An earlier alerting can be achieved by an electronic Identification Friend or Foe (IFF) method. IFF is included in surveillance radars. It triggers off a transponder in an approaching friendly aircraft which transmits a coded response.

There are problems with electronic IFF methods. The codes are easily broken and could be used by hostile aircraft. If codes are frequently changed, friendly aircraft from a number of countries and services may have wrongly coded transponders, or, in aircraft returning from a mission, they may be damaged. Jamming is also a possibility. A mistake would be costly.

FIG. 10.3 The British Javelin shoulder launched SAGW
*(Short Brothers Ltd)*

FIG. 10.4 The Swedish Giraffe Tactical Control Radar
*(Ericssons AB)*

## Warning

After detection and identification the alerting phase ends when it communicates the information it has gathered about the approaching aircraft to firing units and control centres. A reliable, electronic warfare resistant, wide coverage communications system is required to carry the information.

## Control Centres

The importance of the communications network is even more apparent when the role of the control centres is studied. Like the radar systems, the control centres vary in size and complexity depending on the level at which they operate. There are the underground bunkers beneath the mountains in the United States and the Soviet Union which control the strategic scene. At the battlefield level, in NATO and the Warsaw pact, there are hardened bunkers, capable of operating through NBC attacks. Below this, but still comprehensive, are mobile Control and Reporting Posts (RPs), which are part of the Tactical Air Control System (TACS). The centres become smaller and more mobile as their span of control reduces until a battery command post of a light air defence battery is reached. At this stage the mobility may be provided by a Jeep or Landrover.

FIG. 10.5 The Plessey/ITT-Gilfillan A-320 long range electron scanning radar *(Plessey Radar Ltd)*

Whatever the level, the functions of control are similar. They are to give the required current order, which may be 'weapons tight' for example; they update the states of readiness and allocate targets to weapons.

As part of the control procedure, the threat must be analysed. If reaction times are to be effective, this can only be done by computer at any level where air defence cover is being provided. Then the target is allocated to an appropriate weapon system or site.

The computer can again be involved at this stage, but a human being is often required to make the decisions. The allocation will be dependent upon the degree and type of threat the aircraft present and the availability of weapon systems.

## Communications

Mention has already been made of the importance of a reliable and comprehensive communications system: it must be already apparent that an air defence system relies upon it.

At strategic levels satellite communications are normal. At theatre levels tropospheric scatter may well be used in addition to land line. Down at unit level, net radio will be the mainstay. Its function is to enable orders and information to flow from alerting units to control centres, between control centres and the firing units. When the information reaches the firing unit, it should be sufficient to allow the Fire Control (FC) radars to acquire the target.

## Acquisition

Acquisition can be carried out, for self defence weapons, visually. Medium and high level targets are all acquired by radar. They search the area indicated by the TC radars. When the FC radar acquires a target, its purpose is to provide sufficient information for the tracker to locate and lock on to the target. The tracker may be radar or optical, especially in systems which have a low and medium level capability. The Franco-German Roland, the British Rapier, the Russian SA-8 Gecko, and the Canadian Forces ADATS, pictured in Figure 10.6 are all examples of SAGW which transfer to optical tracking when tey have acquired the target by radar.

When it has locked on to the target, the firing unit requires some time to compute a launch time and angle.

## Launch

### Timing

The launch time, once the tracker is locked on, is a function of the target's speed and flight path allied to the missile's speed and range. The aim is to destroy the target before it can release its own weapons. To achieve this, the SAGW needs to be launched when the hostile aircraft is some 4km away in the case of a low level attack, but, when the attack comes in at a medium level, the distance may need to be some 50km.

In most systems there is an automatic method to prevent launch until the target is within range. Once launched, the SAGW must be guided and controlled to its target. The methods of guidance and control have been dealt with in Chapters 5 and 6. Now we will look at the types of guidance and control used by some operational weapons systems and by some well on into development.

FIG. 10.6 The Canadian Forces ADATS on M113
*(The Plessey Company plc)*

## Guidance and Control

### Methods Used

Of all missiles, SAGW use the widest variety of guidance and control methods. Like ATGW, they use SACLOS, semi-automatic homing and passive homing. In addition they use Automatic Command to Line of Sight (ACLOS), beam riding and Command Off the Line of Sight (COLOS). Many of the higher level systems use a combination of more than one method of guidance.

### Self Defence Weapons

The smallest, handiest SAGW are used for self defence and work in the low to medium levels. The Russian SA-7 Grail claims an altitude of 1,500m and a range of approximately 5km. The British Javelin has the same altitude and a range of 7km. The Swedish Rb79 altitude is published as 3,000m with a range of 3 to 5km. The United States has the Stinger, pictured in Figure 10.7, which probably has an altitude and range similar to the British Javelin. All these weapons can be fitted on ships and, in the case of the Stinger on helicopters, as can be seen in Figure 10.8.

Operationally there is an important division between SAGW in this category. Grail and Stinger are fire and forget missiles. They achieve this important ability by having IR heat seeking homing heads. They are easy to operate and the training effort required is not great. However, they are probably not quite so effective when attacking an approaching aircraft head-on though Stinger's IR homing head is sufficiently sensitive to home on an approaching target. Javelin is a SACLOS weapon and a forward hitter. If alerted in time and is well sited, it should be able to destroy aircraft before they release their weapons. On the other hand it demands a high level of training and the concentration of the operator throughout the engagement. The Rb70 pictured in Figure 10.9, is also a forward hitter, but its guidance is achieved by laser beam riding.

The control of this class of missiles, in all cases, is through small wings, usually set forward with rear mounted fins to provide stability.

### *Medium and High Level Weapons*

Examples of medium and high level weapons are Roland, Rapier (pictured in Figure 10.10), and SA-8 Gecko. It was mentioned earlier that all these systems acquire their targets by radar, but track optically. The outline of the method used is illustrated diagrammatically in Figure 10.11, but the detail varies from system to system.

In all cases, after the radar has acquired the target, the optical sight is also aimed at the target. On Roland, this is performed manually and on Rapier it is automatic. When the missile is launched, the optical sight tracks the target. Signals from the missile are monitored and appropriate error signals are generated. The command radio signals to correct the missile flight path are sent from the tracker computer.

In the case of Roland, the missile signals are generated by an IR source and the missile's deviation from line is measured by an IR goniometer. This is not unlike the system used on the Milan ATGW which is also produced by Euromissile. Rapier has a television device with a vidocon tube: it senses when the bright flare image of the missile is not focused on the centre of the tube.

An optical tracking method is only of use when visibility is good. In theatres of operation such as Europe, where there is frequent low cloud cover, it can often not be used. Blindfire systems using radar tracking, have been developed for both Rapier and Roland. In both cases, as illustrated diagrammatically in Figure 10.12, the radar tracks the target missile.

FIG. 10.7 The United States Stinger *(General Dynamics)*

FIG. 10.8  The Stinger fitted (inboard) to the Apache helicopter
*(General Dynamics)*

FIG. 10.9  The Swedish Rb70 *(Bofors Ordnance)*

FIG. 10.10  British Towed Rapier in its 'Dark fire' Configuration
including an electro-optical tracker and surveillance radar
*(British Aerospace)*

The Roland missile emits signals from a beacon which indicates its deviation from the radar beam which is tracking the target. Up to now, both Roland and Rapier have been using SACLOS guidance, but Blindfire Rapier uses an ACLOS differential tracking method. Both target and missile are tracked and the error signals are generated. This information is used by the tracker computer to generate the guidance signals which re-passed to the missile over a radio command link. The missile is then automatically commanded to follow the radar sight line. A study of the Gecko, shown in Figure 10.13, indicates that it has a low light level television, optical guidance and a radar proportional navigation blindfire capacity. On this basis its operation appears similar to the Rapier, but its packaging on the vehicle is more similar to Roland. Its estimated altitude is similar to that of Roland at approximately 6,000m. Rapier's altitude is 4,000m.

Most missiles in this size are controlled by moveable cruciform fins which are either canard, or set further back. Roland is an exception: it uses a deflector in its motor efflux.

### High and Very High Level

NATOs high level and very high level cover has been provided for some years by a combination of the United States Nike-Hercules and Hawk. These missiles can reach altitudes of over 50,000m. The Nike-Hercules has a range

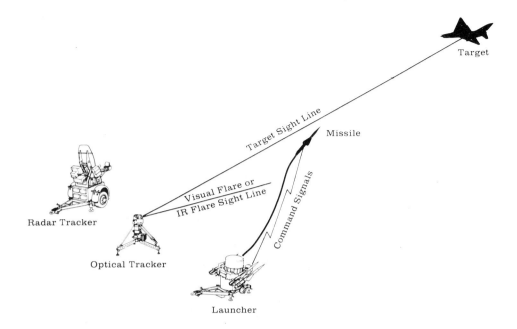

FIG. 10.11 Optical guidance similar to that used on Rapier and Roland

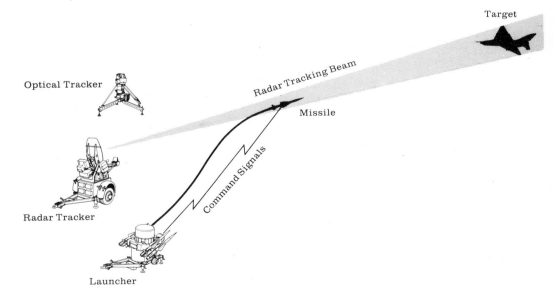

FIG. 10.12 Radar guidance similar to that used on Rapier and Roland

of 150 km and the Hawk some 30 km. Such systems have their fire control on separate vehicles from the missile launchers and the fire control area is often separated by a few kilometers from the launch area. The Hawk, as an example, has four radars. One is a pulse acquisition radar which provides medium level cover. The second is a CW acquisition radar to provide low level cover. The third is a CW high power target illuminating radar. The fourth provides the range to the target. Hawk's guidance is CW semi-active homing. Nike-Hercules is a full command system.

FIG. 10.13 The Rusian SA-8 Gecko

It may be interesting to compare these SAGW with the United States Patriot which is now in NATO. It replaces the Nike and the Hawk. It has a phased array radar, which can be seen in Figure 10.14. This one radar is capable of detecting, tracking and guiding several missiles at a time. The guidance is basically COLOS, but it is enhanced by a Track Via Missile (TVM) radar fitted in the missile. It detects radar energy reflected from the target aircraft, from which it calculates the angle between the missile and the target. This information is then transmitted to the ground. The guidance computer converts these error signals into control signals which are then transmitted back to the missile. Like Hawk, Patriot has a low, medium and high level capability.

FIG. 10.14  The United States Patriot phased array radar system
*(The Raytheon Company)*

It would be incomplete if mention were not made of the Russian SAGW which extend their range and altitude beyond that of Gecko. The mainstays have been the SA-6 Gainful, made famous in the Yom Kippur war, and the SA-4 Ganef. The Gainful's maximum altitude is believed to be in the region of 15,000m and its range is probably 60km. The guidance is guessed to be CW semi-active homing. Ganef is larger, and probably extends the cover to 24,000m altitude and 70m range. Both work in batteries with six tracked launcher vehicles. The Russian S-4 Ganef has two tracked fire control vehicles, a tracked vehicle with a target acquisition radar and a command and signal truck. Each Ganef launcher carries only two missiles compared with the three on the Gainful launcher. These larger, high level missiles all use fins or wings for control.

FIG. 10.15 The Russian S-4 Ganef

## Destruction

The design of warheads is covered in Chapter 8 of this book. Small, self defence SAGW rely on small fragmentation warheads of approximately 2 -2½ kg weight and a direct hit. At the next stage the size and type of warhead depends on whether the warhead is designed to detonate on impact or in proximity to the target. A good comparison in this respect is between Rapier, Roland and Gecko. Rapier is a hittile and so has a simple blast warhead of under 1 kg weight. That of Roland weighs over 6 kg, is described in the open press as a hollow charge multiple effect warhead, and has a lethal radius of over 6m when its proximity fuze detonates it. Gecko is said to have a fragmentation or blast warhead in the region of 45 kg and it has a proximity fuze. Obviously a hittile with a smaller warhead can be smaller and lighter. The approximate missile weights are Rapier 44 kg, Roland 63 kg and Gecko 190 kg. Their comparative sizes, to scale, are illustrated in Figure 10.16.

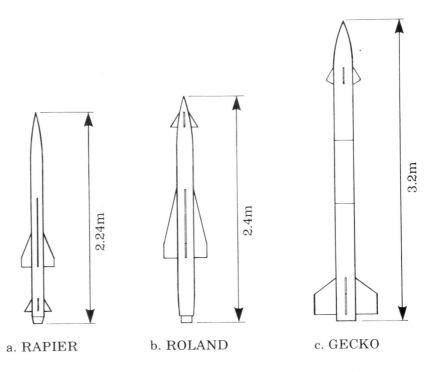

a. RAPIER            b. ROLAND            c. GECKO

FIG. 10.16 Comparative sizes of Rapier, Roland and Gecko SAGW

Although some of the overall size and weight differences can be attributed to speed and range, it indicates that a more mobile, smaller, cheaper missile can be made if it can be made into a hittile. Higher level SAGW have not attempted this, as yet. They rely on blast and fragmentation warheads in the order of 50 kg to 100 kg and the largest may even have optional nuclear warheads.

Although the old Bloodhound and Thunderbird missiles had continuous rod warheads, land based missiles seem to have shunned them more recently. This may be because their lethal zone is restricted to an area perpendicular to the axis of the charge, with consequent fuzing limitations.

## Electronic Warfare

### Electronic Counter Measures

In a field of warfare dominated by electronic devices it is to be expected that electronic warfare would play a large part and Chapter 7 has covered this subject. As will be quickly recognised by any student of the Middle East Israeli-Arab wars, ECM can be decisive. In the Yom Kippur war, it took some time before the Israeli air force found an answer to the Syrian and Egyptian manned SA-6 Gainful SAGW. By the end of that war, they were using decoys and helicopters to warn aircraft of the enemy missile launch. By the 1982 war in the Lebanon, the Israelis were better prepared. From press reports, it would appear that they found out the frequencies used by the Syrian manned SAGW system, often by the use of RPVs and then jammed them before attacking and destroying them with such devastating success.

Radars and communication links can be jammed by airborne jammers and form more distant ground based jammers. Tracking radars in missiles may be defeated by jammers or defeated by screening with such devices as 'window'. Infra-red trackers or homing devices can be confused or decoyed by IR flares which have now been seen commonly on films of air attacks.

## Electronic Counter-Counter Measures (ECCM)

A basic ECCM measure is to ensure that the communication and IR frequencies are kept secure: an attacker will put much effort into gaining information about them in peace and war. Antennas can be designed to work on very narrow beams, with small side lobes to minimise the effect of jamming. In addition, powerful transmitters and relatively insensitive receivers can also reduce the effectiveness of jamming. The ability to change frequency often and quickly is also very important.

## Further Measures

It is possible to carry on this measure and counter measure to a very great extent. Security classifications do not allow discussion of it in any depth, but it is certainly worth going to considerable lengths when the protection of aircraft worth many millions of pounds is involved.

## The Future

The Patriot system is the clearest guide we have at the moment to what the future form of SGW systems will be. Advanced phased array radars will replace the present radars with their cumbersome rotating or nodding heads. If hittiles can be made with a high probability of hit, then the missiles themselves will become smaller. The continuous electronic warfare battle of measure and counter-measure will certainly continue.

# 11.
# Surface-to-Surface Guided Weapons

This is a short chapter because, although some SSGW contain some of the most advanced components to be found in weapons, the system is simple in concept. Also the operational requirement for the battlefield, as will be explained, is not complex.

Strategic missiles will be mentioned briefly in order to put tactical, or battlefield, missiles into context. At the other end of the spectrum, free flight rockets (FFR) will be mentioned, because they overlap in range and effect. The chapter could not be complete if, cruise missiles were not also covered. They can be strategic or battlefield weapons.

## Classifications

In descending order, first there are orbital bombardment systems, which may be deployed but are beyond the scope of a book on battlefield weapons. Then there are strategic missiles and they are normally sub-divided by their range capabilities:

> Intercontinental Ballistic Missiles (ICBM 7,000 - 15,000 km
> Intermediate Range Ballistic Missiles (IRBM) 4,000 - 6,000 km
> Medium Range Ballistic Missiles (MRBM) approximately 2,000 km.

Below these come the tactical SSGW and finally, at the bottom, come the FFR.

## Free Flight Rockets

FFR are dealt with more fully in the Guns and Mortars Volume of this series. They are included here for the sake of completeness and as a useful reference point from which to study tactical SSGW.

### *Development*

A study of history shows that rockets have been used in wars for a much longer span of time than guns. Their origin goes back to China, but their heyday was in the eighteeenth and nineteenth centuries when muzzle loading cannon had a slow rate of fire, were inaccurate and were short on range. The manufacturing and engineering skills developed during the industrial revolution resulted in accurate guns. After that, the use of rockets was restricted to shock action when a sudden heavy weight of fire was required. They were used in the D Day landings; the German Army in the 1939 - 45 war had its Nebelwerfer and the Russians had their Stalin Organs, which created such demoralisation of their foes. The United States Army also introduced a multiple rocket system in World War II.

FIG. 11.1  Czechoslovakian M70 MLRS

## *The Present*

The Russians maintained their interest in multi-launched rocket systems (MLRS) and have fielded their 122mm BM21. The Czechosolvakian M70, shown in Figure 11.1 is an improved version of it. A battalion of eighteen BM21 is able to put 30,000 lbs of HE in a target area within 30 seconds. It is the ability to put a massive salvo suddenly onto a target, before the enemy can go to ground that makes such systems so effective. After the war the Western Block afforded less priority to such weapons, although some development took place in Europe. It is only recently that the United States has developed and is bringing into service their MLRS shown in Figure 11.2

Both the Eastern and Western Bloc have maintained an interest in single larger rockets: the United States Honest John and the Russian Frog now being replaced by the SS21, are results of it. Their published ranges are 32 km for Honest John and 60 km for Frog 7.

FIG. 11.2  The United States MLRS
*(The Vought Corporation)*

## The Need for Guidance

### Accuracy

In a modern FFR, accuracies of 1% of range are possible. Still this means that at 30 km a rocket would miss by 300m and at 60 km by 600m. Such inaccuracy demands guidance at longer ranges. The exact range at which this becomes necessary is debatable and much depends upon the warhead. Both the Soviet Frog 7 and American Honest John can fit nuclear in addition to HE warheads. Even so, a miss by 600m could be significant.

### Cost

When it is necessary to have guidance, missiles become expensive. Their very expense precludes their use for HE warheads, which have a limited effect, so they tend to be reserved for the nuclear role. The end logic of this argument is that even tactical SSGW are a part of the nuclear capability, and consequently part of the deterrent logic. This means that they must be considered in that context.

## Tactical SSGW Perspective

### Membership of the Club

It is known that China, France, the United Kingdom, the United States and USSR all have guided weapons armed with nuclear warheads. There are persistent rumours in the media and press that Israel and South Africa may have a similar capability.

### Mutual Assured Destruction

The mighty ICBMs, in sufficient numbers and sufficiently protected, provide the all important credible second strike capability and with it, mutual assured destruction (MAD) on which present nuclear deterrence is based. These monsters have such ranges as the 13,000 km claimed for the United States Minuteman III and 12,000 km which is the published range of the Soviet SS18. They all have inertial guidance, described in Chapter 5, and their control is normally effected by gimballed nozzles. They have, too, some form of terminal guidance to effect greater accuracy. Mention of one system will be made when discussing tactical SSGW later. Their warheads are invariably nuclear: the Russian warheads tend to be in the megaton range; Western Bloc warheads are in the kiloton range. Both blocs now fit several multiple independently targetted re-entry vehicles (MIRVs) in the place of the old single warhead. Rocket propulsion is used and, although many still have liquid fuels, most new missiles have solid fuel rockets.

## Tactical (?) SSGW

### Grey Areas

In theory, the Soviet SS20 is a MRBM with a range in the region of 4,000 km. It is mounted on a mobile launcher and its warhead probably has three MIRVs each giving a yield of 150 KT. It can affect what is happening on the battlefield, but is probably better described as a theatre weapon. It is easy to see why it makes the nuclear escalation logic totter and why this category of SSGW has been the first to be the subject of an abolition treaty.

The United States and the USSR may regard strategic weapons as those with which their homelands may be attacked and all others as tactical weapons. It is not so easy for those countries likely to be fought over to draw such a clear distinction. What a foreign army commander considers to be a tactical nuclear weapon, landing outside Leipzig or Hannover, may not be seen in the same light by the civilian inhabitants of those cities!

## *Ranges*

For now, let us take, as an arbitrary rule, that tactical or battlefield SSGW are those which may be deployed with field armies. They may have ranges up to approximately 2,000 km. On the European scale, this is well into the international field, but although deployed with field armies their initial release will certainly not be under the control of battlefield commanders.

FIG. 11.3 The Unit States Pershing II *(Martin Marietta)*

At the top of the scale, Pershing II, pictured in Figure 11.3, which is the subject of so much protest and negotiation, is stated to have a range of approximately 1,800 km. The Russian Scaleboard probably has a range of some 800 km and their Scud B is in the region of 270 km. At the bottom end of the range scale are the United States Lance and the French Pluton, pictured in Figure 11.4, which can reach out to a maximum of some 120 km.

FIG 11.4  The French Pluton SSGW

### Warheads

The warhead yields of battlefield SSGW are small in comparison with ICBMs, but it is important not to forget the effect of even a small nuclear warhead. The press gives the warhead size for Pluton as 10 KT or 25 KT, Lance as 10 KT and that for Pershing II up to 400 KT. The yields of Russian warheads are not known, but if the trend on their ICBMs is followed, it is to be expected that they will be larger than those of the Western Bloc. Scaleboard is rumoured to have a 1 MT warhead which may be replaced by three MIRVs.

### Guidance and Control

All battlefield SSGW have some form of inertial guidnace, which has been explained in Chapter 5. In this section we will look at two variations which are used in Lance and Pershing II. Lance, pictured in Figure 11.5, has a strap-down system, which means that the sensors are fixed to the main framework: the alternative would be to mount them on a stabilised table. Thrust alignment errors are cancelled out by spinning the missile with the aid of two tangential jets.

a. Lance                         b. Improved Lance

Fig. 11.5 The United States Lance *(The Vought Corporation)*

Side winds cause Lance, and all SSGW, considerable problems whilst they are within the atmosphere at the beginning and end of their trajectories. Figure 11.6 illustrates the problem.

The centre of pressure lies behind the centre of gravity, so a side wind tends to point the missile into the wind. The thrust of the motor is greater than the wind effect and the missile moves towards the direction of the wind. This turning is sensed by Lance's gyroscopes and an error signal is produced. The missile is thus prevented from turning, so it stays on line and drifts sideways at the same velocity as the wind. A low gain autopilot now turns the missile slightly into the wind to adjust for the drift.

The control of Lance is a form of thrust vector control. Four valves are placed at $90^0$ intervals around the nozzle of the booster motor: they inject fuel, on command, into the exhaust stream, so causing side forces. Large rear-mounted fins provide stability.

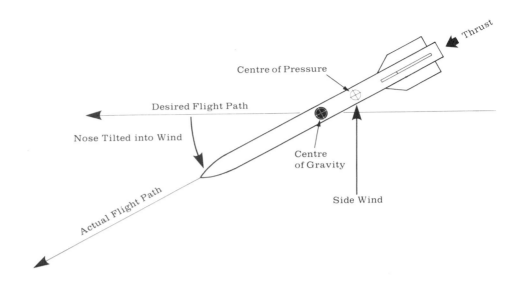

FIG. 11.6  The effect of side winds on SSGW

Pershing II has an inertial guidance system using a stabilised table. However, one of the improvements required from it, over Pershing I, is greater accuracy, so a terminal guidance system has been added. It is named Radar Area Guidance (RADAG). Before launch, it is programmed with a digitalised picture of the target area. As it approaches the target, its radar compares the picture it sees with it. The error signals generated by the comparison process are used to update the inertial guidance system.

The control of Pershing II in the longitudinal roll axis is effected by vanes; pitch and yaw axes are controlled by a swivelling nozzle.

Pershing and the other missiles we have discussed so far are successors of the German V2. There is, however, another line of development from the other German wartime missile.

## Cruise Missiles

### Background

The first operational cruise missiles were the V1 'Doodlebugs' which were used against England in 1944. They were successful to a degree, but their loss rate rose to approximately 70%. Their vulnerability was caused first by their straight flight path, which made them easy to track by the radar defences. Secondly, the latest fighter aircraft of the time were faster than they were and could catch them.

Since that time, both the Eastern and Western Blocs have continued to develop forms of stand-off or flying bombs launched from aircraft. But it was not until the late 1970s that the juxtaposition of developments in micro-electronics, computers and small turbofan engines made possible the modern cruise missile. The result is something more like an unmanned disposable aircraft than a flying bomb. Cruise missiles can now be air launched from aircraft (ALCM), launched from submarines or ships (SLCM) or from the ground (GLCM) as shown in Figure 11.7.

FIG. 11.7 United States Tomahawk cruise missile being launched
*(General Dynamics)*

## Guidance and Control

One problem to be solved was guidance. Some United States cruise missiles are stated to have a range of 2,500 km for ALCM and 600 km for GLCM. These are self imposed range limitations for SALT reasons, and they could be extended. The point is that cruise missiles, which probably travel at slightly below Mach 1, may take several hours to reach their target. An

inertial guidance system used in a SSGW would be expected to have a drift of
several hundreds of metres during each hour. Such an error is not a problem
for SSGW with a normal flight time of a few tens of minutes at the most, but
it is unsatisfactory for a cruise missile. Some form of correction is
occasionally necessary during the flight. The system used is Terrain Contour
Matching (TERCOM).

TERCOM requires good topographical knowledge of the ground under the
flight path and of the target area. Based on that knowledge, terrain details of
map sections, called matrices, of the ground over which the cruise missile is to
pass, is stored in digitalised form in an onboard computer. The missile is then
programmed to fly over the matrices: the concept is illustrated in Figure 11.8.

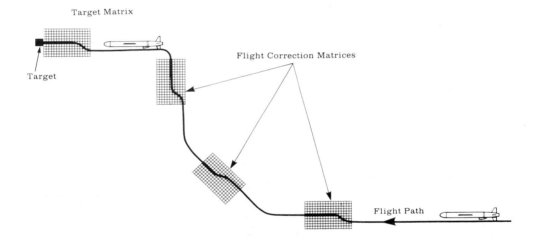

Target Matrix

Flight Correction Matrices

Target

Flight Path

FIG. 11.8  Concept of TERCOM

When not over an area covered by a hostile air defence system, the missile
will fly at its economic cruising height of 5,000 to 10,000 ft, but in hostile air
space it will come down to a height of 50 to 300 ft above ground level: its
exact height will depend on the roughness of the terrain. Whilst over a
matrix, a radar altimeter in the missile compares the terrain with the stored
information. When a match is achieved, a firm position fix is known and the
flight path can be adjusted accordingly. The changes in direction shown in
the flight path are to confuse enemy radar detection and to disguise its
ultimate target. The accuracy of the guidance is claimed to be an impressive
12m at the target.

The control is by aerodynamic surfaces: a cruise missile has wings and tail aerofoils similar to a manned aircraft.

## Propulsion

Most cruise missiles are launched from a container by a solid propellant booster. Figure 11.7 shows this stage. After launch, the booster is jettisoned, an air scoop drops into position and a small low consumption turbofan engine takes over and drives the missile to its target. The scoop can be seen in position towards the bottom of the GLCM Tomahawk shown in flight in Figure 11.9. The wings and rudders, which spring out after launch, are also visible.

FIG. 11.9  Cruise missile in flight *(General Dynamics)*

## Warheads

Nuclear warheads on cruise missiles will probably be of approximately 200KT yield. Other warheads containing sub-munitions are also options.

## Role of Battlefield SSGW and GLCM

It must be stressed again that although battlefield SSGW and GLCM are, in theory, tactical weapons, they are mainly, as we have seen, part of the nuclear deerrent. Apart from their size and mobility, they are very little different from the strategic weapons with which they form a nuclear escalation logic.

# Self Test Questions

## CHAPTER 2

QUESTION 1    Explain the principle of jet propulsion.

Answer    ..............................................

..............................................

..............................................

QUESTION 2    What is the function of the thrust of a jet engine in a missile flying straight and level?

Answer    ..............................................

..............................................

QUESTION 3    Can a ramjet-propelled missile fly at a velocity greater than the velocity of the propulsive jet?

Answer    ..............................................

..............................................

..............................................

QUESTION 4    List types of propulsion unit in ascending order of jet velocity.

Answer    ..............................................

..............................................

QUESTION 5    When kerosine is burned in a gas-turbine engine combustor does the pressure of the flowing gas rise, fall or remain constant?

Answer    ..............................................

ANSWERS ON PAGES 251-2

**QUESTION 7**    Name two techniques of forming double-base propellant charges and say for which type of charge each is particularly suited.

Answer    ............................................

............................................

............................................

............................................

............................................

............................................

**QUESTION 8**    Why is an air-breathing jet propulsion engine's thrust more susceptible to degradation of, say, nozzle performance than is a rocket motor's thrust?

Answer    ............................................

............................................

............................................

............................................

............................................

............................................

**QUESTION 9**    Give reasons for choosing a solid-propellant rocket motor for an anti-tank missile such as Swingfire.

Answer    ............................................

............................................

............................................

............................................

............................................

QUESTION 10   List well-known missiles employing

    (a)  liquid-propellant engine,
    (b)  dual-thrust solid-propellant motor,
    (c)  ramjet engine,
    (d)  ramrocket engine,
    (e)  turbojet engine,
    (f)  turbofan engine.

    Answer    ..........................................

    ..........................................

    ..........................................

    ..........................................

    ..........................................

    ..........................................

## CHAPTER 3

No Questions

## CHAPTER 4

QUESTION 1   What is meant by the phrase 'a normal acceleration of 5g'?

    Answer    ........................................

    ........................................

    ........................................

    ........................................

QUESTION 2   Explain the purposes of stringers and frames in a missile body.

    Answer    ........................................

    ........................................

    ........................................

ANSWERS ON PAGES 252-3

QUESTION 3    Why do most missiles have cruciform wing and tail
              surfaces?

              Answer        ...............................................

QUESTION 4    What is a shock wave?

              Answer        ...............................................

                            ...............................................

QUESTION 5    What are the significant differences between subsonic and
              supersonic missiles?

              Answer        ...............................................

                            ...............................................

                            ...............................................

QUESTION 6    List some of the advantages of slender wings. What is their
              main disadvantage?

              Answer        ...............................................

                            ...............................................

                            ...............................................

                            ...............................................

QUESTION 7    Explain why it is that a subsonic missile has a forward
              speed at which the drag is a minimum.

              Answer        ...............................................

                            ...............................................

                            ...............................................

                            ...............................................

                            ...............................................

QUESTION 8    Why are hemispherical noses on missiles acceptable at subsonic speeds but aerodynamically undesirable at supersonic speeds?

Answer    .............................................

.............................................

.............................................

.............................................

QUESTION 9    What is meant by static stability and why is it important for missile control?

Answer    .............................................

.............................................

.............................................

.............................................

QUESTION 10   List some of the aerodynamic advantages and disadvantages of canard vis-a-vis tailed configurations.

Answer    .............................................

.............................................

.............................................

.............................................

.............................................

## CHAPTER 5

QUESTION 1    Why do GW have a larger SSKP than unguided weapons?

Answer    .............................................

.............................................

ANSWERS ON PAGES 253-4

QUESTION 2     Why do GOT systems usually have a dedicated surveillance system?

Answer     .............................................

.............................................

.............................................

.............................................

QUESTION 3     What characterises a homing missile?

Answer     .............................................

.............................................

.............................................

QUESTION 4     What is a cruise missile?

Answer     .............................................

.............................................

QUESTION 5     Why do semi-active homing systems need two target trackers?

Answer     .............................................

.............................................

.............................................

QUESTION 6     What is the main disadvantage of an MCLOS system?

Answer     .............................................

.............................................

QUESTION 7     What essential instruments are used in an IN missile?

Answer     .............................................

.............................................

QUESTION 8    How many satellites must be seen by a missile using GPS guidance?

Answer    ..............................................

QUESTION 9    Why are COLOS systems susceptible to enemy jamming?

Answer    ..............................................

..............................................

..............................................

..............................................

QUESTION 10    Why are two stage compound systems becoming of increasing importance?

Answer    ..............................................

..............................................

..............................................

## CHAPTER 6

QUESTION 1    In what circumstances is a missile likely to have to pull large g's?

Answer    ..............................................

..............................................

..............................................

QUESTION 2    What factors can make the manoeuvrability of a given missile change during flight?

Answer    ..............................................

..............................................

..............................................

..............................................

ANSWERS ON PAGES 254-5

**QUESTION 3**     What is the outstanding characteristic of Thrust Vector Control?

Answer     ...............................................

...............................................

**QUESTION 4**     If Thrust Vector Control is the sole method of manoeuvring a missile, can one have a simple boost-coast propulsion motor?

Answer     ...............................................

...............................................

**QUESTION 5**     Enumerate the main characteristics of wing control.

Answer    (a)    .......................................

(b)    .......................................

(c)    .......................................

...............................................

**QUESTION 6**     What advantages are there in favour of canard controls?

Answer    (a)    .......................................

(b)    .......................................

...............................................

**QUESTION 7**     Give two advantages and one disadvantage of polar control.

Answer    (a)    .......................................

(b)    .......................................

(c)    .......................................

...............................................

**QUESTION 8**     Do all LOS and homing missiles require a roll position gyro?

Answer        ..............................................

              ..............................................

              ..............................................

              ..............................................

QUESTION 9    What is the main design objective for a lateral autopilot?

              Answer        ...........................................

                            ...........................................

                            ...........................................

QUESTION 10   Does a simple directional autopilot eliminate dispersion due
              to a sidewind. If not, why?

              Answer        ...........................................

                            ...........................................

                            ...........................................

## CHAPTER 7

No Questions

## CHAPTER 8

QUESTION 1    Why is an external warhead large compared with the small
              internal type?

              Answer        ..........................................

                            ..........................................

                            ..........................................

QUESTION 2    What do you understand by warhead effectiveness?

              Answer        ..........................................

ANSWERS ON PAGES 255-6

GW—I

QUESTION 3      Why are warheads less robust than conventional projectiles?

Answer      . . . . . . . . . . . . . . . . . . . . . . . . . . . . . . . . . . . . . . . . .

. . . . . . . . . . . . . . . . . . . . . . . . . . . . . . . . . . . . . . . . .

QUESTION 4      What effect has altitude and water on explosive warhead
performance?

Answer      . . . . . . . . . . . . . . . . . . . . . . . . . . . . . . . . . . . . . . . .

QUESTION 5      Pre-formed, fire formed and natural fragmenting warheads
are placed in descending order of efficiency. Why are there
differences?

Answer      . . . . . . . . . . . . . . . . . . . . . . . . . . . . . . . . . . . . . . .

. . . . . . . . . . . . . . . . . . . . . . . . . . . . . . . . . . . . . . .

. . . . . . . . . . . . . . . . . . . . . . . . . . . . . . . . . . . . . . .

. . . . . . . . . . . . . . . . . . . . . . . . . . . . . . . . . . . . . . .

. . . . . . . . . . . . . . . . . . . . . . . . . . . . . . . . . . . . . . .

QUESTION 6      Why is a discreet rod warhead less effective than a
continuous rod type?

Answer      . . . . . . . . . . . . . . . . . . . . . . . . . . . . . . . . . . . . . . .

. . . . . . . . . . . . . . . . . . . . . . . . . . . . . . . . . . . . . . .

. . . . . . . . . . . . . . . . . . . . . . . . . . . . . . . . . . . . . . .

QUESTION 7      Explain why wave shaping is necessary in some warheads?

Answer      . . . . . . . . . . . . . . . . . . . . . . . . . . . . . . . . . . . . . . .

QUESTION 8      How does a HESH warhead function?

Answer      . . . . . . . . . . . . . . . . . . . . . . . . . . . . . . . . . . . . . . .

. . . . . . . . . . . . . . . . . . . . . . . . . . . . . . . . . . . . . . .

. . . . . . . . . . . . . . . . . . . . . . . . . . . . . . . . . . . . . . . . . .

. . . . . . . . . . . . . . . . . . . . . . . . . . . . . . . . . . . . . . . . . .

QUESTION 9    Define a Safety and Arming Mechanism.

Answer        . . . . . . . . . . . . . . . . . . . . . . . . . . . . . . . . . . . . . . . . .

. . . . . . . . . . . . . . . . . . . . . . . . . . . . . . . . . . . . . . . . .

. . . . . . . . . . . . . . . . . . . . . . . . . . . . . . . . . . . . . . . . .

. . . . . . . . . . . . . . . . . . . . . . . . . . . . . . . . . . . . . . . . .

. . . . . . . . . . . . . . . . . . . . . . . . . . . . . . . . . . . . . . . . .

QUESTION 10   List the basic safety requirements of a Safety and Arming
Mechanism.

Answer        . . . . . . . . . . . . . . . . . . . . . . . . . . . . . . . . . . . . . . . . .

. . . . . . . . . . . . . . . . . . . . . . . . . . . . . . . . . . . . . . . . .

. . . . . . . . . . . . . . . . . . . . . . . . . . . . . . . . . . . . . . . . .

. . . . . . . . . . . . . . . . . . . . . . . . . . . . . . . . . . . . . . . . .

## CHAPTER 9

QUESTION 1    Give two characteristics of a LAW or ATGW which affect
their overall size and weight.

Answer    (a)  . . . . . . . . . . . . . . . . . . . . . . . . . . . . . . . . . . . . .

(b)  . . . . . . . . . . . . . . . . . . . . . . . . . . . . . . . . . . . . .

. . . . . . . . . . . . . . . . . . . . . . . . . . . . . . . . . . . . .

QUESTION 2    What type of warhead is employed on most LAW and
ATGW? Give the reason.

Answer        . . . . . . . . . . . . . . . . . . . . . . . . . . . . . . . . . . . . .

. . . . . . . . . . . . . . . . . . . . . . . . . . . . . . . . . . . . .

ANSWERS ON PAGES 256-7

. . . . . . . . . . . . . . . . . . . . . . . . . . . . . . . . . . . . . . . . . . . .

. . . . . . . . . . . . . . . . . . . . . . . . . . . . . . . . . . . . . . . . . . . .

QUESTION 3    Give three characteristics of a LAW or ATGW which the
              selection of the sighting system affect?

              Answer    (a)   . . . . . . . . . . . . . . . . . . . . . . . . . . . . . . . . . . . . . . . . . .

                        (b)   . . . . . . . . . . . . . . . . . . . . . . . . . . . . . . . . . . . . . . . . . .

                        (c)   . . . . . . . . . . . . . . . . . . . . . . . . . . . . . . . . . . . . . . . . . .

QUESTION 4    Why is a rocket launcher normally longer than a recoilless
              weapon?

              Answer    . . . . . . . . . . . . . . . . . . . . . . . . . . . . . . . . . . . . . . . . . . . .

                        . . . . . . . . . . . . . . . . . . . . . . . . . . . . . . . . . . . . . . . . . . . .

                        . . . . . . . . . . . . . . . . . . . . . . . . . . . . . . . . . . . . . . . . . . . .

                        . . . . . . . . . . . . . . . . . . . . . . . . . . . . . . . . . . . . . . . . . . . .

                        . . . . . . . . . . . . . . . . . . . . . . . . . . . . . . . . . . . . . . . . . . . .

QUESTION 5    What is the disadvantage inherent in the method of over-
              coming backblast which is illustrated in Figure 7.6?

              Answer    . . . . . . . . . . . . . . . . . . . . . . . . . . . . . . . . . . . . . . . . . . . .

                        . . . . . . . . . . . . . . . . . . . . . . . . . . . . . . . . . . . . . . . . . . . .

                        . . . . . . . . . . . . . . . . . . . . . . . . . . . . . . . . . . . . . . . . . . . .

QUESTION 6    How do the Milan ATGW and the Russian RPG7 LAW
              overcome the danger of injury to the firer when the missiles
              leave the launchers?

              Answer    . . . . . . . . . . . . . . . . . . . . . . . . . . . . . . . . . . . . . . . . . . . .

                        . . . . . . . . . . . . . . . . . . . . . . . . . . . . . . . . . . . . . . . . . . . .

                        . . . . . . . . . . . . . . . . . . . . . . . . . . . . . . . . . . . . . . . . . . . .

QUESTION 7    Give two advantages which MCLOS systems enjoy over SACLOS systems.

    Answer    (a)    .......................................

                              .......................................

                              .......................................

                (b)    .......................................

                              .......................................

                              .......................................

QUESTION 8    Why are thermal imaging sights more suitable for ATGW than Image Intensifier sights?

    Answer    (a)    .......................................

                              .......................................

                (b)    .......................................

                              .......................................

                  ....

QUESTION 9    Give four factors which affect the range of an ATGW.

    Answer    (a)    .......................................

                (b)    .......................................

                (c)    .......................................

                (d)    .......................................

QUESTION 10    Will an ATGW with a separated fin capability have a longer or shorter minimum range than one which does not have it? Give reasons.

    Answer    .......................................

                              .......................................

. . . . . . . . . . . . . . . . . . . . . . . . . . . . . . . . . . . . . . . . . . . . . . . . .

. . . . . . . . . . . . . . . . . . . . . . . . . . . . . . . . . . . . . . . . . . . . . . . . .

## CHAPTER 10

QUESTION 1     What are the five agreed NATO names for the height bands
               covered by SAGW?

               Answer     (a)    . . . . . . . . . . . . . . . . . . . . . . . . . . . . . . . . . . . . . . . . . . .

                          (b)    . . . . . . . . . . . . . . . . . . . . . . . . . . . . . . . . . . . . . . . . . . .

                          (c)    . . . . . . . . . . . . . . . . . . . . . . . . . . . . . . . . . . . . . . . . . . .

                          (d)    . . . . . . . . . . . . . . . . . . . . . . . . . . . . . . . . . . . . . . . . . . .

                          (e)    . . . . . . . . . . . . . . . . . . . . . . . . . . . . . . . . . . . . . . . . . . .

QUESTION 2     What are the two main requirements to ensure that guns
               are effective in an air defence role?

               Answer     (a)    . . . . . . . . . . . . . . . . . . . . . . . . . . . . . . . . . . . . . . . . . . .

                          (b)    . . . . . . . . . . . . . . . . . . . . . . . . . . . . . . . . . . . . . . . . . . .

QUESTION 3     What are four main elements of an air defence system?

               Answer     (a)    . . . . . . . . . . . . . . . . . . . . . . . . . . . . . . . . . . . . . . . . . . .

                          (b)    . . . . . . . . . . . . . . . . . . . . . . . . . . . . . . . . . . . . . . . . . . .

                          (c)    . . . . . . . . . . . . . . . . . . . . . . . . . . . . . . . . . . . . . . . . . . .

                          (d)    . . . . . . . . . . . . . . . . . . . . . . . . . . . . . . . . . . . . . . . . . . .

QUESTION 4     What are the main functions of any control centre?

               Answer     (a)    . . . . . . . . . . . . . . . . . . . . . . . . . . . . . . . . . . . . . . . . . . .

                          (b)    . . . . . . . . . . . . . . . . . . . . . . . . . . . . . . . . . . . . . . . . . . .

                          (c)    . . . . . . . . . . . . . . . . . . . . . . . . . . . . . . . . . . . . . . . . . . .

ANSWERS ON PAGES 257-8

QUESTION 5    What is the function of a FC radar?

              Answer      ...........................................

                          ...........................................

              ...........

QUESTION 6    What determines the launch time once the tracker has
              locked on to the target?

              Answer      ...........................................

                          ...........................................

                          ...........................................

                          ...........................................

QUESTION 7    Give a major reason why Rapier is smaller than Roland
              and Gecko?

              Answer      ...........................................

                          ...........................................

                          ...........................................

QUESTION 8    What are the functions of the four radars used in the Hawk
              system?

              Answer    (a)  .......................................

                        (b)  .......................................

                        (c)  .......................................

                        (d)  .......................................

QUESTION 9    How many and what types of radar does Patriot use to
              carry out the same function?

              Answer      ...........................................

                          ...........................................

QUESTION 10   What is the limitation of a continuous rod warhead?

Answer      .........................................

.........................................

.........................................

.........................................

## CHAPTER 11

QUESTION 1    What are the three normal classifications of strategic
missiles?

Answer      .........................................

.........................................

.........................................

QUESTION 2    What is the approximate range limit for FFR and why is it
probably not worth extending their range?

Answer      .........................................

.........................................

.........................................

QUESTION 3    What form of guidance is normally used in long range
SSGW?

Answer      .........................................

QUESTION 4    Give the published ranges of:

(a)  Pershing II
(b)  Scaleboard
(c)  Pluton

Answer    (a)   ...................................

(b)   ...................................

(c)   ...................................

ANSWERS ON PAGES 258-9

QUESTION 5    What form of guidance is employed in the Lance missile?

Answer    .............................................

.............................................

QUESTION 6    In what way do side winds affect the accuracy of SSGW?

Answer    .............................................

.............................................

.............................................

QUESTION 7    How is the accuracy of Pershing II improved beyond that normally possible with inertial guidance?

Answer    .............................................

.............................................

.............................................

QUESTION 8    In what three main fields of technology did improvement benefit the development of cruise missiles?

Answer    .............................................

.............................................

(a)    .............................................

(b)    .............................................

(c)    .............................................

QUESTION 9    What form of guidance is used in American cruise missiles? Give an outline of its concept.

Answer    .............................................

.............................................

.............................................

QUESTION 10   What is the propulsion system of a GLCM?

Answer       ...............................................

             ...............................................

             ...............................................

# Answers to Self Test Questions

## CHAPTER 2

Pages 233-5

QUESTION 1    The principle of jet propulsion is to create a useful propulsive force through the reaction to the creation of a high-velocity jet.

QUESTION 2    Its function is to counteract exactly the aerodynamic drag on the missile.

QUESTION 3    No. It is impossible to create a useful forward force when using the surrounding medium as the propulsive medium unless the jet velocity exceeds the forward speed.

QUESTION 4    Turbofan, turbojet, ramjet, ramrocket, solid-rocket, liquid rocket.

QUESTION 5    The pressure of the flowing gas falls slightly.

QUESTION 6    'Pressure recovery' is the term used to describe how well the intake slows down the captured airstream, exchanging velocity for pressure rise.

QUESTION 7    The two techniques are casting and extruding. Casting is likely to be used for very large diameter charges and for those whose cross-section prevents extrusion while extrusion tends to be used for producing the smaller sizes.

QUESTION 8    Deficiencies in the performance of components such as compressor, turbine or nozzle reduce the gross thrust. Because the net thrust of an air-breathing engine is the difference between the gross thrust and the ram drag, the reduction in net thrust is more marked than the reduction in gross thrust alone. Hence the air-breather's greater sensitivity to loss of component performance.

QUESTION 9      In terms of pure propulsive efficiency, the rocket motor is
                not well matched to a slow missile such as the Swingfire.
                However, it is the lightest, simplest, most compact and
                convenient propulsion unit available.

QUESTION 10     (a)  Lance
                (b)  Rapier, Swingfire
                (c)  Bloodhound, Sea Dart
                (d)  A.S.6.
                (e)  Harpoon
                (f)  Tomahawk, ALCM

## CHAPTER 3

No Questions

## CHAPTER 4

Pages 235-7

QUESTION 1      An acceleration of $5 \times 9.81$ m/s$^2$ at right angles to the line
                of flight. Under these conditions a missile would be flying
                in a curved path. All the missile components appear to
                resist this manoeuvre with a force equal to five times their
                individual weights.

QUESTION 2      The frames prevent the circular shape of the missile outer
                skin from being flattened and the stringers resist buckling
                of the skin between the frames.

QUESTION 3      Because they may be required to move suddenly in any
                direction.

QUESTION 4      A sudden pressure rise heralding the approach of an object
                travelling at supersonic speed.

QUESTION 5      Subsonic missiles tend to have rounded noses, large wings
                and small motors (because their drag is relatively small).
                Supersonic missiles have pointed noses, small wings and
                large motors.

QUESTION 6      Slender wings are structurally more efficient, easier to
                handle and not liable to stall. They also exhibit similar
                aerodynamic characteristics at both subsonic and low
                supersonic speeds. Their main disadvantage is that they
                have a large drag.

QUESTION 7    Because the drag at supersonic speeds is effectively in two parts. One part of the drag force on the missile increases with speed squared as the missile increases speed. The other part reduces as speed squared as the missile increases speed. When these are added together the result is a dip in the drag curve where the drag is a minimum.

QUESTION 8    Hemispherical noses on missiles at subsonic speeds have little drag because the air flows smoothly around them. At supersonic speeds, the presence of the shock wave causes very high drag unless the nose is pointed.

QUESTION 9    Static stability is a measure of the tendency for an object to return to its original position when it has been disturbed. It also quantifies the size of a deliberate disturbance which will be needed to produce a given result, hence its importance for the missile control.

QUESTION 10   Canard controls give a faster and usually a larger response to a particular control input. They suffer from aerodynamic complications when used to roll the misile. There may also be some resistance from the guidance or warhead specialists to the positioning of control surfaces near to the nose of the missile.

## CHAPTER 5

Pages 237-9

QUESTION 1    Because they use a closed loop system.

QUESTION 2    Because GOT systems normally engage targets of opportunity where continuous watch is necessary together with rapid transfer of the target to the weapon system.

QUESTION 3    A GOT missile which contains the target tracker in the missile itself. They nearly always use a PN trajectory.

QUESTION 4    a missile which travels at constant height and constant speed for most of the time.

QUESTION 5    One tracker is needed to keep the target illuminating beam on target. The guidance tracker in the missile measures rate of turn of sight line.

QUESTION 6    The difficulty in training and maintaining the skill of the operator.

QUESTION 7     Gyroscopes and accelerometers.

QUESTION 8     At least four.

QUESTION 9     Direction and range of both target and missile from the
tracking station must be known at all times. It is relatively
easy for jamming to deny range information.

QUESTION 10    The development of small sensors and microprocessors
permits the use of smart homing heads in small battlefield
systems.

## *CHAPTER 6*

Pages 239-41

QUESTION 1     The likely circumstances are:

(a)  fast targets and fast missiles;
(b)  short impact ranges;
(c)  situations when the target tends to be 'crossing' rather
than approaching more or less straight ahead.

QUESTION 2     The factors are:

(a)  changes height and speed (strictly speaking Mach
Number if the missile is supersonic).
(b)  changes in the size of the static margin due to changes
in the position of the centre of pressure and centre of
gravity;
(c)  changes in the missile mass.

QUESTION 3     High manoeuvrability can be obtained in the boost phase.

QUESTION 4     No, the motor has to be thrusting right up to impact.

QUESTION 5     Wing control:

(a)  reduces body incidence;
(b)  requires heavy servos and heavier wings;
(c)  is inefficient as the lift from the missile body is not
fully utilised.

QUESTION 6     The advantages are:

(a)  the initial manoeuvre is the intended direction;
(b)  the normal force from the canard controls adds to that
from the missile body and wings.

QUESTION 7     The advantages are:

(a) it saves weight and drag;
(b) the missile takes up less space.

The disadvantage is:

(c) the missile is not as responsive as missiles with two pairs of controls and lifting surfaces.

QUESTION 8     All LOS missiles require a roll position gyro to use with a roll position gyro (or with a resolver if it is fully rolling). It is not essential with a homing missile.

QUESTION 9     To make the missile 'g' response as a result of a control surface movement more consistent.

QUESTION 10     No, because a directional gyro senses the angular position (ie direction) of the missile, not the direction in which it is moving.

## CHAPTER 7

No Questions

## CHAPTER 8

Pages 241-3

QUESTION 1     Blast effects fall off rapidly with distance, therefore a large quantity of explosive is needed for an external WH whilst an internal WH which penetrates the target, needs only a small amount.

QUESTION 2     The effect the WH has on the target.

QUESTION 3     Because the launch forces acting on the WH are much lower than in a gun.

QUESTION 4     Altitude decreases the effect, water can enhance it.

QUESTION 5     Pre-formed absorb little or no explosive force when being separated from the casing. Fire-formed require some force to complete their separation. Natural fragments are created by the utilisation of a larger amount of the available explosive force to break open the case.

QUESTION 6    Because the rod generally acts as a small fragment as it
              tends to topple and loses its potential to slice through a
              target which a continuous rod is designed to do.

QUESTION 7    To ensure that the detonation effect is simultaneously
              applied over the entire area of projected contents.

QUESTION 8    It squashes or collapses on to the target and is initiated by
              the base fuze resulting in scabbing effect inside the target
              brought about by reversal of the pressure wave at change of
              density.

QUESTION 9    A safety and arming mechanism consists of an arrange-
              ment of explosive components and safety devices designed
              to ensure safety up to a certain time after launch. It also
              ensures the completeness of the explosive train and
              responds to the fuze signal in a positive way to function
              the WH.

QUESTION 10   Fail safe, visual indications of arm/non arm state,
              compatibility, no possibility of mal-assembly.

## CHAPTER 9

Pages 243-5

QUESTION 1    The two main characteristics which affect the overall size
              and weight of a LAW or ATGW are:

              (a)  the warhead size;
              (b)  the range of the missile which, in turn, decides the size
                   of the propulsion system.

QUESTION 2    The type of warhead normally used on LAW and ATGW is
              hollow charge (HEAT). This type is used because it is much
              lighter than any other.

QUESTION 3    The type of sighting system selected affects:

              (a)  the effective range;
              (b)  the choice between a re-usable or a disposable weapon;
              (c)  the simplicity of training.

QUESTION 4    A rocket launcher is normally longer than a recoilless
              weapon because the rocket must be all burnt before it leaves
              the launcher. If it is not, the efflux may well injure the firer.

QUESTION 5    The disadvantage inherent in the method illustrated in Figure 7.6 is that the compensating mass is added weight.

QUESTION 6    Both have initial charges which launch the missiles clear of the launchers before the rocket motors ignite.

QUESTION 7    (a)  A MCLOS system has an inherently better accuracy than a SACLOS system, which becomes more important as range increases.
              (b)  A MCLOS system is not so easily decoyed as a SACLOS system.

QUESTION 8    (a)  Image intensifiers do not match the range of ATGW so well as Thermal Imagers.
              (b)  Thermal Imagers can see through poor weather and battlefield smog. Image Intensifiers can not.

QUESTION 9    Four factors which affect the range of an ATGW are:

              (a)  the weight of the warhead;
              (b)  the amount of propellant;
              (c)  the time of flight;
              (d)  the predicted visibility.

QUESTION 10   An ATGW with a separated fire capability will have a longer minimum range. The reason is apparent from a study of Figure 7.12 and 7.13.

## CHAPTER 10
Pages 246-8

QUESTION 1    The five agreed NATO names for height bands are:

|     |                 |                  |
|-----|-----------------|------------------|
| (a) | very low level  | below 150m       |
| (b) | low level       | 150 - 600m       |
| (c) | medium level    | 600 - 7,500m     |
| (d) | high level      | 7,500 - 15,000m  |
| (e) | very high level | above 15,000m    |

QUESTION 2    The two requirements to ensure that guns are effective in air defence role are:

              (a)  high rate of fire;
              (b)  effective, and therefore expensive, fire control system.

QUESTION 3    Four main elements of an air defence system are:

(a)  detection system;
(b)  acquisition system;
(c)  launching system;
(d)  control system.

QUESTION 4    The main functions of a control centre are:

(a)  give the current control order;
(b)  up-date the state of readiness;
(c)  allocate targets to weapons.

QUESTION 5    A FC radar's function is to provide sufficient information for the tracker to locate and lock on to the target

QUESTION 6    When the tracker has locked on to the target the launch time is a function of the speed and flight path allied to the missile's speed and range.

QUESTION 7    Rapier is a hittile, whereas Roland and Gecko use proximity fuses. Speed and range also affect size.

QUESTION 8    The functions of the four Hawk radars are:

(a)  acquisition at medium level;
(b)  acquisition at low level;
(c)  target illuminating;
(d)  range.

QUESTION 9    Patriot uses a single phased array radar to carry out all four functions.

QUESTION 10   The lethal zone of a continuous rod warhead is limited to an area perpendicular to the axis of the charge.

## CHAPTER 11

Pages 248-9

QUESTION 1    (a)  Intercontinental Ballistic Missiles (ICBM). Range 7,000 - 15,000 km.
              (b)  Intermediate Range Ballistic Missiles (IRBM). Range 4,000 - 6,000 km.
              (c)  Medium Range Ballistic Missiles (MRBM). Range approximately 2,000 km.

QUESTION 2    Frog 7 has a range of 60 km. Beyond that the accuracy of 1% of range is not sufficient for effective results.

QUESTION 3    Long range SSGW employ inertial navigation.

QUESTION 4    (a)  Pershing II — approx. 1,800 km.
              (b)  Scaleboard — approx.   800 km.
              (c)  Pluton       — approx.   120 km.

              These are ranges given in open publications. They are only intended to give an impression of their capability. The figures should not be quoted authoritatively.

QUESTION 5    The Lance missile used a strap down version of guidance.

QUESTION 6    Because the centre of pressure of a SSGW is behind the centre of gravity, a side wind causes the nose to turn into the wind (see Figure 9.6).

QUESTION 7    Pershing II has a terminal guidance system named Radar Area Guidance (RADAG). Its outline operating procedure is given in the text.

QUESTION 8    Developments in the following three main fields of technology came together to make possible the development of cruise missiles:

              (a)  micro-electronics;
              (b)  computers;
              (c)  small turbofan engines.

QUESTION 9    The guidance system used in American cruise missiles is Terrain Contour Matching (TERCOM). Its concept is shown in Figure 9.9.

QUESTION 10   A GLCM is launched using a solid propellant booster. When that is jettisoned a small turbofan engine takes over.

# Glossary of Terms and Abbreviations

**A**

**AAGW**

Air-to-air guided weapon, a dogfight weapon.

**ACLOS**

Automatic Command to Line of Sight.

**Active homing**

Missiles carry a power source to illuminate the target

**Actuator**

A device, either linear or rotary, for moving the fins or jetavator of a missile. Can be hydraulic, pneumatic (hot or cold gas) or electrical.

**Aerodynamic centre**

The point on lifting surface about which there is no change in overturning moment with change in lift.

**Aerofoil section**

The cross-sectional shape of a wing designed to produce lift but little drag.

**AHGW**

Anti helicopter GW.

**Airframe**

The components which make up the structure of the missile including wings and control surfaces.

**ALCM**

Air Launched Cruise Missile.

**AOA**

Area of Authority.

**ARM**

Anti-Radar Missile

**ASGW**

Air-to-Surface Guided Weapons

**ASPJ**

Airborne self protection jammer.

**ATGW**

Anti-Tank Guided Weapon.

**Autopilot**

There is no universally agreed definition of an autopilot, but usually it is understood to mean a system for controlling the flight path of a missile, either by moving aerodynamic surfaces or by thrust vector control. Accelerometers and gyroscopes are used to measure the actual flight path through electronic circuitry. The whole makes a closed loop system. (Not all missiles use autopilots).

**Autopilot – Lateral autopilot**

An autopilot for controlling the lateral acceleration or 'g' of a missile. A cartesian missile, if it uses an autopilot at all, would usually use two: one for controlling the 'g' in the pitch plane and another for controlling the 'g' in the yaw plane.

**AUW**

All-up weight, ie launch mass.

**AWACS**

Airborne Warning and Control System.

**B**

**Ballistic missile**

Missile which follows a near ballistic or free fall path.

**Ballistic trajectory**

Path followed by a body moving under gravity only.

**Bar**

Pressure unit approximately equal to atmospheric pressure at sea level.

**Beacon**

Flare, flash tube, or radio transmitter at the rear of a missile.

**Beetle tank**

An early German guided weapon in the form of a crawling bomb.

**Bi-propellant**

Separate fuel and oxidant (oxidiser).

**Black Chaff**

Chaff optimized to absorb EMR.

**Blast**

A destructive wave produced in the surrounding atmosphere by an explosion or detonation. The blast includes a shock front, high pressure gas behind the shock front and a varification following the high pressure.

**BMEWS**

Ballistic Missile Early Warning System.

**Bomblet**

A small container carrying its own complete initiation system.

**Boost coast**

A single motor missile unpowered for most of its flight.

**Boost sustain**

A missile with two stage propulsion. Essential for TVC.

**Boundary layer**

The layer of air close to the surface of the missile in which shear stresses are important.

**Bypass duct**

An annular passage surrounding the core of a turbine aero-engine; a portion of the air ingested passes through this duct, by passing the engine core.

**C**

**C**

Velocity of light: $3 \times 10^8$m per sec.

**Canard**

A missile configuration in which the control surfaces are positioned forward of the main lifting surfaces.

**Cartesian control**

A system of guidance/control in which steering signals are produced by the guidance system and implemented by the control system in an up-down, left-right manner.

**Case-bonded charge**

A propellant charge which is formed in and bonded (with adhesive) to the motor case.

**Centre of pressure**

The point through which an aerodynamic load must act to provide the moment which it causes.

**Chaff**

Also called 'window'. Thin strips of metal-coated plastic dispersed in bundles to decoy radar.

**Characteristic velocity**

The ratio of the product of chamber (combustor) pressure and nozzle throat area and propellant mass flow rate.

**Choking**

The phenomenon of the maximum mass flow which may pass through a nozzle for given upstream conditions.

**Cigarette burner**

A solid propellant configuration in which the propellant burns longitudinally at an end face.

**Circus**

Number of jamming aircraft on a 'race track'.

**CL**

Command link. The communication channel between guidance computer and missile.

**CLGP**

Cannon launched guided projectile. USA term for GLGP.

**CLOS**

Command to Line of Sight Guidance.

**Closed Loop System**

negative feedback system in which the output automatically aligns itself with the demanded input by making the error become zero.

**COLOS**

Command Off the Line of Sight.

**Command guidance**

A form of guidance in which the guidance computer is separated from the missile.

**Command link**

Wire, optical fibre, radio beam or laser beam command channel to missile.

**Composite**

A type of heterogeneous propellant composed primarily of ammonium perchlorate as oxidant and a polymerisable binder as fuel.

**Compression**

The opposite of an expansion.

**Continuous rod**

A guided missile warhead configuration consisting of a series of steel rods longitudinally encasing an explosive charge. The rods are joined at alternate ends and create an expanding hoop on warhead detonation.

**CRP**

Control and Reporting System

**Cryogenic**

Description sometimes applied to an exceptionally low temperature liquified gas.

**Cruise missile**

A missile which flies most of the time at constant speed and constant height.

**Cruise trajectory**

Constant speed, constant height path.


**D**

**Decoy**

False target provided by enemy to deceive radar or optical sensor.

**Dedicated surveillance**

A system exclusive to a particular guided weapon system.

**Design point**
>    A fixed flight condition at which engine performance parameters
>    are optimised.

**Detonation**
>    An exothermic reaction wave which follows and also maintains a
>    shock front in an explosive.

**Detonator**
>    An explosive device for starting detonation.

**Discrete rod**
>    A long rod of metal designed to penetrate a target.

**Double base**
>    A type of homogeneous colloidal propellant composed primarily of
>    nitrocellulose and nitroglycerine.

**Drone**
>    A UMA with pre-programmed flight path.

**Dual-thrust motor**
>    A solid-propellant motor giving a short duration – high thrust,
>    followed by a longer duration – low thrust; it is a booster/
>    sustainer design.

**E**

**ECM**
>    Electronic Counter Measures.

**ECCM**
>    Electronic Counter Counter Measure.

**EMR**
>    Electromagnetic radiation ie light, IR, MMW, Radar waves, radio
>    waves.

**Engine**
>    A liquid-propellant rocket or an airbreather.

**EPJ**
>    Escort protection jammer.

**ESM**

>  Electronic Support Measures. The detection and location of enemy transmitters.

**EW**

>  Electronic Warfare.

**Expansion**

>  Process undergone by a gas in which the density falls or the pressure falls (or both).

**Explosive**

>  A chemical substance or mixture which, when suitably initiated, can react to produce an explosion.

**Extrusion**

>  To press out through a shaped orifice.

**F**

**$\dot{F}$ (F dot)**

>  Rate of turn of flight path.

**FC radar**

>  Fire Control radar.

**FFR**

>  Free Flight Rocket.

**FGA**

>  Fighter Ground Attack.

**Fin**

>  Control surface of missile.

**Fin servo**

>  Closed Loop Control System which makes the position of the fin follow the demand.

**Fixed location end point**

>  The point to which a GOLIS missile is guided.

**FOV**

>  Field of view

**Fragmentation**
>    The shattering of a munition casing caused by an explosive charge.

**Fuze**

>    An electronic device used in a missile capable of sensing or detecting the target. Normally does not include explosive components, unlike artillery fuze systems.

## G

**General surveillance**
>    A form of surveillance system gathering information for several different purposes.

**GLCM**
>    Ground Launched Cruise Missile.

**GLGP**
>    Gun Launched Guided Projectile.

**GOLIS**
>    Guide Onto Location in Space

**GOT**
>    Guide Onto Target.

**GPS**
>    Global Positioning System.

**Gravity**
>    Force of gravity or acceleration due to gravity loosely used as a unit. Force or latax of so many 'g'. Strictly 9.81m per sec.

**Gross thrust**
>    The product of jet velocity and gas mass flow-rate.

**Guidance loop**
>    The essential closed loop system of a guided weapon.

**GW**
>    Guided Weapon.

# H

**HE**

High Explosive. Any explosive which is capable of detonation when suitably initiated.

**HEAT**

High Explosive Anti-Tank.

**HESH**

High Explosive Squash Head.

**HI**

A high altitude segment of a flight path.

**Hittile**

A missile which is so accurate that it is not worth fitting a proximity fuse.

**Homing Guidance**

A GOT system in which the missile carries the target tracker.

**Hypergolic**

The description of liquid fuel and oxidant which ignite on contact.

# I

**ICBM**

Intercontinental Ballistic Missile.

**IFF**

Identification Friend or Foe.

**IG**

Inertial Guidance. A system in which missile displacement is measured by the double integration of accelerometer signals.

**Igniter**

A device for starting burning or deflagration.

**Ignition**

The start of burning.

**Impulse**

The integral of rocket motor thrust with respect to time

**IN**

Inertial Navigation. (See IG).

**Incidence**

The angle between the missile or one of its component parts and the missile flight path.

**Initiator**

A device for setting off explosive or pyrotechnics, eg a detonator or igniter.

**IR**

Infra-red electromagnetic radiation.

**IRBM**

Intermediate Range Ballistic Missile.

**Iron bomb**

USA name for a conventional free fall aerial bomb.

**J**

**Jammer**

Radar, radio or laser transmitter intended to confuse or deceive enemy receivers.

**K**

**K**

PN constant. The radio of F/S.

**L**

**Laser**

Light amplification by stimulated emission of radiation. A coherent light or IR transmitter.

**Latax**

Lateral acceleration. The result of a pitch or yaw demand on an air-frame.

**LAW**

Light Anti-Armour Weapon.

**LO**

A low altitude segment of flight path.

**LOAL**

Lock On After Launch.

**LOBL**

Lock On Before Launch.

**Loose charge**

A propellant charge which is made separately and inserted (cartridge style) into the motor case.

**LOS**

Line of Sight. The line between track point and the target at any instant.

**LOSBER**

LOS Beam Rider.

**LWR**

Laser Warning Receiver.


**M**

**Mach number**

The speed of a missile divided by the ambient speed of round.

**MAD**

Mutually Assured Destruction.

**MBT**

Main Battle Tank

**MCLOS**

Manual Command to Line of Sight.

**MHz**

Megahertz: $10^6$Hz.

**Micrometre**

Sometimes called micron. $10^{-6}$m. Symbol $\mu$m sometimes used.

**MIRV**

Multiple Independently targetted Re-entry Vehicle.

**Missile**
> A device propelled through the air.

**MG**
> Machine Gun

**MLRS**
> Multi-Launch Rocket System.

**MMW**
> Millimetre wave

**Momentum**
> The product of mass and velocity.

**Motor**
> A solid-propellant rocket.

**MRBM**
> Medium Range Ballistic Missile.

**N**

**NADGE**
> NATO Air Defence Ground Environment.

**NATINADS**
> NATO Integrated Air Defence System.

**Net thrust**
> Gross thrust minus inlet momentum drag.

**Neutral Point**
> The position of the centre of gravity on the longitudinal axis of a missile which will give neutral static stability.

**Newton's Second Law**
> Force is proportional to rate of change of momentum.

**Newton's Third Law**
> Action versus reaction are equal and opposite.

**NG**
> Navigational Guidance. A missile containing the guidance computer also carries instruments which measure the artificial or natural environment of the missile.

**Noise jammer**

Confusion to victim receiver caused by a total confusion of signals – random noise.

**Nozzle**

An orifice with (nearly always) a convergent-divergent profile through which the propulsive gas is accelerated and discharged.

# O

**One-dimensional**

A type of flow in which it is assumed that the fluid properties are constant across the flow.

**Optical fibre**

Thin, string-like optical wave guide which transmits signals in the form of pulses of light.

**Oxidant**

The component of a bi-propellant combination which supports the combustion of the fuel.

# P

**Passive homing**

A homing missile which tracks natural energy coming from the target.

**Perfect gas**

A thermodynamically 'ideal' gas.

**PGM**

Precision Guided Munition. A compound guided weapon with terminal homing.

**Pitot intake**

A carefully designed open-ended duct; pod-mounted aero-engines exhibit good examples.

**PN**

Proportional Navigation. Used for most homing systems. The rate of turn of flight path is made proportional to the rate of turn of sight line.

**Polar Control (often called 'twist and steer')**

A system of guidance/control when steering signals are produced by the guidance system and implemented by the control system such that the missile rolls so that its lifting surfaces lie in a given plane, and then manoeuvres perpendicular to that plane.

**Power**

The measure of the energy available from an explosive.

**Propellant mass fraction**

Ratio of propellant mass to launch mass of missile (or stage of missile).

**Propulsive efficiency**

The effectiveness of conversion of jet kinetic energy into propulsive power.

# R

**RADAG**

Radar Area Guidance

**Ram effect**

The pressure increase obtained in an air-breathing engine intake by virtue of its forward motion.

**Ramjet**

The simplest (in terms of moving parts) of all air-breathing engines in which the compression is produced by the 'ram' or forward velocity pressure in the intake; combustion downstream of the intake thus gives the high velocity jet.

**Rapier**

A British low level SAGW.

**Rear Controls (sometimes called 'Tail Controls')**

A method of steering a missile by moving small aerodynamic surfaces placed as far to the rear of the missile as possible.

**REC**

Radio Electronic Combat. English translation of the Russian equivalent of EW.

**Repeater Jammer**

Deceives victim receiver by transmitting a deformed copy of the expected signal.

**Reticle**

An optical disc with some areas transparent and some opaque. Used in IR trackers.

**Retro lamp**

A form of jammer used to dazzle a misile operator.

**RMSMD**

Root Mean Square Miss Distance. A statistical measure of lack of accuracy.

**Roll position stabilisation**

A missile which does not roll as it flies.

**Roll reference**

Position datum for the roll angle of a missile. Provided by gyros or external signals.

**RPV**

Remotely Piloted Vehicle.

**S**
**$\dot{S}$ (S dot)**

Rate of turn of sight line.

**SACLOS**

Semi-Active Command to Line of Sight.

**SAGW**

Surface-to-Air Guided weapon.

**SALT**

Strategic Arms Limitation Talks.

**SAM**

Surface-to-Air Missile.

**Seeker**

American term for homing head.

**Semi-active homing**

A homing missile system in which the target is illuminated by a radar or laser which is not in the missile itself.

Sensitivity

> A measure of the relative ease with which reliable functioning may be assured in different explosives or explosive systems under the intended conditions of use.

SFPA

> Staring Focal Plane Array. A modern form of IR imaging detector.

Shaped charge

> An explosive charge shaped to concentrate its effect when detonated. The effect of the charge is enhanced by the addition of a metal liner.

Shock

> A discontinuity (in supersonic flow) across which there is a step rise in gas pressure and step fall in velocity.

SIJ

> Stand in or stand forward jammer.

SLGM

> Submarine Launched Guided Missile.

SMCLOS

> Semi Manual Command to LOS.

SOJ

> Stand Off jammer

Span

> The distance from one wing tip to another, measured at right angles to the body centre line.

Specific fuel consumption (sfc)

> An air-breathing engine performance parameter defined as fuel flow rate divided by net thrust.

Specific impulse

> A rocket motor performance parameter, defined as fuel flow rate divided by the propellant mass flow rate.

SR

> Surveillance Radar.

SSGW

> Surface-to-Surface Guided Weapon.

**SSKP**

Single Shot Kill Probability. A statistical measure of lethality.

**Stall**

The phenomenon which causes a missile or aeroplane to lose height because of a loss of lift and an increase in drag.

**Star-centre**

A common solid propellant configuration which gives nominally constant thrust throughout the burn time as the propellant burns in an outwards direction from a star-shaped central conduit.

**Static margin**

The distance along the fore-and-aft axis of the missile between the centre of pressure and centre of gravity.

**Static pressure**

The pressure of a flowing gas exclusive of any dynamic component due to its velocity.

**Striker**

A version of the British Combat Reconnaissance Vehicle (Tracked) fitted with Swingfire.

**Subsonic**

A velocity less than the local velocity of sound.

**Supersonic**

A velocity greater than the local velocity of sound.

**Sweepback**

The angling rearwards of the leading edge of a wing.

**Swingfire**

An ATGW using MCLOS guidance.

**T**

**TACS**

Tactical Air Control System.

**TBJ**

Target Borne Jammer.

**TC Radar**
> Tactical Control Radar.

**TERCOM**
> Terrain Contour Matching.

**TGSM**
> Terminally Guided Sub Munition.

**Thermal efficiency**
> The effectiveness of conversion of fuel energy into jet kinetic energy.

**Throat (choke)**
> The minimum cross-section area of a nozzle, either convergent only or convergent-divergent.

**Thrust coefficient**
> The ratio of the thrust and the product of chamber (combustor) pressure and nozzle throat area.

**Thrust vector control (TVC)**
> A method of steering a missile by altering the direction of the thrust of the propulsion motor.

**TSPM**
> Tank Self Protection Missile.

**Turbofan**
> A dual-flow derivative of the turbojet incorporating a bypass in which part of the entering air is compressed to a lesser extent than the air going through the combustor and which ultimately rejoins the hot flow prior to expansion through the nozzle.

**Turbojet**
> The simplest form of mono-flow gas-turbine jet engine with relatively low frontal area and high jet velocity.

**TVC**
> Thrust Vector Control.

**TVM**
> Track Via Missile

**Twist and Steer**
> A missile which banks and steers like a manned aircraft. Polar control.

## U

**UMA**

Unmanned Aircraft.

## V

**V1**

An early German cruise missile, developed and employed in World War II.

**V2**

An early German ballistic missile, developed and employed in World War II.

**Velocity of Detonation (V of D).**

This is the speed at which a detonation wave progresses through an explosive.

**Viscosity**

A measure of the tendency of a fluid to ahere to a surface in motion through it.

## W

**Wavelength**

Distance advanced by EMR during the time of one cycle. Usual symbol $\lambda$.

**Weapons Tight**

No launch of weapons permitted unless target is definitely identified as hostile.

**Wing controls**

A method of steering a missile by moving the main lifting surfaces of the missile. These surfaces are usually placed slightly ahead of the centre of gravity of the missile.

**Wire control**

A command link using a wire or wires.

# Bibliography

Barrere M., Jaumotte A., de Venbeke B.F., Vanden Kerckhove J., "Rocket Propulsion", Elsevier Publishing Co., Amsterdam.

Cohen H., Rogers G.F.C., Saravanamuttoo H.I.H., "Gas Turbine Theory", Longman Group Ltd., London.

Edwards C.S., "The Story of Strapdown Inertial Systems", British Technical Journal 1, 1979.

Garnell P., "Guided Weapon Control Systems", 2nd Edition, Pergamon Press, 1980.

Hill P.G., Peterson C.R., "Mechanics and Thermodynamics of Propulsion", Addison-Wesley Publishing Co. Inc., New York.

Lancaster O.E., "Jet Propulsion Engines", Vol XII, "High Speed Aerodynamics and Jet Propulsion", OVP, London.

Liepmann H.W., Roshko A., "Elements of Gas Dynamics", John Wiley & Sons, New York.

Royal Air Force, "RAF Standard Trade Notes", AP3302 Part 3.

Sutton G.P., Ross D.M., "Rocket Propulsion Elements", John Wiley & Sons, New York.

Williams F.A., Barrere M., Huang N.C., "Fundamental Aspects of Solid Propellant Rockets", Technivision Services, Slough, England.

# Index